Reading Matters

Laraine E. Flemming

Houghton Mifflin Company
Boston   New York

Publisher: Patricia A. Coryell
Senior Sponsoring Editor: Lisa Kimball
Development Editor: Kellie Cardone
Editorial Assistant: Peter Mooney
Senior Project Editor: Margaret Park Bridges
Senior Manufacturing Coordinator: Marie Barnes
Marketing Manager: Annamarie Rice
Marketing Associate: Laura Hemrika

Cover image: © 2002 STOCKART.COM, Geoffrey Zipoli

Library of Congress Control Number: 2002109444

ISBN: 0-618-25661-X

123456789-MV-08 07 06 05 04

Contents

Part III   Making a Match Between the Reader and the Text   **77**

Unit I   The Mysteries of Memory   **78**

Unit II   Media Watch   **147**

Unit III   Terrorism Invades America   **220**

Preface

Good readers are flexible readers. They use a variety of different comprehension and critical reading strategies, mixing and matching them in order to better adapt to the text they are reading. Yet it's always been clear to me that few of the students I taught over the years knew the importance of reading flexibility. If anything, they seemed unaware of the many different strategies available. For that matter, they didn't really understand how to adapt the strategies they knew to different reading assignments. Those students are the reason I wrote this book.

In very concrete terms, *Reading Matters* shows students precisely what the phrase "flexible reading" means when applied to different assignments. After a brief but comprehensive review of the strategies skilled readers use to construct meaning, students learn how to adapt those strategies to four units of themed readings. The readings are excerpted from textbooks, magazines, and newspapers, and there are specific pre-reading pointers about how to approach each one.

Special Features

Thematically Linked Readings
Each unit of readings focuses on one topic or issue. Unit I explains how human memory both records and distorts reality. Unit II zeroes in on the media to suggest that journalists today are coming under some very harsh and deserved scrutiny. Unit III describes what it means to live with the threat of terrorism, while Unit IV considers the place of civil liberties in a nation under siege.

Emphasis on Synthesizing
Because the readings linked by a common theme encourage students to constantly synthesize different ideas on the same topic, they are an important feature of the book. The ability to synthesize is a critical reading skill, and students need to make connections between different points of view as often as possible. *Reading Matters* gives them plenty of chances to do precisely that.

Concise and Comprehensive Review
Although *Reading Matters* was designed to be used in an intermediate to advanced reading class, the book makes no assumptions about its users' background knowledge. **Parts I** and **II, Getting Down to Basics**

and **Strategy Tune-Up,** offer a brief but thorough review of the terminology and skills used in the questions accompanying the readings.

Lengthy Textbook Selections

Student readers definitely need numerous chances to hone their skills on brief passages or selections. But at some point, they have to work with longer selections that more closely resemble the textbook assignments that confront them on a regular basis. *Reading Matters* gives students the opportunity to work with a variety of textbook selections.

Pointers on Adapting to Different Texts

Each reading begins with a list of specific text features and suggested reader responses. The goal of these suggestions is to help students become expert readers who know how to shift gears depending on the material they are assigned.

Drawing Conclusions

The assignments and questions that conclude each reading ask students to go beyond the author's explicit statements to infer what the same author might have to say about issues not directly mentioned in the reading itself.

Two Kinds of Exercises Accompanying Extended Readings

Although the first set of questions accompanying the readings relies solely on multiple choice, the second set of critical reading questions is far more open-ended, and students are asked to come up with their own answers rather than selecting one of the author's.

Focus on Current Affairs

It's not by coincidence that *Reading Matters* focuses on issues like the threat of terrorism and the appropriate response to that threat. Most students want to participate in discussions of concern to their country, but they often lack the knowledge that would enable them to do so. *Reading Matters* purposely focuses on topical issues in an effort to make students aware that reading can help them develop informed opinions, and those opinions will allow them to participate in discussions going on across the country. In other words, the book answers the question that students don't usually pose but often want to ask: Why bother to read?

Exit Exam Format

Because many state exit exams require students to choose among four possible choices, the majority of questions in *Reading Matters* ask students to choose from among four answers.

Vocabulary Instruction

Every reading begins with a review of the vocabulary students will encounter in the selection. Thus they get to see new words defined in isolation *and* placed in a larger context.

Emphasis on Memory

It's no coincidence that the first unit of readings focuses on the workings of memory. Readings 1 and 2, in particular, emphasize not just how memory works but how it can be made to work better. While students are practicing their reading skills, they are also learning how to effectively store and later recall new information.

Flexible Format

The book's format is carefully designed so that the text can be used in any number of ways. Instructors can follow the book's sequence or skip around to suit their students' specific needs.

Also Available by the Author

Laraine Flemming is the author of a three-book series that begins with *Reading Keys*, a text that offers instruction in basic reading skills such as using context, reading for main idea, identifying supporting details, and recognizing organizational patterns. Explanations in this book are extremely brief yet very clear. To aid comprehension, all explanations are consistently punctuated by numerous reviews and reminders. The text includes a large number of carefully sequenced and imaginative exercises, which allow students to master the material in small, incremental bites.

Reading for Results picks up where *Readings Keys* leaves off, slightly increasing the level of difficulty in both explanations and exercises. Students work with longer passages and get a deeper sense of what it means to understand and evaluate an author's work. They also get a chapter-long introduction to the essentials of critical thinking with particular emphasis on purpose, tone, argument, and bias.

For those teaching a slightly more advanced reading course, *Reading for Thinking* begins with a review of the concepts and skills covered in *Reading for Results,* but it quickly moves to an expanded discussion of the critical thinking skills summarized at the end of *Reading for Results. Reading for Thinking* places special emphasis on the analysis of extended arguments and the detection of faulty reasoning. All three books in the series reflect my long-time use of lively topics chosen to stimulate students' interest in reading.

Software for Independent Learning

Getting Focused is an interactive software program covering the same skills taught in *Reading for Results*. The program begins by teaching students how to distinguish between general and specific language, then uses those two terms to guide students step by step through the basics of comprehension and critical reading. Graphically attractive and easy to navigate, *Getting Focused* allows for both individualized instruction and independent learning.

Acknowledgments

As always, my reviewers were an enormous help in the writing of this book, and my thanks go to Kathleen S. Britton of Florence–Darlington Technical College, Helen Carr of San Antonio College, Joan E. Hellman of The Community College of Baltimore County–Catonsville, Susan Messina of Solano Community College, and Deborah Spradlin of Tyler Junior College.

Thanks, too, to the instructors who have accessed my website at *http://users.dhp.com/~laflemm* and offered me suggestions via e-mail. Your comments have been of great value. I appreciate your taking the time to send them. My hope is that you will take the time to do the same for this new book and forward to me any comments or questions you might have.

Wishing you much success with *Reading Matters*,
Laraine Flemming

Part I

Getting Down to Basics

Even if you skim just a few pages of this book, you'll quickly notice that it places a heavy emphasis on reading flexibility. You are, that is, consistently encouraged to adapt your reading strategies and skills to the particular characteristics of the text you are reading.

This emphasis is not meant, however, to suggest that you need to develop a whole new set of reading strategies for every assignment. On the contrary, skillful readers master a number of basic techniques. Then they mix and match to suit the particular text they are reading. Thus, it seems sensible to start with a review of the essential strategies you'll make use of in the pages that follow. Then we can talk about how to use these skills with maximum efficiency and flexibility.

Strategy 1   ## Use Questions to Discover the Main Idea

For almost any college reading assignment, you'll need to determine the overall or general main idea for the entire reading as well as the main idea of each individual paragraph. Determining the main idea of the entire reading will help you see how the individual parts of the reading fit together. Determining the main idea of each paragraph will show you how the author supports his or her overall point.

To discover the main idea of the entire reading, you need to identify the topic and the main idea. You can do that by asking two key questions paragraph by paragraph:

> **1.** To describe the topic, ask: What person, place, event, or idea do most of the sentences refer to either directly or indirectly?
> **2.** To determine the main idea, ask: What idea about that topic gets the most explanation or development?

As the topics and main ideas of the individual paragraphs become clearer in your mind, you need to ask yourself the next key question:

> What is the overall or central main idea of the entire reading?

Most of the individual paragraphs in a reading act as **supporting details** that explain, illustrate, or prove one or two central points, or main ideas. Your initial, most basic goals of reading are to (1) discover what overall point the author wants to make and (2) establish the kind of support offered by the details.

Strategy 2   ## Look for Sentences That Summarize Main Ideas

Particularly in textbooks, writers make heavy use of topic sentences and thesis statements. **Topic sentences** are general sentences that "language," or put into words, the main idea of a paragraph. **Thesis statements** do the same for longer readings, essays, and articles. Here's a paragraph that opens with an underlined topic sentence:

> <u>Human beings have a deep-seated tendency to see meaning in the ordinary variations that are bound to appear in a small number of subjects or samples.</u> To illustrate, most basketball players and fans believe that

players have hot and cold streaks in shooting. In a paper titled "The Hot Hand in Basketball," cognitive psychologist Amos Tversky and two other researchers analyzed the shooting of individual players in more than eighty games played by three separate basketball teams. It turned out that basketball players—even famed "streak shooters"—have no more runs of hits or misses than would be expected by chance. Yet when interviewed, players, fans, and coaches all insisted that players had hot or cold streaks where they were fated to make the shot or bound to miss.

(Adapted from Atul Gawande, "The Cancer-Cluster Myth," in *The Best American Science and Nature Writing,* 2000, p. 72.)

In this case, the topic sentence is the very first sentence in the paragraph. It's there to sum up the point of the entire passage: We like to see patterns or meaning where none really exists. Particularly in textbooks, topic sentences are likely to open paragraphs, and thesis statements are likely to start off chapter sections. However, be aware: Outside the context of textbooks, topic sentences can move around a good deal. So, too, can thesis statements.

Strategy 3

Determine What Questions the Supporting Details Answer

As you already know, writers don't just introduce topic sentences and then leave it up to readers to figure out how these sentences can be supported, explained, or proven. Instead, they back up their ideas with **supporting details** that anticipate and answer the questions readers might raise. Here's an example:

In the 1930s, when the United States was in the grip of a severe economic depression, Americans found hope in a scrawny brown racehorse named Seabiscuit. Although Seabiscuit had started his racing life as an apparently hopeless loser, he ended it as one of the biggest winners the horseracing world had ever seen. When he was bought by millionaire Charles Howard in 1936, Seabiscuit was a three-year-old colt that had run and lost most of his forty-three races. Although everyone seemed to think he had potential, the horse continued to lose even the easiest races. Hoping to improve Seabiscuit's performance, Howard hired trainer Tom Smith, who magically transformed the shy colt. In less than a year, Seabiscuit started winning races and setting track records. By November of 1938, he was ready for his race against War Admiral, the number one racehorse in America. In just two short years, Seabiscuit and his scrappy rise to fame had become so well known that the race had close to one-third of the nation glued to their radios, waiting to hear the outcome. The listeners weren't disappointed. Against all odds, Seabiscuit won.

As you can tell from this paragraph, the author uses dates and events to zero in on two questions readers might raise: "Why was Seabiscuit considered a hopeless loser?" and "How did he become a winner?" When you finish the paragraph, you should recall enough of the supporting details to answer, at least generally, both of those questions. Otherwise, you haven't fully understood the author's message.

Make Paraphrasing a Habit

When the page is right in front of their eyes, readers often assume they've understood the author's meaning. However, when they close the book and try to remember what the author said, those same readers are likely to discover that the meaning was not so clear after all.

To monitor, or check, your comprehension as you read, periodically see if you can **paraphrase** the main idea, and maybe a supporting detail or two, from the paragraph or passage you've just finished. Try, that is, to express the author's ideas using your own words. If you can paraphrase what you've read, then you have really grasped the author's meaning. In addition, while searching for words to replace the author's, you have forced your brain to process the information in depth, giving your mind a chance to store the information in long-term memory.

Be Ready to Draw Inferences

Writers sometimes suggest rather than state their ideas: They say just enough so that readers have the basis to make or draw an inference. An **inference** is an educated guess about what a person implies but doesn't directly state. For an illustration, read the following passage. Then decide what you think is the implied main idea of the paragraph.

Many people think of divorce as a modern ill, brought on by a decline in moral values. But, in fact, the first divorce is said to have occurred around 230 B.C. For that matter, there is plenty of evidence showing that the men of ancient Rome frequently divorced wives who could not bear children. Sometimes they even divorced and remarried just to gain political power. It's probably no coincidence, therefore, that the power-hungry generals Pompey and Mark Antony had no less than five wives apiece. The great Roman orator Cicero had a very specific, if less professional, reason for divorcing his first wife, Terentia. She was the wealthier of the two, and Cicero claimed that Terentia was not providing adequately for himself and their daughter, Tullia. But Cicero wasn't satisfied with his second wife, Publilia, either. He divorced her when Tullia died, claiming that Publilia did not adequately grieve for his daughter. During Cicero's time, women also had access to divorce as long as they had their fathers' approval. However, not many men were willing to make divorce easy for women, even if the women were their daughters. Thus, wives were far less likely to abandon their husbands than the other way around.

Which main idea is implied by the author?

a. It's incorrect to assume that the women of ancient Rome never had access to divorce; they had the opportunity but just didn't use it.
b. Although it's often assumed that divorce is a modern invention, it was actually quite common among the ancient Romans.

Answer *a* won't work because you can't use it to sum up the paragraph, which covers more than divorce for ancient Roman women. Inference *a* also distorts the section of the paragraph dealing with Roman women since the paragraph says women weren't generally allowed to get a divorce. Answer *a* makes it sound as if women chose not to get a divorce. Answer *b* is the right choice because it could be used to summarize the entire paragraph, and it doesn't distort or contradict anything said in the paragraph.

When you infer a main idea implied by the author, remember these four points:

1. An implied main idea should summarize the paragraph just like a topic sentence would.
2. The implied main idea has to be solidly based on the statements that the author actually makes.
3. It should be based more on the author's words than on what you know, feel, or think about the topic.
4. An implied main idea should never be contradicted by a statement in the paragraph.

Strategy 6

Let Transitions Be Your Guide

Transitions are verbal signposts that signal how an author's train of thought will develop. They can help you navigate your way through even the most complicated prose. Thus, be on the watch for words like those listed in the box below.*

Common Transitional Signals

Transitions indicating an addition to the original train of thought:
also, in addition, further, furthermore, last, likewise, moreover, not surprisingly, similarly, first, firstly,[†] second, secondly,[†] too, what's more

Transitions indicating that the author is changing, challenging, or contradicting the original train of thought:
although, after all, but, in (by) contrast, however, nevertheless, nonetheless, on the contrary, yet, still, despite that fact, rather, on the other hand, regardless, surprisingly, actually, conversely, unlike, in reality, fortunately though

Transitions signaling that the author is pointing out similarities:
similarly, likewise, by the same token, in the same vein

Transitions that introduce examples and illustrations:
for example, for instance, specifically, in other words, that is, as in, to illustrate

Transitions that introduce the effects of some cause:
as a result, consequently, thus, therefore, hence, in response

Transitions that trace the order of events:
currently, during that time, in the year, at that point, at that moment, after that event, in the meantime, in the interim, following, before, next, soon

Strategy 7

Read to Uncover Patterns

The more you recognize the patterns of organization that underlie a reading, the more easily you can mentally store and remember the

---

* As you'll see from the list, some transitions can fill two different functions.
† Many handbooks for college composition frown on the use of *firstly* and *secondly*, so you should probably avoid using these words. However, you will see them in print.

information presented by those patterns. Thus, when you read, be on the lookout for the five common patterns of organization listed below:

1. *Definition:* The author opens by defining a word or term. The definition is followed by additional information such as the word's origin, an explanation of how the word differs from other words, or an illustration of the word in context.
2. *Time order:* Step by step or date by date, the writer tells readers how something works or how a situation, person, or idea developed over time.
3. *Comparison and contrast:* The writer explains or argues a point by explaining how two topics are similar or different.
4. *Cause and effect:* The writer explains how one event (the cause) leads to another (the effect). Sometimes the writer explains how one effect has several causes or how one cause has several effects.
5. *Classification:* The author explains how some larger group can be broken down into two or more subgroups, each with its own set of characteristics.

Strategy 8

Pay Attention to Tone

Sometimes the way a writer says something is as important as the actual point he or she wants to make. Thus, experienced readers are careful to attend to the **tone,** or feeling, conveyed through a writer's selection of details and choice of words. Depending on the subject matter and what the author wants to say about it, tone can vary a lot—from coolly **objective,** or unemotional, to enthusiastic and supportive or mistrustful and critical. Listed below are some common tones writers are likely to assume.

Words That Describe Tone

admiring	cautious
amused	cheerful
annoyed	confident
angry	cool
appalled	critical
astonished	disapproving
awed (filled with wonder)	disgusted

disrespectful	nostalgic (looking fondly
dumbfounded (very	toward the past)
surprised)	objective
embarrassed	outraged
engaged (deeply	passionate
involved)	puzzled
enthusiastic	regretful
horrified	sad
humorous	sarcastic
insulted	shocked
insulting	skeptical
ironic (saying the opposite	solemn
of what is intended)	sorrowful
joyful	sure
neutral	surprised

Strategy 9

Get a Sense of the Writer's Purpose

Overall, most writing falls into two kinds: **writing meant to inform** and **writing meant to persuade.** Although both purposes can be present in one piece of writing, one purpose will usually dominate, or outweigh, the other. Once you decide the author's primary purpose, you are in a better position to evaluate the writer's work. For example, if you are fairly sure that the purpose is mainly to inform, then you can decide if tone and purpose match. For example, if an author's purpose seems mainly to inform, then he or she should not be using any emotional tone. The tone should remain fairly cool and objective. If you notice that the choice of words is heavily charged with positive or negative connotations, or associations, then you can be pretty sure that the author's **bias,** or personal leaning, is creeping into the discussion.

Clues to Purpose

Informative Writing

- appears in textbooks, newspapers, lab reports, research findings, case studies, and reference works.
- employs a title that names or describes a topic.

- states or suggests a main idea that describes a situation, event, person, concept, or experience without making any judgment.
- relies more on factual than on connotative or emotional language.
- employs more statements of fact than statements of opinion.
- reflects an emotionally neutral tone.
- reveals little or nothing about the author's personal feelings.
- includes both the pros and cons of a given issue.

Persuasive Writing

- appears in newspaper editorials, political pamphlets, opinion pieces, and articles or books written to explain the author's position on current or past events.
- employs a title that suggests a point of view.
- states or suggests a main idea identifying an action that needs to be taken or a belief that should be held—or at the very least, considered.
- often leans heavily on highly emotional language.
- relies a good deal on opinions and uses facts mainly to serve these opinions.
- often expresses a strong emotional tone that reveals the author's personal feelings.
- includes only the reasons for taking an action or holding an opinion; explains why arguments against that action or opinion are not sound.
- frequently includes rhetorical questions that require no answer because the response is obvious.

Strategy 10   Analyze Arguments

Arguments are everywhere in prose. They are most obvious in newspaper editorials, where writers offer an opinion and try to convince readers to share it. But arguments also appear in magazines and on television. They are even in textbooks. However, before you let yourself be convinced by an argument, you need to analyze it. First, filter out the opinion that lies at the heart of the argument. Then evaluate the evidence used to support it. Here to illustrate is an argument against believing in psychics:

> Although a large portion of the American population believes in psychics, there is no hard, scientific evidence that anyone can really predict

the future. In fact, the lack of any relevant proof is a major reason to suspend belief when it comes to those making claims about their extraordinary psychic abilities. Whenever the subject of extrasensory powers comes up, someone usually has a friend or relative who visited a psychic and was astonished to discover how amazingly accurate he or she was! The problem with these stories, however, is that they have never been verified, nor have the predictions been repeated under the eyes of skeptical observers. In fact, those who lay claim to psychic gifts often insist that a skeptic's presence is the real reason why psychics can't prove their powers' existence. In other words, psychics can't offer hard evidence of extrasensory abilities to anyone, who doesn't already believe in their existence. This means that psychics' powers can be tested only by those already inclined to believe these powers exist. No wonder, then, that members of the scientific community are, for the most part, skeptical when it comes to the claims of psychics.

When you spot an argument like this one, you need to immediately start jotting notes in the margin. These notes should reduce the argument to its bare bones: (1) the writer's opinion, (2) the reasons or evidence in support of that opinion, and (3) any response to possible objections (this last element may or may not be present). Here's how the argument in the previous passage breaks down into those three elements:

Opinion	It's a mistake to believe in psychics.
Reason	There is no hard evidence proving their existence.
Response to opposition	Anecdotes don't count because the experiences haven't been repeated before or verified by skeptics.

Let's take aim at the argument above. After all, shouldn't the author tell readers how he knows there's no "hard, scientific evidence." Statements like that need to be *attributed*. That is, the writer needs to give a source or basis, perhaps a reference to a study that reviewed a good deal of research on psychics. Lack of attribution is a common mistake among writers overly determined to persuade, so be on the lookout for this error (as well as those listed on pages 11–12). But before you figure out what's wrong with an argument, you always need to *analyze* it by reducing it to its essential parts as we have done here.

Strategy 11   Be on the Lookout for Errors in Arguments

Eager to argue their point, writers sometimes get carried away, and their reasoning becomes careless. Experienced readers realize how common this is. Therefore, they are always on the lookout for errors like the ones outlined in the chart below:

Error	Definition	Example
Hasty generalization	The writer introduces a broad generalization that applies to large numbers and offers one or two examples as proof.	Our educational system is a disaster. My nephew is in the sixth grade, and he can't write a sentence without making a mistake.
Circular argument	The writer's opinion and reason for holding it are one and the same.	Pit bulls are dangerous animals that should not be kept as pets because they are capable of doing great harm.
Irrelevant reason	The writer supplies a reason. Unfortunately, it isn't related to the topic at hand.	We need to make it much more difficult to obtain a divorce. Look how the divorce rates in Europe are climbing.
Confusing coincidence with cause and effect	Because two events happened around the same time, the writer insists that one caused the other.	Getting a divorce needs to be much more difficult. With the rise in divorce, we've also seen an increase in the number of hyperactive children.
Lack of attribution	The author refers to experts, studies, claims, etc., without giving you any or enough information to check them for yourself.	Studies indicate that children in daycare have higher verbal abilities than those cared for at home.
Overreliance on rhetorical questions	Instead of offering evidence to support an opinion, the author asks questions with obvious answers.	Are we prepared to send our children to schools that have little or no respect for students' individuality?

Error	Definition	Example
Personal attack	The author doesn't support the argument or opinion but instead attacks the opposition.	The governor's arguments against the death penalty are based on nothing but self-interest: He just wants to distract voters from the corruption in his administration.
Appeal to the emotions	The writer doesn't tell you why you should hold a particular opinion. Instead, he or she tries to trigger an emotional response by talking about motherhood, tradition, religion, country, innocent children, etc.	Those demanding an end to the space program need to remember the spirit of adventure on which this country is based.

Strategy 12   Watch for Allusions

Allusions are references to real or fictional people, places, or events that an author uses to create both tone and meaning. For example, Niccolò Machiavelli was a sixteenth-century statesman and writer who suggested that a successful ruler should not be ashamed to pursue power through trickery. Machiavelli's advice apparently made quite an impression. His name is now used to suggest a less than straightforward approach to political behavior. In the sentence that follows, note how the allusions to Abraham Lincoln and Machiavelli serve to give readers a vivid portrait of former president Lyndon Baines Johnson: "*Lincolnesque* in his public statements, Johnson could be positively *Machiavellian* in his behind-the-scenes political maneuvering." While the allusion to Lincoln suggests that Johnson liked to seem honest and forthright in public, the reference to Machiavelli implies that in private Johnson didn't mind using manipulation and trickery to get what he wanted.

Allusions were once used as decorations that showcased the writer's wide learning. But that's no longer how they are employed. Writers now use allusions as a colorful verbal shorthand that calls up a whole set of traits connected to the person, place, or event being mentioned. Make sure you pay attention to any allusions a writer uses.

Strategy 13   Understand the Implications of Similes and Metaphors

Students who take a literature course know that they have to interpret a writer's **similes** (comparisons using the words *like* or *as*) and **metaphors** (implied comparisons). Yet those same students are inclined to skip over similes and metaphors outside the realm of fiction or poetry. And that's a mistake. Writers often use both similes and metaphors to communicate their ideas. For an example, see the brief passage that follows:

> When Scotland was the scene of a horrifying act of school violence in 1996, the immediate reaction was not to make unsubstantiated accusations about the school's failure to protect its children. Instead, there were immediate calls for more gun control—this in a country where guns are about as common as flying pigs. Yet, in fact, the man who killed sixteen children had been the owner of several handguns. The Scots were showing their usual good sense in refusing to draw the most unlikely conclusions and concentrating on the more likely causes of the crime—an unstable man with easy access to an arsenal of weapons.

Skip over the simile that compares the presence of guns in Scotland to the presence of flying pigs, and you are likely to miss the author's point: The Scots in general possess few guns, but if even a few guns are not strictly controlled, tragedy can result. The moral of this story is simple: Don't speed-read when you spot a simile or metaphor. Make sure you understand what the simile or metaphor suggests.

Understanding the Terminology

Here's a list of the terms you'll encounter while answering questions about the readings in parts II and III of this book. Browse through the list and put a check next to any words or phrases you don't already know. Review them in your spare time so you don't have to think twice about their meaning. That will make answering the questions much easier. However, if a term used in a question puzzles you, feel free to refer to these pages.

_____ **Allusions** Allusions are references to people, places, and events. Authors use them to create both tone and meaning. In the following reference, the author alludes to a famous cartoon character to make a point: "She wasn't fooled by his Daffy Duck manner; he was one of the smartest lawyers on Wall Street."

_____ **Attribution** This term refers to the practice of naming the source of a study or claim.

_____ **Bias** Bias in writing reveals the author's personal inclination to favor or criticize a particular idea, action, or event.

____ **Circular reasoning** Writers who employ circular reasoning don't argue their opinions. Instead, they use different words to say the same thing twice.

____ **Connotation** The associations—positive, negative, or neutral—that are attached to a word. For example, the word *muscular* usually has positive connotations: "She had a strong, *muscular* body." The word *musclebound*, however, has negative associations: "Too much weight training had made him *musclebound*." The word *muscle* is almost always neutral in connotation: "She had pulled a *muscle* and was limping."

____ **Denotation** The dictionary meaning of a word. Words that have only a *denotation* carry no emotional impact. The word *table*, for example, can be said over and over without affecting our emotions, whereas the same cannot be said of a word like *love*.

____ **Facts** Statements of fact describe people, things, and events without evaluating or interpreting them. They are not influenced by an author's personal experience or background, and their accuracy can be checked, or verified.

____ **Figurative language** Figurative language makes sense in the imagination rather than in reality. For example, if you say a person "has her head in the clouds," you don't mean her neck and head reach to the sky. You mean that she has a dreamy, impractical nature.

____ **Generalizations** Generalizations sum up or draw conclusions about a number of different, but in some way related, people, places, or events.

____ **Gist** The gist of a reading is the general idea, explained or promoted by the author.

____ **Hasty generalizations** Broad generalizations based on too few examples are considered "hasty."

____ **Icon** In this context, an icon is a graphic symbol used to highlight important material in textbooks.

____ **Implied main idea** The implied main idea of a reading is suggested but not directly stated.

____ **Inappropriate inferences** Inappropriate inferences are conclusions based more on the reader's personal experience than on the author's actual words.

____ **Inferences** Inferences are the conclusions a reader draws about ideas that are implied in a text but not directly stated.

____ **Informative writing** Informative writing describes events or ideas without including personal judgments by the author.

____ **Irony** Writers who use irony say the opposite of what they mean.

____ **Irrelevant evidence** Facts or evidence not related to the idea under discussion.

—— **Metaphor**   Metaphors make comparisons that reveal a hidden similarity between two very different things.

—— **Objective**   Being objective means making judgments without letting your personal bias affect your point of view.

—— **Opinions**   Statements of opinion reflect the author's point of view. Unlike statements of fact, they are shaped by an author's personal experience, training, and background, and they cannot be checked for accuracy.

—— **Paraphrase**   A paraphrase translates an author's ideas into someone else's words without altering or changing the original meaning.

—— **Persuasive writing**   Persuasive writing expresses an opinion that the writer wants readers to share or at least to consider.

—— **Prereading or previewing**   To preread or preview material, look at selected portions of the text before reading it from beginning to end.

—— **Purpose**   An author's purpose is his or her intention in writing. Although there are many reasons why authors write—to criticize, describe, celebrate, amuse, and so on—most of them fall into two general categories: writing to inform or writing to persuade.

—— **Relevant evidence**   Facts or reasons related to the opinion being discussed.

—— **Rhetorical questions**   A question is considered rhetorical when the expected answer is already implied by the person posing the question: "Do you really want to use products that have been tested on suffering animals?"

—— **Similes**   Comparisons using *like* or *as*, similes—like metaphors— reveal an unexpected likeness between two very different things, actions, or ideas.

—— **Slippery slope thinking**   Writers who use this error in logic say that if one event happens, a host of similar but much worse events are bound to follow.

—— **Supporting details**   Supporting details can take many forms. They can be facts, figures, examples, or quotations, but their function is always the same: They anticipate and answer questions readers might have about the reading.

—— **Synthesizing**   In the process of synthesizing, readers find a way to link or connect different sources that discuss the same topic.

—— **Thesis statement**   Thesis statements function like topic sentences but they sum up an entire reading rather than a single paragraph.

____ **Tone** Like tone of voice in speaking, tone in writing is the author's way of expressing his or her attitude toward a particular subject. Depending on the audience and subject matter, a writer's tone can range widely. The same writer can be angry or sarcastic in one context and humorous or lighthearted in another.

____ **Topic sentence** General sentences that sum up the point of a paragraph are called topic sentences.

____ **Transitions**   Transitions are words, phrases, and sentences that signal how the writer's train of thought will develop.

Part II

Strategy Tune-Up

Here are a series of exercises designed to give you practice with the strategies you'll need in order to answer questions about the readings in Part III.

Practice 1

Use Questions to Discover Main Ideas in Paragraphs

Directions: Circle the appropriate letters to identify the topics and main ideas.

1. Tonics—medicines, or remedies believed to have an invigorating effect—were extremely popular throughout the nineteenth century. Magazines of the day were filled with ads touting the effectiveness of tonics for various needs, from restoring hair to eliminating headaches. Although the ads certainly helped, there is probably another, more critical reason why tonics were so in demand: The major ingredient in most of them was alcohol. Some tonics were 80 proof. The high alcohol count may well explain the number of testimonials offered by tonic users. People who swallowed a tonic for, say, depressed spirits or low energy probably did feel more sprightly, at least temporarily. They felt better the same way most people feel better after having a double shot of bourbon. Of course, once the effect of the tonic wore off, those who celebrated its medicinal effects probably had a serious hangover and no particular improvement in their medical condition.

What topic is repeatedly referred to in the paragraph?

   a. medicine in the nineteenth century

   b. bogus remedies for ailments

   c. nineteenth-century tonics

Which idea about the topic gets the most explanation or development?

   a. The nineteenth century was a time when medicine was in its infancy and people believed some ridiculous claims about diseases and their cures.

   b. Nineteenth-century tonics were probably popular not because they did any real good but because they had a high alcohol content.

   c. In the nineteenth century, those who took a tonic in order to improve their health probably ended up with a bad headache.

2. In public and private, John Adams, the second president of the United States, showed the greatest respect for his clever and spirited wife, Abigail. But even though Adams doted on his wife, he wasn't about to let his respect for Abigail's advice influence his attitude toward women's rights. When John was away drafting the Declaration of Independence, Abigail wrote with a request that he "remember the

ladies." Although Abigail distrusted eighteenth-century females who were more interested in politics than family, she still wanted to make sure that women got a share of the new freedoms being promoted by her husband and his fellow rebels. As she wrote to him, "Do not put such unlimited power into the hands of the Husbands. Remember all Men would be tyrants if they could." Abigail even warned John that women would stir up a rebellion if their rights were not acknowledged by direct reference in the Declaration of Independence. John wrote back that her suggestions only made him laugh and that, in any case, women were the more powerful sex and in no particular need of his or anyone else's aid. When the Declaration of Independence was finished, it only made reference to men's need for "Life, Liberty, and the Pursuit of Happiness."

What topic is repeatedly referred to in the paragraph?

a. John Adams

b. the marriage of Abigail and John Adams

c. Abigail's advice to John Adams

Which idea about the topic gets the most explanation or development?

a. For most of their long marriage, Abigail Adams was her husband's closest political adviser.

b. John Adams may have loved Abigail, but he wasn't necessarily interested in her advice about promoting the rights of women.

c. Like most other men of the eighteenth century, John Adams did not take the issue of women's rights very seriously.

3. Following World War I, Congress awarded veterans of the war a bonus payable in 1945. However, when the United States went into a deep economic depression in the thirties, desperate veterans marched on Washington, asking President Hoover to grant that their bonuses be paid early. What's come to be known as the Bonus March seemed to be officially over on June 17, 1932, when Congress refused the veterans' request and most of the ex-soldiers went home. Some five thousand, however, remained and refused to leave. Instead, they set up makeshift tents and camped out to protest their treatment by the government they had served. A few even took over an abandoned Treasury building. By the end of July, Washington authorities were sick of the situation, and they called on the police to evict the veterans, many of whom reacted with

outrage. Shots were fired and two demonstrators were killed. When the police commissioner then asked the federal government for help, President Hoover sent in army troops, including a machine-gun detachment. The troops set fire to the tents. Outraged, the veterans attacked the soldiers. Although no one died in the melee, many veterans received bayonet wounds. Widely blamed for his mishandling of the Bonus Marchers, President Hoover lost his bid for reelection.

What topic is repeatedly referred to in the paragraph?

a. Herbert Hoover's presidency

b. the treatment of World War I veterans

c. Herbert Hoover's treatment of the Bonus Marchers

Which idea about the topic gets the most explanation and development?

a. After World War I, veterans of the war were promised a huge bonus; unfortunately, they couldn't receive it until 1945.

b. Hoover's mishandling of the Bonus March led to violence and bloodshed that probably cost him the presidency.

c. When the U.S. veterans of World War I asked for their bonuses to be paid early, they expected the government to fulfill their request.

4. Most people would probably say that the mass vaccination of children against diseases such as measles and mumps is a huge medical success story. But Barbara Loe Fisher, president of the National Vaccine Information Center, is more cautious, arguing that parents need to be better informed about the possible side effects of childhood vaccinations. Although Fisher acknowledges that vaccines have caused a huge decline in the rate of childhood infectious diseases, she also points out that there has been a simultaneous doubling in the number of children with asthma and learning disabilities. While she does not maintain that the connection between the two is certain, she does believe that the possibility of a connection should be investigated. Fisher is concerned as well that reactions to the vaccines have seldom been studied, mainly because the numbers are not high and doctors don't always report all complaints. Consequently, the Food and Drug Administration is unlikely to spend the money to pursue the potential risks of mass vaccination. Yet Fisher, whose own child went into a convulsion and shock after receiving a vaccination, is determined to change the situation. She believes that parents need to be given more information about the

potential risks of vaccination so they can make informed decisions. As she puts it, her organization is "pro-education and pro-informed consent, not antivaccine."

(*Source of information:* Arthur Allen, "A Shot in the Dark," *New York Times Magazine,* May 5, 2001, p. 31.)

What topic is repeatedly referred to in the paragraph?

   a. the potential risks of vaccinations

   b. National Vaccine Information Center

   c. the Food and Drug Administration's handling of vaccine reactions

Which idea about the topic gets the most explanation and development?

   a. Although many believe mass vaccinations against childhood diseases are a necessity, Barbara Loe Fisher, president of the National Vaccine Information Center, insists they are not because vaccinations can cause reactions that in some cases leave children with serious illnesses.

   b. Although many people believe mass vaccinations against childhood diseases are a boon to children, Barbara Loe Fisher, president of the National Vaccine Information Center, insists parents need to know about the risks along with the benefits.

   c. Although mass vaccinations against childhood diseases have caused a decline in the rate of childhood infectious diseases, Barbara Loe Fisher insists that the risks far outweigh the benefits.

5. For thousands of years, malaria was a mysterious and lethal disease. Doctors theorized that the foul air rising from swamps caused the disease, but they were never able to prove their theory. It wasn't until the close of the nineteenth century that a group of physicians began to understand malaria's true causes. The unraveling of malaria's mystery started with French physician Charles Alphonse Laveran, whose studies of the disease led him to believe that mosquitoes might transmit malarial agents (later called *Plasmodium vivax*). Then, on August 19, 1894, British physician Ronald Ross killed two mosquitoes that had been feeding on the blood of patients infected with malaria. When he examined the insects, he found that the two were indeed malaria carriers. But it would take another physician, Italian zoologist G. B. Grassi, to discover that only one mosquito, the female *Anopheles*, was responsible for spreading the disease far and wide. Because the female *Anopheles* requires blood every seventy-two hours as nourishment for her

eggs, she'll fly great distances in search of a meal. Thus, the *Anopheles*, roaming over large areas, is able to infect equally large numbers of people. Unfortunately, despite the discoveries of Laveran, Ross, and Grassi, control of malaria remains difficult because mosquitoes continuously become immune to the insecticides used to kill them.

What topic is repeatedly referred to in the paragraph?

    a. the symptoms of malaria

    b. the history of malaria

    c. the cause of malaria

Which idea about the topic gets the most explanation and development?

    a. Because the mosquitoes that spread malaria have become immune to the insecticides used to destroy them, the disease is still a threat to millions of people all over the world.

    b. Thanks to G. B. Grassi, we now know how malaria is spread; unfortunately, knowing the cause has not ended the disease's threat.

    c. Because of the work of three different doctors from three different countries, we at least now know how malaria is spread.

Practice 2

Use Questions to Discover Main Ideas in Longer Readings

Directions: Circle the appropriate letters to identify the topics and main ideas.

1. Tracking Cell Phone Users

One obvious benefit of carrying a cell phone is the ability to exchange information with others in a timely manner. Witnesses to an accident, for instance, can instantly call for police officers and ambulances. When people get lost or in trouble, they can notify someone immediately. Indeed, about half of all 911 emergency calls now come from cell phones.

Nonetheless, as far back as 1996, the Federal Communications Commission (FCC) saw a problem beginning to emerge. Although cell phones allowed people to call 911 emergency services right away, these callers could not always report exactly *where* they were. As a result, the FCC mandated that by 2005 wireless communication carriers must develop systems that can tell emergency dispatchers the location of cell phone callers to within a maximum of 150 meters. These new cell phone tracking systems will eventually provide some advantages; however, they also bring with them a few unintentional, but disturbing, disadvantages.

The ability to pinpoint a cell phone's location will certainly help emergency personnel find people in trouble. Many emergency dispatchers listen helplessly to cell phone callers' pleas for help but are unable to pinpoint the callers' locations. Recently, for example, four young people in a boat lost in the mists of Long Island Sound pleaded for help over a cell phone. Rescuers, however, could not locate them, and all four perished.

In response to tragedies like this one, wireless communication companies have begun embedding chips into new cell phones that can read coordinates from the network of satellites that make up the military's global positioning system (GPS). When a caller dials 911, the chip inside the phone searches for the closest satellites, which then provide the caller's latitude and longitude. This information is relayed to the 911 dispatch system, giving emergency personnel more details about the caller's whereabouts. Consequently, police, firefighters, and paramedics can sometimes find people who might otherwise have been lost. In Rhode Island, for example, the Coast Guard has been able to locate several boaters when their cell phones identified their locations. If city maps have been updated with accurate geographic coordinates, the data from cell phones can be translated into street addresses and directions.

Cell phone tracking systems also give parents the ability to track their children's whereabouts. Already, location services that provide kids with GPS bracelets are increasing in popularity in Europe, Japan, and China. In the near future, American parents may be able to monitor their children's locations from afar simply by giving them cell phones.

Yet despite improving 911 response and increasing parents' peace of mind, cell phone tracking systems have also raised concerns about the drawbacks of developing tracking technologies. Although the wireless communication companies claim that their tracking systems work only when a caller dials 911, the American Civil Liberties Union (ACLU) fears that this technology will some day allow the government to monitor the activities of American citizens. Other groups are concerned that tracking systems will allow corporations to manipulate consumers by sending them ads and information based on their nearness to stores or restaurants. Privacy organizations say that law enforcement officials and attorneys will want to gather information about an individual's whereabouts to settle legal cases. In short, people will be able to find each other. And like it or not, court orders may begin to override the right to privacy. Of course, cell phone companies respond to these concerns by reminding consumers that if they don't want to be tracked they can simply turn off their cell phones.

Inevitably, the new tracking technologies will be more widely used in the coming years. Only time will tell if the advantages will outweigh the disadvantages.

(*Source of information:* David LaGesse, "They Know Where You Are," *U.S. News & World Report,* September 8, 2003, p. 32.)

What topic is repeatedly referred to in the reading?

a. the Federal Communications Commission

b. cell phone tracking systems

c. cell phones

Which idea about the topic gets the most explanation and development?

a. Cell phones have made it easier to rescue accident victims.

b. The new tracking technologies for cell phones are plagued by problems.

c. The new cell phone tracking systems have the potential for positive and negative consequences.

2. **The Question of Gay Marriage**

Should gay and lesbian people be permitted to marry? Polls consistently show that our nation is split in half over this issue. Forty-eight percent of those surveyed believe that society will deteriorate if homosexuals are permitted to marry. Fifty percent, however, say that allowing homosexual marriages will improve society or have no ill effect. In fact, among Americans ages 18 to 29, there is a striking amount of support in favor of gay marriage; 67 percent in this age group believe that denying gay people the right to marry is to challenge the democratic traditions on which the country is based.

Opponents of gay marriage argue that gay marriages would destroy the moral foundation upon which our society was built. In response, supporters contend that it seems even more immoral to deny gay people their civil rights because of prejudice. Those who advocate gay unions say that when gay and lesbian citizens are denied the right to marry, they are being discriminated against based on their sexual orientation, a practice that is illegal and unethical. Advocates of gay marriage point out that our democracy guarantees all citizens equal rights; therefore, homosexuals should not be denied the rewards and benefits of marriage enjoyed by heterosexuals. Regardless of sexual orientation, everyone should receive equal protection under the law, including the right to legally marry.

Those who support gay marriage argue that it actually strengthens society's moral foundation rather than destroying it. Marriage encourages individuals to settle down and evolve into responsible, productive members of the community. Therefore, advocates claim, society benefits when homosexuals are encouraged to form permanent unions just as heterosexuals do.

Finally, supporters of gay marriage have pointed out that religious arguments in support of heterosexual-only marriage cannot be applied to this debate. They argue that gay marriage is a matter for the state. Because the U.S. Constitution mandates the separation of church and state, state governments cannot deny citizens their rights based on religious justifications.

Half of all Americans and two-thirds of all young people polled are no longer willing to deny that gay people have the right to marry. As a result, it is very possible that in the future more and more states will begin to allow gays to legally marry.

(*Source of information:* Cathy Lynn Grossman, "Public Opinion Is Divided on Gay Marriages," *USA Today,* October 7, 2003, p. 21A.)

What topic is repeatedly referred to in the reading?

   a. civil rights for homosexuals

   b. homosexual marriage

   c. discrimination against homosexuals

Which idea about the topic gets the most explanation and development?

   a. Opponents of gay marriage insist that homosexual unions will lead to our society's moral decay.

   b. The strongest supporters of homosexual marriage argue that denying gay people the right to marry undermines our democratic traditions.

   c. Polls indicate that gay marriage arouses a good deal of controversy all across the nation.

Practice 3

Look for Topic Sentences That Summarize Main Ideas in Paragraphs

Directions: Read each paragraph. Identify the topic sentence and then decide which statement better paraphrases the main idea.

1. ¹ When royal families make the news these days, it's often for bad or embarrassing reasons. ² Revelations about the less-than-proper behavior of Queen Elizabeth's children and their mates or lovers seem to be a staple of the British media. ³ Similarly, the tabloid press has been covering the shenanigans of the children of Prince Rainier III of Monaco for decades and the Dutch press has recently reported on an heir to the throne who was in love with a mobster's ex-girlfriend. ⁴ But noteworthy exceptions to royal misbehavior are the conduct of King Juan Carlos of Spain and of his wife, Queen Sofia. ⁵ When Francisco Franco, the military dictator who had ruled Spain with an iron fist, selected Juan Carlos as his successor, the Spanish people expected little from the new king because he appeared weak and had lived in impoverished conditions in Rome, Italy. ⁶ But the king did not seek absolute power—he was, in fact, an advocate of a constitutional monarchy, where all political power rests with a democratically elected parliament and the king has only ceremonial functions. ⁷ When Franco's former allies attempted to block the move to a constitutional monarchy in 1981, the king himself rallied the troops in defense of democracy. ⁸ Such actions earned Juan Carlos the everlasting admiration of his subjects.

Topic Sentence _____

Paraphrase

   a. When it comes to the king of Spain, not all the news about royalty is bad.

   b. The media are obsessed with royal families and how they behave.

2. ¹ Tim Berners-Lee invented the tools that form the basis for the World Wide Web (WWW), which is generally known now as "the Web." ² Many believe that the Web's importance may equal that of the printing press. ³ One would assume, then, that his invention brought Berners-Lee fame and fortune—but this is not the case. ⁴ To this day, Berners-Lee has never sought to make money from his ideas, and his name is known mostly to computer experts. ⁵ He created the technology that makes the WWW possible while working as

a consultant for a Swiss firm in the 1980s. [6] Yet, he never claimed ownership of that technology—rather, it is available to everybody for free. [7] Nor did Berners-Lee ever seek the limelight. [8] He later worked at the Massachusetts Institute of Technology in the unglamorous position of director of the WWW Consortium.

Topic Sentence _____

Paraphrase

   a. Thanks to Tim Berners-Lee, the World Wide Web has revolutionized our society in a number of ways.

   b. The inventor of the World Wide Web never became famous or rich because of his invention.

3. [1] Most psychologists no longer believe in the theories promoted by the Viennese physician Sigmund Freud. [2] Yet Freud's theories about the mind and its ills have had a lasting impact on language, and many Freudian concepts have entered everyday speech. [3] It was Freud who first formally outlined the notion of "unconscious" feelings and desires that are hidden from the conscious mind. [4] A *Freudian slip* is a verbal mistake that seems to be accidental yet manages to reveal ideas hidden in the speaker's unconscious mind. [5] Because of Freud, we use the term *repression* when a person unconsciously hides desires or memories from the conscious mind. [6] We also speak of *sublimation,* meaning that someone has translated an unacceptable feeling like sexual attraction toward a family member into a more acceptable form, say a passion for music. [7] One of the most often encountered terms used by Freud is *ego,* which has come to generally denote a person's sense of identity and self-worth.

Topic Sentence _____

Paraphrase

   a. Freud had a lasting influence on our language.

   b. Psychoanalysts do not generally rely on Freudian terminology.

4. [1] Muhammad Ali is perhaps the best-known and best-liked athlete in the world today. [2] But it took a long time for Ali to become a hero. [3] Although he won a gold medal at the Olympics in 1960, the experts didn't think Ali's boxing skills were good enough for a successful career—he did too many things "wrong." [4]Nobody expected him to beat Sonny Liston in the 1964 title fight for the heavyweight crown. When he did, some called it a fluke. [5]Later that year, he offended many by giving up what he called his "slave name" (Cassius Clay) and became a Muslim. [6]Others took exception to Ali's self-promotion and his flippant sense of humor. [7]And then in 1967, Ali refused to join the U.S. Army to serve in the Vietnam War, which he considered ethically wrong. [8]The government prosecuted him for draft evasion, and the boxing commission took his title away. [9]In 1971 the Supreme Court reversed that decision, but by then, Ali had lost more than three years of his career at a time when he was at his prime. [10]Still, Ali accepted all of this with grace. [11]He never sued the government or boxing commission, and over time he reestablished himself as "the Greatest" through a series of extraordinary matches. [12]It is precisely the combination of superior boxing skills, engaging personality, and moral conviction that has earned Ali the admiration of the world.

Topic Sentence _____

Paraphrase

    a. Muhammad Ali was poorly treated by the U.S. government and the boxing commission.

    b. Muhammad Ali reached the current level of admiration only after a long struggle.

5. [1]Among the great inventors who changed modern life forever, the inventor of television, Philo T. Farnsworth, remains mostly unknown to the present day. [2]Farnsworth's anonymity was a result of several factors. [3]For one, Farnsworth, "Philo" to his friends, had few backers and worked out of his own, small laboratory. [4]He obtained patents for his invention, but when the Radio Corporation of America (RCA) planned to manufacture TV sets in the 1930s, it refused to recognize the patents or to pay royalties to Farnsworth. [5]RCA lost the ensuing, lengthy lawsuits, but World War II started soon after; with the outbreak of war, the production of TV sets was halted by the U.S. government. [6]After the war ended, RCA began to market TV sets in earnest. [7]Because Farnsworth's patents had expired, the company promoted some of its employees as the inventors of TV in an extensive public relations campaign. [8]Why didn't Farnsworth respond with his own promotion? [9]He lacked the means, but perhaps more important, he actually didn't like what he saw on TV and forbade its use in his own family. [10]As a result, he died virtually unknown.

Topic Sentence _____

Paraphrase

   a. Philo T. Farnsworth may have invented television, but like Dr. Frankenstein, he wasn't particularly pleased by his creation.

   b. There are several reasons why Philo T. Farnsworth, the inventor of television, remains an obscure figure.

Practice 4

Look for Topic Sentences That Summarize Main Ideas in Paragraphs

Directions: Read each paragraph. Identify the topic sentence and then decide which of the three statements is the best paraphrase.

1. [1]The term *flying saucer* originated with a story pilot Kenneth Arnold told when he returned from a flight that took him over the area around Mount Rainier, Washington, on June 24, 1947. [2]After he had landed, Arnold told airport personnel that during the flight he suddenly noticed a flash of light. [3] When he turned in the direction of the flash, he saw nine silvery objects flying "like a saucer would if you skipped it across the water." [4] When word got out about his story, Arnold was mobbed by reporters wanting to know more about his experience. [5]The term *flying saucers* subsequently appeared in the headline of a newspaper story, and the name took off. [6]As a result of the stories, spotting flying saucers became all the rage; in 1947 alone, more than 850 sightings were reported. [7]In response, the U.S. Air Force felt compelled to launch Project Saucer, which aimed at investigating these reports scientifically.

Topic Sentence _____

Paraphrase

   a. The existence of flying saucers has been confirmed by more than 850 sightings.

   b. The term *flying saucer* derives from the experience of a pilot flying near Mount Rainier in 1947.

   c. Flying saucers are an invention of newspapers.

2. [1]The first astronaut was not a human, but a dog. [2]Her name was Laika, and she was launched into orbit inside a spacecraft as part of the space program of the former Soviet Union. [3]Scientists wanted to find out how space travel affects living creatures, with the ultimate goal of making it safe for people. [4]While in space, Laika was nourished by feeding devices, and her vital signs were monitored and transmitted back to Earth. [5]She died after a week when the oxygen supply of her spacecraft ran out. [6]In fact, Soviet scientists had never planned to get Laika back to Earth safely because they hadn't yet discovered how to do so. [7]In response to worldwide protests, the researchers announced that Laika was never uncomfortable and died painlessly, but few believed the Soviets' claims.

Topic Sentence _____

Paraphrase

    a. A dog was the first living creature to travel in space.

    b. Soviet scientists were irresponsible in letting a dog die in space for lack of oxygen.

    c. The first "astronaut" died during her flight.

3. [1]After the 1941 attack on Pearl Harbor by the Japanese, the U.S. government ordered the army to round up all persons of Japanese ancestry living on the West Coast and hold them in detention camps. [2]The assumption was that any one of these people, regardless of gender, age, or citizenship, was a threat to the security of the country. [3]When asked to register as an American of Japanese ancestry, Gordon Hirabayashi, an American-born U.S. citizen and student at the University of Washington, tried to protest this treatment. [4]Despite a curfew, he appeared with his lawyer at the Seattle FBI office and argued that the registration order was racist and violated his rights under the Constitution. [5]He was promptly arrested and held in jail for five months before he was tried. [6]In court, even the judge showed an open bias for the prosecution, and Hirabayashi was convicted for refusing to register and for breaking curfew. [7]Upon appeal in 1943, the Supreme Court admitted that the detention order was racially motivated, but nevertheless upheld Hirabayashi's conviction. [8]His name was not fully cleared until 1987, when an appellate court ruled that his conviction was based on prejudice rather than military necessity. [9]As the Hirabayashi case shows, wartime hysteria can lead to mistakes at every level of law enforcement.

Topic Sentence _____

Paraphrase

   a. Gordon Hirabayashi was treated unfairly by the courts.

   b. The treatment of U.S. citizens of Japanese ancestry was appalling during World War II.

   c. Hysteria during time of war can cause law enforcement agencies to make mistakes.

4. [1] The "unsinkable" luxury liner *Titanic* sank on April 15, 1912, after hitting an iceberg at full speed. [2] The accepted explanation was that the impact with the iceberg opened a big hole in the ship's hull, causing the ship to flood and ultimately to break into two halves that slid into the icy ocean less than three hours after impact. [3] In 1985, an expedition team found the two pieces standing 2,000 feet apart on the ocean floor under 13,000 feet of water. [4] But photographs showed no sign of a big hole in either half. [5] This new evidence led naval engineers to propose a second explanation for the *Titanic's* sinking. [6] According to their analysis, the ship's hull was made of low-grade steel plates that were likely to become brittle in cold water. [7] The impact with the iceberg caused some plates to fracture, which led to the flooding and ultimate breakup of the hull. [8] The engineers concluded that better material and construction techniques might have prevented the disaster or at least delayed the breakup so that more passengers and crew could have been saved.

Topic Sentence _____

Paraphrase

   a. The discovery of wreckage from the *Titanic* led to a new theory about the cause of its breakup.

   b. We will never know what really caused the *Titanic* to sink.

   c. The safety of ships depends on better construction methods and materials.

5. [1] Roswell, New Mexico, is a mecca for ufologists, people who believe in flying saucers and other unidentified flying objects. [2] It all started in 1947, when—after a night of storm and thunder—Mac Brazel, a local rancher, went out to check on his sheep and found a field strewn with wreckage that looked as if a strange type of aircraft had crashed there. [3] Brazel called in the sheriff, who then called in the military to investigate. [4]Army officials gave several explanations for the incident over the years. [5]Unfortunately, the army's explanations about what happened at Roswell are contradictory, which is the main reason why many ufologists believe to this day that what Brazel found in 1947 were the remainders of a spaceship. [6]Three weeks after the event, the army issued a statement confirming that the wreckage was that of a flying saucer. [7]Shortly afterwards, an army spokesman retracted the earlier statement and claimed instead that the wreckage belonged to a conventional weather balloon. [8]In 1978, a physicist and a writer interviewed witnesses of the 1947 events and found gaps in the army's report. [9]A general was even quoted as saying that the weather balloon story was invented only to "get the press off our backs." [10]The government started a new investigation of the Roswell incident in 1994 and promptly came up with yet another theory. [11]This time, officials claimed that the wreckage came neither from a flying saucer nor from a weather balloon, but from a surveillance balloon used in a top-secret project. [12]It was this need for secrecy that had caused the army to launch the earlier stories. [13]But by then, ufologists were asking themselves, Why should we believe the army this time?

Topic Sentence _____

Paraphrase

  a. Roswell, New Mexico, will ultimately give us the key to understanding UFOs.

  b. People who believe that Roswell was the site of a UFO landing refused to look at all the evidence that undermines their belief.

  c. Because the army offered different versions of what happened in Roswell, believers in UFOs are convinced to this day that a UFO landed there.

Practice 5

Look for Thesis Statements That Summarize Main Ideas in Longer Readings

Directions: Circle the appropriate letter to identify the thesis statement.

1. Where's the Justice?

Next time you are feeling sorry for yourself and think the world is being brutally unfair, stop whining and consider the case of Joseph Amrine, who sits on death row, hoping against hope for a pardon.

In 1985, Amrine was convicted by an all-white jury of killing a fellow prisoner at what was then the Missouri State Penitentiary. Those who were once witnesses against Amrine now say he didn't do it. Moreover, new witnesses have identified another inmate as the real killer. In addition, at least three of the twelve jurors who originally convicted Amrine now believe he is innocent. Yet if Amrine doesn't receive a pardon, he may well be executed, even though, in the words of the *St. Louis Post-Dispatch*, "no evidence is left standing against him."

When the witnesses who originally helped convict Amrine came forward to say they had made a mistake, a federal judge ruled that the witnesses were not credible. These same witnesses were believable enough to get Amrine convicted, but they apparently weren't credible enough to set him free. How's that for legal logic? A three-judge panel also discounted evidence from new witnesses who claim to have seen another prisoner commit the crime for which Amrine was convicted. According to the judges, the new testimony could have been discovered during the original trial but wasn't. Therefore, it doesn't count now. The judges also admit that Amrine might be innocent—but the law's the law.

Think this story can't get any worse? Think again. Panel members generally agreed that Amrine's public defender did a bad job defending him: The lawyer didn't introduce evidence to challenge the prosecution's witnesses, and he failed to interview and prepare defense witnesses. Yet the judges' criticism of the public defender, like all the other evidence that indicates Amrine's innocence, doesn't seem to count because the courts say it doesn't. Joseph Amrine's only hope is that Missouri's pro–death penalty governor ignores the courts and gives him a pardon.*

(*Source of information:* Dave Lindorff, "Too Late to Stop the Hangman?" www.salon.com/news/feature/2002/02/20/amrine.)

Thesis Statement

a. Next time you are feeling sorry for yourself and think the world is being brutally unfair, stop whining and consider the case of Joseph Amrine, who sits on death row, hoping against hope for a pardon.

b. When the witnesses who originally helped convict Amrine came forward to say they had made a mistake, a federal judge ruled that the witnesses were not credible.

c. Joseph Amrine's only hope is that Missouri's pro–death penalty governor ignores the courts and gives him a pardon.

*Joseph Amrine is now a free man.

2. Classifying the Martial Arts

Martial arts can be described and classified in many different ways. Some people categorize them by their country of origin (Japan, China, or Korea). Others categorize martial arts according to style: either striking vs. grappling or hard vs. soft. Martial arts can also be categorized as internal or external. External martial arts are those that rely upon the body's physical parts—the strength, power, and movement of muscles and bones. Karate and tae kwon do, both of which include kicks and punches, are considered to be external martial arts. Internal martial arts are those that rely upon an individual's inner qualities, such as timing, focus, and awareness. Tai chi and aikido are examples of internal martial arts. Neither type is better than the other, and both are effective martial art forms.

A comparison of karate, an external martial art, and aikido, an internal martial art, reveals the major differences between the two different types. The fundamental distinction is in how each type uses force. External martial artists use force against force. In karate, opponents strike at each other directly to stop an attack. They are taught to tense their muscles when striking, both to better absorb the impact of a blow and to cause more damage to the opponent. In contrast, internal martial artists do not meet an opposing force with more force. Instead, they redirect an opponent's attack. In aikido, for example, the martial artist blends with the attack and uses an opponent's body weight and momentum against him or her.

These two different views of force result in different kinds of training and techniques. The external martial arts focus on power from the outside. For example, a student of karate focuses on concentrating the body's power. Training is hard and includes practice in delivering explosive kicks and punches with speed and force. The internal martial arts, on the other hand, focus on power from the inside. Thus, aikido training is more slow, deliberate, and relaxed. The student focuses on developing a calm union of mind and body that allows the martial artist to make conscious, efficient movements.

Finally, the two schools differ in their philosophies and goals. An expert in karate believes in fighting and struggling against an opposing force. This art was originally designed for lethal hand-to-hand combat, based on the theory of "one strike, one kill." The goal of karate, then, is to win by destroying one's opponent. However, the aikido follower believes in acceptance instead of struggle. Instead of fighting, he or she yields to overcome force. The goal is to win without fighting at all.

Thesis Statement

   a. Martial arts can be described and classified in many different ways.

   b. Martial arts can be categorized as internal or external.

   c. The internal martial arts are those that rely on individual's inner qualities such as timing, focus, and awareness.

Practice 6

Identify the Questions Answered by Supporting Details

Directions: For each passage, circle the letter of the correct main idea. Then circle the letter of the question that is *not* answered by the supporting details.

1. Gambling researchers say that of the estimated 8 million compulsive gamblers in the United States, fully 1 million are teenagers. Most live far from casinos, so they favor sports betting, card playing, and lotteries. Once bitten by the gambling bug, many later move on to casinos and racetrack betting. "We have always seen compulsive gambling as a problem of older people," says Jean Falzon, the executive director of the National Council on Problem Gambling, based in New York City. "Now we are finding that adolescent compulsive gambling is far more pervasive than we had thought." Just ten years ago, teenage gambling did not register even a blip on the roster of social ills. Today gambling counselors say an average of 7 percent of their caseloads involve teenagers. New studies indicate that teenage vulnerability to compulsive gambling hits every economic stratum and ethnic group. After surveying 2,700 high school students in four states, California psychologist Durand Jacobs concluded that students are 2½ times as likely as adults to become problem gamblers. In another study, Henry Lesieur, a sociologist at St. John's University in New York, found eight times as many gambling addicts among college students as among adults.

(*Source of information:* Ricardo Chavira, "The Rise of Teenage Gambling," *Time*, February 25, 1991, p. 78.)

Main Idea

   a. Overall, teenagers make up the majority of compulsive gamblers.

   b. Compulsive gambling among teenagers has become a serious problem.

Which question is *not* anticipated and answered by the supporting details?

    a. What research suggests that teenage gambling is a serious problem?

    b. What causes a teenager to become a compulsive gambler?

    c. Has compulsive gambling always been a problem among teenagers?

2. Music, sacred or otherwise, pervaded every walk of twelfth-century life, although very little survives, and what does is so poorly preserved that we can only guess at how it should be played. Nevertheless, we do have examples of the hymns that were sung in churches, the songs that were sung by soldiers, and the multipart songs that originated in Wales and were sung for pleasure in castles and manor houses. Carols had not yet become purely associated with Christmas but were sung and danced to celebrate a variety of holy days and even the coming of spring. *Sirventes* were songs of a satirical nature, often only of topical interest, which is why they too were rarely written down, but they were highly popular.

(Adapted from Alison Weir, *Eleanor of Aquitaine: A Life,* p. 112.)

Main Idea

    a. In the twelfth century, music seemed to be everywhere.

    b. Sacred music was an essential part of daily life in the twelfth century.

Which question is *not* anticipated and answered by the supporting details?

    a. What kind of music pervaded every aspect of twelfth-century life?

    b. Where was the music of the twelfth century played or sung?

    c. Who were the great musicians of the twelfth century?

3. Fears about terrorism are likely to encourage the use of a sweeping eavesdropping system called Echelon. Echelon is the National Security Agency's top-secret global wiretapping network. It was developed, and is now operated, as a joint effort by the U.S. National Security Agency and the intelligence operations of England, Canada, Australia, and New Zealand. For a long time, there were rumors about Echelon's enormous surveillance capabilities, but many people doubted its existence. However, a report by the European Parliament in July of 2001 confirmed that Echelon is real and that it is capable of intercepting just about any telephone conversation, e-mail, Internet connection, or fax worldwide. Reportedly, Echelon works like a global police scanner that searches out the presence of specific key words like *bomb* or *hijack*.

Main Idea

   a. Anxious about the threat of terrorism, we may be forced to illegally invade the privacy of U.S. citizens.

   b. Due to fears about terrorism, the surveillance system called Echelon may be put to greater use than ever before.

Which question is *not* anticipated and answered by the supporting details?

   a. What is Echelon?

   b. How will Echelon affect our civil rights?

   c. Who controls Echelon?

4. Medieval society was strictly ordered: Serfs* and peasants served their masters, while their masters served greater lords and ladies, and everyone served the king. Within this feudal system, the wife—no matter what her social station—was obedient to her husband. As the thirteenth-century English jurist Henry de Bracton formulated it, a woman was obliged to obey her husband in everything, as long as he did not order her to do something in violation of Divine Law. Bracton relates a case in which a wife and husband forged a royal document. Although the husband was hanged, the wife was acquitted on the grounds that she had simply followed her husband's orders. Both French and English law went so far as to declare that a woman who killed her husband should be tried for treason, rather than the lesser crime of felony, since she had taken the life of her lord and master. In other words, a woman who attacked her husband was also attacking the nation.

(Adapted from Marilyn Yalom, *A History of the Wife*. New York: Perennial Books, 2001, p. 46.)

Main Idea

   a. During medieval times, it was acceptable for a husband to use physical punishment as a way of controlling his wife.

   b. Medieval society observed a strict hierarchical order that extended to the relations between husband and wife.

*Serfs: agricultural laborers owned by the person in possession of the property on which the serfs worked.

Which question is *not* anticipated and answered by the supporting details?

    a. How did the hierarchical organization of medieval society affect marital relations?

    b. How do we know that the medieval belief in hierarchy extended even to marriage?

    c. How did women feel about being in a strictly hierarchical relationship with men as their rulers?

5. The fast-food industry is at least partially responsible for the sharp increase in the number of obese Americans. In 1970, Americans ate $6 billion worth of burgers, French fries, and other fast-food items. By 2000, that figure had soared to $110 billion. At the same time, obesity rates have gone through the roof. Today, 61 percent of adults are either overweight or obese, and the number of obese children has tripled since 1970. Obviously, the trend to "super-size" fast-food portions is at least partly to blame for this obesity epidemic. One fast-food meal can contain 1,600 calories, which is more than many people should consume in an entire day. Fast-food restaurants are encouraging Americans to become fat by providing them with too many calories at once.

Main Idea

    a. The super-sizing of food portions is occurring throughout the fast-food industry.

    b. Thanks to the consumption of calorie-rich fast food, Americans are experiencing an obesity explosion.

Which question is *not* anticipated and answered by the supporting details?

    a. What portion of the American population is obese?

    b. Why did the fast-food industry decide to super-size portions?

    c. How has the fast-food industry contributed to obesity in America?

Practice 7

Be Ready to Draw Inferences

Directions: Circle the letter of the main idea implied by the paragraph.

1. According to a 2002 Harris poll, 96 percent of Americans feel good about their relations with their families, while 93 percent are satisfied with their homes. The poll also revealed that 88 percent of

Americans feel good about their social lives, 86 percent feel good about their health, and 84 percent are content with their standard of living. Some 82 percent are satisfied with the city or town in which they live. And a whopping 92 percent of Americans report feeling positive about the overall quality of their lives.

(*Source of information:* Humphrey Taylor, "The Harris Poll Annual 'Feel Good Index,'" July 3, 2002, www.harrisinteractive.com/harris_poll/index.asp?PID=309.)

Implied Main Idea

a. A recent Harris poll indicates that most Americans are happy with their lives.

b. A recent Harris poll suggests that Americans would not change anything about their lives.

2. If you want to catch someone in a lie, you can talk the person into taking a lie detector test. These tests are effective in measuring signs of nervousness (breathing rate, heart rate, and amount of perspiration), which all tend to increase when we lie. However, because other factors (such as room temperature) can also produce these kinds of physical changes, lie detector results can be misleading. Another alternative for unmasking a liar is "face reading." Because the muscles of the face are connected to the areas of the brain that handle emotions, even really good liars cannot control brief "microexpressions" that offer a glimpse into their true feelings. There are also facial expressions, like those accompanying true sadness, that are very difficult to fake, so you can learn to interpret the presence or absence of different facial muscle movements. Of course, these movements are often barely noticeable, so you have to be trained in what to look for. Yet another method for catching liars is computer voice analysis. Software programs such as the Verdicator allow you to record the suspected liar's voice and then analyze its tone. The stress of lying usually affects the voice, allowing the program to accurately assess the possibility of dishonesty. The disadvantage of this technology is its $2,500 price tag.

(*Source of information:* James Geary, "How to Spot a Liar," *Time Europe*, March 13, 2000, www.time.com/time/europe/magazine/2000/313/lies.html.)

Implied Main Idea

a. The three methods for exposing a liar effectively analyze different kinds of physical changes, but all three have disadvantages.

b. The Verdicator is the only really accurate method of catching a liar.

3. Most fishing-boat operators are not required to have a license or safety training. Likewise, most crew members receive no training or certification. Nor are there safety standards for the design or maintenance of fishing boats. Therefore, on many fishing boats, safety equipment—such as life rafts and life vests—is either broken or missing altogether. Furthermore, fishing seasons are limited for certain fish species, fish prices are low, and competition in the fishing industry continues to increase. Therefore, fishermen feel pressured to work even in bad weather, when rough seas make flooding, capsizing, or being swept overboard more likely. As a result, 152 out of every 100,000 fishermen are killed on the job each year. That rate is nine times higher than the fatality rate for firefighters and police officers.

(*Source of information:* Gary Stoller, "Despite Law, Fishermen Face Deadliest Job Risks," *USA Today,* March 12, 2003, 1A.)

Implied Main Idea

a. Most fishermen would abandon their profession if they could afford to do so.

b. A number of factors make fishing the most dangerous profession of all.

4. Do boys and girls who watch a lot of violent television shows really grow up to be more violent adults? In a rare long-term study that began in the late 1970s, researchers interviewed 329 six- to nine-year-old children and rated their exposure to violence based on the TV shows they liked to watch. The participants were interviewed again in their early twenties. Researchers also checked the participants' criminal records and talked to their spouses and friends. The male participants who watched the most TV violence were twice as likely as the other men to have physically assaulted their wives during an argument. They were also more likely than the other participants in the study to have physically assaulted another adult, committed a crime, or broken a traffic law. The female participants who had watched the most TV violence were twice as likely as the other women to have hurled something at their husbands during an argument. And they, too, were more likely to have physically assaulted another adult or broken a law.

(*Source of information:* "Study: Children's Viewing Linked to TV Violence," *USA Today,* March 9, 2003, www.usatoday.com/news/health/2003-03-09-tv-violence_x.htm.)

Implied Main Idea

a. A long-term study suggests that children who watch violent TV shows exhibit more aggressive behavior in adulthood.

b. You can't use a single study to prove a connection between watching television and being prone to violence.

5. Which is better for you: jogging or brisk walking? Both types of exercise provide an excellent aerobic workout that will strengthen your heart and lungs. Both also improve muscle tone, increase energy, and reduce stress. However, you'll have to walk longer— about forty-five minutes at five miles per hour—to get the same health benefits as twenty to thirty minutes of jogging. You'll also have to walk longer to burn more calories for weight loss. If a 150-pound person walks briskly for four miles, he or she will burn about 340 calories. If that person jogs the same distance, he or she will burn 450 calories. But jogging does not necessarily burn more fat than walking does. Research indicates that jogging burns carbohydrates primarily, whereas walking burns stored fat. Yet, jogging does increase the body's metabolism, so stored fat continues to burn long after the workout. Walking, though, is easier on the knees, hips, feet, shins, and back. Jogging is a high-impact exercise that is much harder on the joints, increasing the risk of injury.

(*Sources of information:* Carol Krucoff, "Speed Walking vs. Jogging," *FamilyFun,* www.familyfun.go.com/yourtime/fitness/expert/dony0800bwks_jogwalk/; and Texas Medical Center, "Walking vs. Jogging," www.tmc.edu/health_briefs/6_15_00-jogging.html.)

Implied Main Idea

a. Both walking and jogging improve physical fitness, but each has its disadvantages.

b. If you want to exercise in order to lose weight, jogging is probably the most effective exercise there is.

Practice 8   ## Be Ready to Draw Inferences

Directions: Circle the letter of the main idea implied by the paragraph.

1. Telling lies is one way of avoiding trouble. As a matter of fact, surveys show that about 41 percent of lies are told to protect ourselves when we misbehave. For example, we might tell a loved one that we were stuck in traffic when we were actually having a beer with friends. Another 14 percent of fibs are the "little white lies" that protect people's feelings and keep relations friendly. For instance, we tell a friend that a new hairstyle is becoming even when it isn't. Occasionally, telling lies to ourselves is good for our health. One study showed that patients who remained in a state of denial about the dangers of upcoming surgery actually had fewer complications than patients who were worried about the consequences. In another study of breast cancer patients, most of the women who denied that

they were ill were still alive. The majority of women who had accepted their illness had died. And don't forget the emotional benefits of telling lies. If we lie to ourselves about how much it hurts when other people reject us, or if we lie to ourselves about being glad that the people who left us are gone, then we're likely to cope better with the pain and recover more quickly.

(*Source of information:* James Geary, "Deceitful Minds," *Time Europe,* March 13, 2000, www. time.com/time/europe/magazine/2000/313/deceit.html.)

Implied Main Idea

a. Telling lies may help us survive a devastating disease, but it won't do much to improve our reputations.

b. Telling lies offers several benefits.

c. Denial is good for our health.

2. In a study at the University of North Carolina–Chapel Hill, fifty couples who were either married or romantically involved held hands while watching a ten-minute video and then hugged their partners for twenty seconds. During that time, another 85 people sat quietly without their partners. Next, all 185 participants were asked to tell a story about a recent stressful occurrence in their lives. Immediately after telling their stories, the heart rate of the people who had *not* held hands or received a hug increased by ten beats per minute. The heart rate of those who had just had physical contact with a loved one increased only five beats per minute. Also, the blood pressure of those who had not touched their partners rose significantly. As a matter of fact, the increase was double that of the individuals who had received a hug.

(*Source of information:* Marilyn Elias, "Study: Hugs Warm the Heart, and May Protect It," *USA Today,* March 9, 2003, www.usatoday.com/news/health/2003-03-09-hug-usat_x.htm.)

Implied Main Idea

a. One study suggests that loving physical contact reduces the harmful physical effects of stress.

b. Married people are better able to handle stress than are those who are single.

c. Hugs can lower blood pressure.

3. Most cars get an average of 23.6 miles per gallon, and the most fuel-efficient automobiles, such as Volkswagens, get between 40 and 50 miles per gallon. But sport utility vehicles (SUVs) are gas-guzzlers. King-size SUVs like the Ford Expedition and the Lincoln Navigator get a mere 12 miles per gallon or less in city driving and

only 17 miles per gallon in highway driving. And the smaller SUVs get a maximum of 18 miles per gallon. This unnecessary need for more gasoline ensures that America will remain dependent on an often unstable Middle East for our oil supply. SUVs are also a danger to other drivers on the road. In 2002, government safety testers smashed a Chevrolet Trailblazer into the side of a Honda Accord at 40 miles per hour. The collision "killed" the dummy in the Accord. Furthermore, in SUV-car collisions, there are sixteen times as many fatalities in the cars as in the SUVs. What's more, SUVs are a danger to their own drivers. Because of their height and size, these vehicles are three times more likely than cars to roll over—the leading cause of vehicle-related deaths.

(*Sources of information:* "Fuel Efficient Vehicles Outnumbered by Gas Guzzlers in U.S. Showrooms," *CNN.com*, October 2, 2000, www.cnn.com/2000/US/10/02/epa.mileage.ap/; Richard J. Newman, "Big, Bad Brutes?" *U.S. News and World Report*, March 10, 2003, pp. 43–44; and Curtis Rist, "Roll Over, Newton," *Discover*, April 2001, www.discover.com/apr_01/featnewton.html.)

Implied Main Idea

a. Sport utility vehicles cause a number of serious problems.

b. Currently there is a massive attempt to discredit SUVs.

c. Because of their many drawbacks, SUVs are becoming less popular with consumers.

4. The average Australian, Canadian, Japanese, and Mexican employee works about 100 hours (or two and a half weeks) less per year than the average American worker. British workers put in about 250 hours (more than five weeks) less than American workers, and Germans work approximately 500 hours (more than twelve weeks) less than Americans work. Most American workers take, on average, only two weeks' vacation per year, while European workers take four to six weeks. In other countries, such as France, the workweek is only thirty-five hours long, compared to a forty-hour workweek in the United States.

(*Source of information:* Porter Anderson, "Study: U.S. Employees Put in Most Hours," *CNN.com*, August 31, 2001, www.cnn.com/2001/CAREER/trends/08/30/ilo.study.)

Implied Main Idea

a. American workers want to work more hours than do workers in other industrialized countries.

b. Americans work longer hours than workers in other industrialized nations.

c. American are more productive than workers in other industrialized countries.

5. Sixty-five million years ago, a giant asteroid hit Earth and probably caused the extinction of the dinosaurs. How likely is it that another huge asteroid could impact our planet and wipe out the human race? Since 1993, NASA and the Air Force have been collaborating to identify all nearby asteroids with a diameter of at least one-sixth of a mile. So far, they've found 700 out of an estimated 1,100, and none of them seems to be heading toward us. As a matter of fact, our closest call with an asteroid was in 1994, when a thirty-foot rock passed by 65,000 miles away. However, if we do find an asteroid to be on a collision-course with Earth, we will have decades to figure out what to do about it. Already, scientists have been working on ways to deflect or destroy asteroids. In 2001, for example, NASA landed a probe on an asteroid, proving that we have the technology to either plant a bomb or fire thrusters that could alter the asteroid's path.

(*Sources of information:* Dan Vergano, "Much Ado About Asteroids," *USA Today,* March 11, 2003, p. 9D; and Kurt Jensen, "Some Hits and Misses," *USA Today,* March 11, 2003, p. 9D.)

Implied Main Idea

a. There's a high probability that Earth will be hit by another asteriod in the next century.

b. It's unlikely that a huge asteroid will strike Earth and cause the extinction of the human race.

c. NASA has overestimated the threat posed by asteroids.

Practice 9

Be Ready to Draw Inferences

Directions: Circle the letter of the main idea implied by the paragraph.

1. Researchers at the University of California at Los Angeles wanted to find out if keeping a secret has any effect on one's physical health. They studied a group of gay men who had tested positive for HIV but were otherwise healthy. Some of these men were keeping their sexual preference secret from their friends, family, and co-workers. Others were open about their homosexual identities. After nine years, researchers found that the HIV disease progressed more rapidly in the men who were concealing their sexual orientation. As a matter of fact, the men who had maintained the highest level of concealment also had the highest rate of illness and death.

(*Source of information:* Norman Anderson with P. Elizabeth Anderson, "Secrets and Lies," *Psychology Today,* March/April 2003, pp. 60–64.)

Implied Main Idea

a. Studies suggest that keeping secrets does not seem to affect one's physical health.

b. Keeping secrets causes physical harm.

c. People who can't keep a secret seem to have more health problems than people who can.

d. At least one study suggests that keeping serious secrets can prove harmful.

2. In 2001, Alabama Chief Justice Roy Moore installed a 5,280-pound granite carving of the Bible's Ten Commandments inside a government judicial building. Moore described this monument as a symbol of the divine basis for law in a country that was founded upon Judeo-Christian principles. The American Civil Liberties Union and other opponents of the monument argued that it should be removed because it clearly violated the First Amendment to the U.S. Constitution, which says that the government can "make no law respecting an establishment of religion." Moore and his supporters countered that the Constitution's authors were mostly religious men who did not intend to exclude all mention of God from the government they created. As a matter of fact, Moore and others argued, the carving of the Ten Commandments was just one of many public acknowledgments of God. They pointed out that the Declaration of Independence refers to God; our national motto is "In God We Trust"; the presidential oath of office includes the phrase "so help me God"; Congress begins its workday with a prayer to God, and even the U.S. Supreme Court begins its sitting with "God save the United States and this honorable court." They also argued that judicial courts permit religious symbols such as Christmas trees and menorahs to be part of holiday displays on public properties. The monument's opponents, however, insisted that such symbols do not promote a particular set of beliefs; in contrast, the main purpose of the Ten Commandments carving was to advance a specific religion.

(*Sources of information:* Larry Copeland, "10 Commandments Appeal Fails," *USA Today,* August 21, 2003, p. 1A, www.usatoday.com/usatonline/20030821/5428594s.htm; Rob Schenk, "U.S. Answers to Higher Law," *USA Today,* August 13, 2003, www.usatoday. com/news/ opinion/editorials/2003-08-13-oppose-usat_x.htm; and "Judge Rules 10 Commandments Monument Violates Constitution," November 18, 2002, http://stacks.msnbc.com/ local/wvtm/ al393461.asp.)

Implied Main Idea

a. A monument of the Ten Commandments was an appropriate addition to an Alabama judicial building.

b. A monument of the Ten Commandments was an inappropriate addition to an Alabama judicial building.

c. A monument of the Ten Commandments installed inside an Alabama judicial building provoked controversy about its appropriateness.

d. Chief Justice Roy Moore was wrong to blur the separation between church and state.

3. One old wives' tale says that you should not swim for an hour after you eat or you'll get cramps. Today, medical researchers call this sound advice, for they have found that when the blood in your body is diverted to your digestive system, there's not as much blood available for the muscles needed to swim, increasing the possibility of cramping. Another old wives' tale, however, warns children not to go outside with wet hair, for they'll catch a cold. One modern researcher has immersed hundreds of subjects in icy water for hours on end, and has found that these chilly baths have never caused a cold for any of the participants. The old wives did get it right, though, when they advised chicken soup for curing a cold. Medical researchers have found that the ingredients in chicken soup inhibit the migration of cells that cause congestion, reduce mucus, and loosen congestion. But when it comes to putting butter on a burn, the old wives were wrong again. Modern science has shown that butter does not stop the burning, soothe the skin, or prevent tissue damage, as the old wives claimed it would.

(*Source of information:* Judy Waytiuk, "The Truth About Old Wives' Tales," *Reader's Digest Canada,* 2001, www.readersdigest.ca.mag/2001/12/old_wive.html.)

Implied Main Idea

a. Modern researchers have proven that old wives' tales are scientifically accurate.

b. Modern researchers have proven that old wives' tales are not scientifically accurate.

c. Modern researchers have proven that some old wives' tales are scientifically accurate and some are not.

d. Old wives' tales about not swimming after eating have been supported by modern scientific research.

4. Many people, even those who care nothing about birds in general, love hummingbirds because these colorful little creatures are so tiny and cute. However, a typical hummingbird has a demanding metabolism, for its heart beats more than 1,200 times a minute and its wings move at more than 2,000 revolutions per minute. For the energy it needs to survive, it must consume 7 to 12 calories by drawing nectar from about 1,000 different flowers every day. This amount

is the equivalent of a 180-pound human consuming 204,300 calories, or 171 pounds of hamburger, on a daily basis. Not surprisingly, once a male hummingbird has located a good food source, such as a feeder or a flower patch, it fiercely guards its territory and fights off rivals. It vocalizes threats, chases intruders, and will not hesitate to collide with other birds in the air, claw them, or use its bill as a weapon. Hummingbirds can even intimidate hawks and other birds a hundred times their size.

(*Source of information:* Richard Coniff, "So Tiny, So Sweet . . . So MEAN," *Smithsonian*, September 2000, pp. 72–81.)

Implied Main Idea

a. Hummingbirds' beauty makes up for their nasty nature.

b. Hummingbirds only seem cute and sweet; they're actually mean and aggressive.

c. Of all the birds, hummingbirds are the most amazing.

d. People should put out more feeders for hummingbirds to help them survive.

5. King Tutankhamen, or King Tut, the famous 18th Dynasty Egyptian king whose mummy and treasure-filled tomb were discovered in 1922, was only about eighteen years old when he died more than 3,000 years ago. Was he murdered? X-rays taken of the mummy in 1963 show a possible blood clot at the lower base of King Tut's skull, which could have been caused by a violent blow to the head. The x-rays also revealed not only breaks in the thin bones about Tut's eyes but also a condition that prevented Tut from turning his head without moving his entire torso. Thus it would have been easy to sneak up behind him. Archaeological evidence also indicates that after her husband's death, Tut's queen sent a letter to a neighboring king begging him to send one of his sons for her to marry. That king complied with her request, but the prince was ambushed and killed while on his way to Egypt. Soon afterward, Tut's widow was forced to marry Aye, her husband's elderly adviser, who then became the new king. After her second marriage, however, the Egyptian queen herself disappeared from all historical records.

(*Sources of information:* Lee Krystek, "The Death of King Tut: Was It Murder?" Museum of Unnatural History, www.unmuseum.org/tutmurder.htm; and "Who Killed King Tut?" *Time for Kids*, September 27, 2002, www.timeforkids.com/TFK/magazines/printout/0,12479,353755,00.html.)

Implied Main Idea

a. Evidence indicates that King Tut may have been murdered with a blow to the head.

    b. Evidence indicates that a neighboring king probably murdered King Tut by crushing his skull.

    c. Evidence indicates that King Tut's death was due to natural causes that may never be fully understood.

    d. X-rays prove that Egypt's King Tut was a murder victim.

Practice 10 — Read to Uncover Patterns in Paragraphs

Directions: Identify the pattern or patterns organizing each paragraph by circling the appropriate letter(s).

1. *Pathogens* are parasites that enter the body and use its cells or tissue for their own reproduction. During this process, they damage or destroy the cells or tissue. An *infectious disease* is an illness caused by a pathogen. The most common pathogens are viruses and bacteria, which differ from each other in important ways. A *virus* is tiny (about one thousand times smaller than a human hair) and cannot reproduce outside a living cell. The virus must invade the cells of another organism in order to multiply, which can lead to serious diseases in plants, animals, and humans. A *bacterium*, in contrast, is a complete living cell ten times as large as a virus; some bacteria even consist of several cells. Not all bacteria are dangerous—in fact, many play an important part in maintaining life on Earth. For example, bacteria are essential in the decomposition of organic wastes and dead bodies, a process that frees elements needed by other organisms and returns them to the environment. Bacteria can also be used to remove pollutants from air, water, or soil.

    a. definition

    b. time order

    c. comparison and contrast

    d. cause and effect

    e. classification

2. Plate tectonics, a theory developed in the 1960s, provides a convincing explanation for the causes of an earthquake. According to this theory, Earth's outer crust (the continents and ocean floors) sits on top of plates of rock that enclose the interior like the cracked shell of a hard-boiled egg. The individual plates are in constant

motion and may get jammed. This results in great strains at the edges, eventually causing the plates to fracture. As the plates break free, energy is released in the form of seismic waves that move upward through the crust and spread out, causing the ground to shake suddenly and—possibly—with great force. If this happens beneath the sea, the damage is usually small, but on land, the results can be devastating. For example, an earthquake in China on June 27, 1976, killed between 250,000 and 750,000 people.

a. definition

b. time order

c. comparison and contrast

d. cause and effect

e. classification

3. In 1961, Project Apollo was launched by President Kennedy, who wanted to land a person on the moon and return him safely to Earth. By then, the U.S. space program had put several satellites into orbit around Earth and learned how to send a person into space and back. Project Apollo was to build on this experience and to develop—through a series of missions of increasing difficulty—the technology needed for a moon landing. But the program started with a disaster when, on January 27, 1967, the three astronauts of *Apollo 1* died in a fire that consumed their spacecraft during a launch-pad test. Only a year and a half later, however, on October 11, 1968, *Apollo 7* successfully carried a crew into an orbit around Earth and returned it safely. Two months later, *Apollo 8* took its crew into orbit around the moon. In March and May 1968, *Apollo 9* and *Apollo 10* tested the lunar module, a vehicle designed to carry an astronaut from an orbiting spacecraft to the surface of the moon and back to the craft. These experiments came to a successful conclusion with *Apollo 11* on July 20, 1969. On that day, astronauts Neil Armstrong and Edwin "Buzz" Aldrin landed the lunar module *Eagle* on the moon in an area called the Sea of Tranquility

a. definition

b. time order

c. comparison and contrast

d. cause and effect

e. classification

4. Employees receive their salaries or wages directly. In addition, they may receive *benefits* paid for fully or in part by their employer. These benefits fall into several categories. One is an *insurance package* consisting of a health plan, life insurance, and—possibly—a dental plan. In addition, employers must provide *unemployment insurance* as well as *workers compensation insurance*, which covers job-related injuries or disabilities. A second group of benefits may consist of a *pension and retirement program*. A company must make contributions to its employees' Social Security accounts; some employers offer an additional pension or retirement package paid for wholly or in part by the employers. A third benefit category is *pay for time not worked*, which may include paid vacations, holidays, and sick leave. A fourth category, *quality of life benefits*, may include child care, a cafeteria plan, exercise and other recreational facilities, or a credit union. In the end, the total benefit package an employer provides depends not only on the financial situation of the company, but also on the type of employee it wants to attract.

   a. definition

   b. time order

   c. comparison and contrast

   d. cause and effect

   e. classification

5. Bill Clinton, the forty-second president of the United States, is remembered as "the Comeback Kid" because he survived—as a politician—several setbacks that would have ended the careers of most other elected officials. He lost his first political race in 1974, when he ran for Congress. But two years later, Clinton was elected attorney general of Arkansas; in 1978 he became governor of that state. He lost his bid for reelection in 1980, only to win the governorship back in 1982. His presidential campaign got off to a bumpy start in 1991 amid rumors about his personal life; however, Clinton proved to be an able campaigner, winning the Democratic primary and subsequently the presidency in 1992. Some of his sweeping proposals ran into stiff opposition from Republicans and parts of the public, and in the midterm elections of 1994, the Republicans won control of both houses of Congress. His chances for reelection appeared slim, but Clinton learned how to pursue smaller objectives successfully. Helped also by a booming economy, he was elected in 1996 to a second term by a landslide. True to form, he found himself again in trouble when he misrepresented—under oath—his affair with a White House intern. Clinton was impeached but not

convicted, and stayed in office. His popularity remained high throughout this scandal and for the rest of his presidency, then declined again as a result of some controversial pardons he announced during his last days in office. Still, even that mishap didn't put a stop to his career. He has since signed a multimillion-dollar book contract, commands high fees as a speaker, and may even obtain a lucrative TV contract.

a. definition

b. time order

c. comparison and contrast

d. cause and effect

e. classification

Practice 11

Read to Uncover Patterns in Longer Readings

Directions: Identify the patterns organizing the reading by circling the appropriate letter(s).

1. Connecting Mind and Body

Can your thoughts affect your body's ability to fight off disease? Scientists have been accumulating evidence suggesting that your mind does indeed exert a direct influence upon your immune system. Recent studies have shown, for example, that depressed people have a greater risk for heart disease. Other research has indicated that wounds suffered by women coping with the stress of Alzheimer's disease do not heal as fast as wounds suffered by women who do not have Alzheimer's. Additional studies have indicated that people who are under stress get colds and the flu more often; also, their symptoms are more severe.

As a result, researchers at the University of Wisconsin decided to investigate whether negative emotions reduce the effectiveness of people's immune systems. These researchers first attached fifty-two women ranging in age from fifty-seven to sixty to an electroencephalogram (EEG) machine, which measures brain activity. Next, they asked the women to write about positive and negative events in their lives. The women were directed first to think about a period of intense joy for one minute and then spend five minutes writing about that experience. Then they were asked to think and write about a period of extreme sadness, fear, or anger. While they were writing, the EEG machine measured how much activity was occurring in the right prefrontal cortex, the area of the brain that is involved in emotional responses involving anger, fear, and sadness. Finally, researchers gave each of the women a flu shot.

Six months later, researchers measured the level of antibodies, disease-fighting substances, in the women's bodies. They found that women whose prefrontal cortex had been most active as they were thinking about intensely negative emotional experiences had the lowest level of antibodies. Thus, negative emotions appeared to weaken their immunity. This result led the scientists to speculate that negative thinking interferes with the prefrontal cortex's communication with the body's stress and immune systems. While this particular experiment did not compare activity in the brain's left prefrontal cortex (the area associated with positive emotions) to antibody levels, researchers theorize that positive thinking is likely to have the opposite effect by producing a stronger immune response.

(*Source of information:* Erica Goode, "Power of Positive Thinking May Have a Health Benefit, Study Says," *New York Times*, September 2, 2003, www.nytimes.com.)

a. definition

b. time order

c. comparison and contrast

d. cause and effect

e. classification

2. **Frida Kahlo's Painful Inspiration**
The talented and tormented artist Frida Kahlo was born in 1907 in a suburb of Mexico City. At age six, she contracted polio, which left her right leg and foot thin and stunted. In spite of her disability, however, Kahlo became a tomboy, preferring boys' games like soccer, boxing, wrestling, and swimming. In 1922, at the age of fifteen, Kahlo entered a mostly male preparatory school, where she took courses in biology, zoology, and anatomy in preparation for becoming a doctor.

Then, on September 17, 1925, she was involved in an accident that completely altered the course of her life. The bus she was riding home from school collided with a trolley car, killing several passengers. A broken metal handrail pierced and crushed eighteen-year-old Kahlo's pelvis. Her spine was fractured in three places, and her right leg and foot were broken. She was not expected to live. However, she spent a month in the hospital and endured the first of many operations. Afterwards, clad in a plaster body cast, she spent three months at home in bed, unable to return to school.

While confined to her bed, she began to paint. When she recovered and grew stronger, she found a new interest in politics and joined the Communist Party. In 1928, she met fellow artist Diego Rivera at a party. They began a courtship and married in 1929. In 1930, the couple went to the United States, where they spent three years in San Francisco, Detroit, and New York City while Rivera painted his famed murals and displayed his work in shows. Kahlo, too, was painting; however, she was not only dealing with the incessant pain in her injured right foot and leg, but she was also suffering from a devastating series of miscarriages and medically necessary abortions. She longed to have a child, so she succumbed to deep despair and depression every time she lost another baby. It was in Detroit after yet another miscarriage that her distinctive style began to emerge with her painting of herself, naked and crying, in a blood-soaked bed.

More pain awaited her when she returned to Mexico. Her mother had died, and her husband, who had always been notorious for his extramarital affairs, became involved with a series of other women. In 1934, Kahlo was hospitalized three times after succumbing to stress-related illnesses, and she separated from Rivera.

From 1937 to 1938, however, Kahlo entered a productive artistic period fed by her friendships with exiled Russian revolutionary Leon Trotsky and French artist André Breton and his wife. In the summer of 1938, Kahlo sold her first paintings to American actor Edward G. Robinson, and shows of her work in New York City and France soon followed. Despite her artistic success, her personal life was still unsettled, and she finally agreed to divorce her unfaithful husband in 1939. She painted intensely, including a portrait of herself wearing a dress torn open to reveal a broken heart. Her health deteriorated, and when her doctor diagnosed her as having "a crisis of nerves," Kahlo agreed to reconcile with Rivera. The couple remarried in 1940.

Unfortunately, Rivera was still unfaithful; husband and wife continued to fight, and Kahlo engaged in extramarital affairs of her own. During the last ten years of her life, her physical condition continued to worsen, and she was forced to endure several surgeries on her back, foot, and leg. In 1953, her right leg was amputated below the knee. During this time, she became addicted to alcohol and painkilling drugs. Yet in that year she was finally honored with her first one-woman show in her own city. Ordered by doctors not to leave her bed, she had the bed, with her in it, carried to the show's opening night so that she would not miss her long-awaited triumph. Despite her weakened physical condition and her emotional turmoil, she continued to remain acive in politics, too. Only eight days before her death, she attended a protest of 10,000 people in Mexico City. She was only forty-seven years old when she died of a pulmonary embolism on July 13, 1954.

Like many artists, Kahlo did not sell many paintings in her lifetime. However, she is recognized today as a significant twentieth-century artist, and her paintings are now sold at auction for millions of dollars. As one organizer of a 1993 exhibition of Kahlo's work pointed out, "Kahlo made personal women's experiences serious subjects for art, but . . . her paintings transcend gender boundaries. Intimate and powerful, they demand that viewers—men and women—be moved by them."

(*Source of information:* Phyllis Tuchman, "Frida Kahlo," *Smithsonian*, November 2002, pp. 50–59.)

a. definition

b. time order

c. comparison and contrast

d. cause and effect

e. classification

Let Transitions Be Your Guide

Directions: Circle the transitions that introduce either the main idea or supporting details. If there is a transitional sentence, underline it.

1. Most people know that dolphins have been trained to entertain humans at aquarium shows and in swim-with-dolphins programs. But many people are not aware that dolphins' intelligence and capabilities also make them a valuable component of the U.S. military. In 1960, the Navy's Marine Mammal Program began to train dolphins to detect underwater threats to military vessels. During the Vietnam War and Operation Desert Storm, these creatures used their natural sonar abilities to search for scuba divers trying to plant explosives on the underside of American ships. During the 1991 war with Iraq, dolphins located and marked submerged mines that could blow up the Navy's vessels. Sensors mounted to the

animals' fins recorded their responses to the things they encountered as they swam, allowing U.S. forces to pinpoint the location of
potential dangers.

(*Sources of information:* "Dolphins Aid Iraq Mine-Clearance," *CNN.com,* March 26, 2003,
www.cnn.com/2003/ WORLD/meast/03/26/sprj.irq.ummqasr/index.html; and Tim Friend, "A
Wartime First: Dolphins Called to Clear Mines," *USA Today,* March 27, 2003, p. 8D.)

2. Many sun worshippers believe that using a tanning bed is safer than
    getting a tan by lying outside in the sun. They are, however, mis-
    taken: Tanning beds are every bit as dangerous to your health as the
    sun's natural radiation is. The ultraviolet light of tanning beds dam-
    ages the skin just as sunlight does, causing premature aging. The
    radiation from tanning beds has also been linked to the development
    of melanoma, the most serious form of skin cancer, which causes
    almost 8,000 deaths per year. What's more, tanning beds' ultraviolet
    radiation also appears to have a damaging effect on the immune
    system. Not surprisingly, the American Medical Association has for
    years been urging people to stop using tanning beds.

    (*Source of information:* American Academy of Dermatology, *The Darker Side of Tanning,* 1996,
    www.aad.org/pamphlets/darker.html.)

3. Mixed-breed mutts have always been relegated to the lower classes
    of the dog world. Recently, however, several varieties of trendy new
    hybrid dogs have been raising the status of some mixed breeds from
    mongrel to that of designer dog. Canines like the schnoodle, a mix
    between a schnauzer and a poodle, are becoming popular because
    they don't shed and don't require the regular grooming that a pure-
    bred poodle needs. They also do not suffer from the health prob-
    lems that often plague purebred pups. Labradoodles, a mixture of
    Labrador and poodle that sells for about $850 each, are intelligent
    and good with children. And several other combinations—such as
    the cockapoo (cocker spaniel and poodle), the yorkipoo (Yorkshire
    terrier and poodle), and goldendoodle (golden retriever and poo-
    dle)—are all the rage because they, too, are proving to be smart,
    family-friendly pets.

    (*Source of information:* Amy Saltzman, "Oodles of Schnoodles," *U.S. News and World Report,*
    March 31, 2003, p. D8, www.usnews.com/usnews/issue/030331/misc/31dogs.div.htm.)

4. American citizens should support government-funded research
    into the development of affordable hydrogen-powered engines.
    Creating vehicles that run on hydrogen instead of gasoline is, first
    of all, essential to our national security. Currently, the United States
    relies on foreign sources for 55 percent of its oil, and that figure is
    expected to rise to 68 percent by 2025. Two-thirds of that oil is used
    for transportation costs. Therefore, replacing our gasoline engines
    with hydrogen-powered engines will reduce, or even eliminate, the

danger that comes from continuing to rely on foreign suppliers for our energy needs. Switching to hydrogen-powered vehicles will also benefit the environment. Unlike gasoline engines, hydrogen fuel cells produce only water as a waste product, so they will reduce air pollution and the gases that contribute to global warming.

(*Sources of information:* U.S. Department of Energy, *FreedomCAR and Fuel Initiative,* February 5, 2003, www.eere.energy.gov/hydrogenfuel/; and "Shoot for the Moon," *USA Today,* March 11, 2003, p. 11A.)

5. The flu is generally thought of as a short-term illness that goes away after a patient spends a few miserable days in bed. This is not always the case, though. In reality, several twentieth-century flu pandemics, or widespread epidemics, actually killed millions of people. In 1918–1919, the Spanish influenza was responsible for the deaths of as many as forty million people, half a million of them in the United States alone. This disease affected everyone, not just high-risk groups like children and the elderly. As a matter of fact, the mortality rate was highest among twenty- to fifty-year-old adults. Several subsequent pandemics, including the 1957–1958 Asian flu and the 1968 Hong Kong flu, were not quite as deadly as the Spanish flu. However, both of these outbreaks killed more than one million people each.

(*Sources of information:* "Mystery Illness Revives Epidemic Worries," *New York Times,* March 27, 2003, www.nytimes.com; and Centers for Disease Control, *Pandemics and Pandemic Scares in the Twentieth Century,* www.cdc.gov/od/nvpo/pandemics/flu3.htm#8.)

| Practice 13 | ## Pay Attention to Tone |

Directions: Circle the appropriate letter to identify the tone of the paragraph.

1. About 1.5 million Americans are allergic to peanuts. Exposure to peanuts can be life-threatening for these unfortunate people, because their bodies can overreact by closing down their airways, leading to suffocation. As a matter of fact, more than 150 people die tragically every year due to an accidental encounter with peanuts or with foods that contain them. Fortunately, though, researchers have been developing promising new experimental compounds that reduce the severity of the body's allergic reaction. Although these new drugs will not cure the allergy, they are the first real treatment ever created. Therefore, they definitely offer hope to those who live in fear of a peanut-triggered attack. Soon, for the very first time, peanut allergy sufferers may finally have access to an anti-

dote that will provide them with much-needed relief and peace of mind.

(*Source of information:* Christine Gorman, "Fighting Over Peanuts," *Time*, March 17, 2003, www.time.com.)

Tone

    a. neutral

    b. critical

    c. hopeful

    d. skeptical

2. Actor-comedian George Lopez deserves to be congratulated for bringing to television one of the first Latino comedy hits. His major-network sitcom *George Lopez* features a Latino family. The show brings a fresh new diversity to TV comedy by focusing candidly on the daily struggles of working-class minorities. Lopez has perfected his role as a likable but burdened father who manages to find humor even in the most painful situations and weighty issues. Thanks to its superb writing and Lopez's comedic talents, the show is always witty without being harsh or preachy. It's no wonder that his hilarious but thought-provoking performance has earned him both popular and critical success.

(*Source of information:* James Poniewozik, "Prime Time Therapy," *Time*, March 24, 2003, www.time.com.)

Tone

    a. neutral

    b. critical

    c. admiring

    d. skeptical

3. Can someone please explain to me the lure of reality-based television shows? Given their high ratings, there must be something to them, but no matter how hard I try, I cannot discover their virtues. Take, for example, *The Bachelor*. Week after week, what drew viewers to the spectacle of attractive, perhaps intelligent, young women openly competing for the affections of a mildly attractive young man. And certainly *The Bachelorette* wasn't any better. If anything, the dialogue was worse, as the contestants endlessly mulled over one another's flaws using the tired language of pop psychology: "I don't think she will choose him; he's just not in touch with his emotions." The main criterion for the success of these shows—and

this includes *American Idol,* which is not, despite the claims of its defenders, about finding new talent—is the competitors' willingness to face the prospect of humiliation before a huge viewing audience: "My dear young woman, you are seriously in need of a bra, and your voice is perhaps the worst I have ever heard." Sad as it may seem, television audiences tune in to reality programming week after week to see not who wins but who gets cut from the show and whether the person making an exit weeps or becomes enraged. Fans of reality television must feel that they themselves have no life. They need to tune into the lives of others in hope of having an intense emotional experience. It's hard to tell, then, what's more pathetic: reality programming or the people who watch it.

Tone

    a. neutral

    b. disgusted

    c. humorous

    d. hopeful

4. Eighteen states now require high school students who want a diploma to pass an exit exam, a test designed to make sure that graduates have mastered a certain level of knowledge. But these tests are unfair. They are punishing students for the state's failure to provide quality education. Schools all over the country are underfunded, overcrowded, and neglected. Many kids do not have teachers with experience or even the proper credentials, and they do not have access to counselors. School classrooms are rundown, and there aren't enough textbooks for everyone. Yet, students are still expected to somehow learn in these substandard environments, and when they don't, they pay the price by being denied a diploma. Exit exams should not even be a consideration until all of our country's students are provided with the fundamental educational resources they need in order to learn.

(*Source of information:* Abdi Soltani, "Tests Punish Students," *USA Today,* June 20, 2003, p. 14A, www.usatoday.com/usatonline/20030620/5261827s.htm.)

Tone

    a. neutral

    b. critical

    c. angry

    d. humorous

5. In 1955, writer and dictionary editor Albert H. Morehead identified some gaps in our language that needed to be filled by new words. He said, for example, that we need a dignified substitute for the words *boyfriend* and *girlfriend* when talking about mature men and women who are involved in a committed relationship but not married. For example, it seems silly to call the man my mother-in-law is seeing her *boyfriend,* when she is sixty and he is sixty-five. Yet that's what we say for lack of a better word. Morehead also correctly pointed out that we really needed a word meaning "to state your opinion." We can say *opine,* but that sounds pretentious, and most people would laugh in response. And why don't we have a word, as Morehead insisted we should, to indicate that we are listening to what someone is saying without indicating that we are in agreement. *Yes* is the word we usually use, but that suggests we agree with what the person has said (and maybe we don't). Our only other option is to grunt, but that seems rather crude. Where is a word to identify brothers and sisters without identifying their gender? Of course, we have *siblings,* but that sounds like a word from a textbook. What's even more odd is that Morehead pointed out these gaps in the language almost fifty years ago, and they still haven't been filled. When a need for a word arises, don't speakers usually come up with a new word which then becomes part of the language?

(*Source of information:* Allan Metcalf, *Predicting New Words,* p. 75.)

Tone

    a. neutral

    b. humorous

    c. skeptical

    d. puzzled

Practice 14   **Identify the Author's Purpose**

Directions: Circle the appropriate letter to identify the writer's purpose.

1. The term *artificial intelligence* was coined in 1956. It refers to a computer's ability to perform higher intellectual tasks characteristic of the human brain. These tasks include reasoning, making decisions, and learning from experience. High-speed computers with a lot of memory capacity and the right programming are using artificial intelligence to play games, solve problems, and understand language. For example, an IBM computer beat world champion Garry Kasparov in a 1997 chess match. Artificial intelligence gives a jet airplane's computers the ability to study the plane's instrument readings and tell the pilot how to land in a fog. Also, smart computers are learning how to talk and how to diagnose medical problems by analyzing a patient's symptoms.

Purpose

a. The writer wants to inform readers about artificial intelligence.

b. The writer wants to convince readers that the artificial intelligence of computers has benefited humanity.

2. Animal rights groups like the People for the Ethical Treatment of Animals (PETA) would have us believe that wearing hats or coats trimmed with fur is morally wrong. However, fur garments are, in actuality, perfectly acceptable. Animals are clearly lesser creatures that God put on this planet for the use and benefit of mankind. We use animals for food and for leather to make products like furniture, shoes, and wallets, and we use them for medical research into diseases like cancer and AIDS. The majority of people accept these uses of animals, so why should they oppose the wearing of fur? If we're going to eat animals, it stands to reason that we should also use them to keep ourselves warm. As a matter of fact, fur is Nature's answer to winter, for there is no better protection in cold weather. Plus, when we buy fur, we help support thousands of human beings whose livelihood and cultures depend upon the fur trade. If people stopped wearing fur, many of these people would no longer be able to feed their children. But perhaps the best reason to wear fur is your right to make your own choice about what you want to wear on your own body. According to the Fur Information Council of America, 86 percent of consumers support freedom of choice when it comes to deciding whether to buy or wear fur, and 92 percent oppose the tactics used by animal rights activists to try to deter you from making up your own mind. So, if you like wearing fur, you should not let others prevent you from exercising your personal rights.

(*Source of information:* Fur Information Council of America, www.fur.org/fica2003/faqs/talk.asp.)

Purpose

a. The writer wants to inform readers about the controversy surrounding the wearing of fur.

b. The writer wants to persuade readers that there is nothing wrong with wearing fur.

3. More than half of the adult population of the United States is over-weight, with more than one-fifth seriously obese. Who is to blame? A prime target is restaurants, especially fast-food chains, which are serving portions of ever-increasing size. An order of fries is now twice as big as it was fifteen years ago, and a double cheeseburger now contains all of the calories an adult would need for an entire day. Fast-food outlets clearly do this to attract customers, but does this make them responsible for the obesity that's sweeping the country? Anyone who argues this way neglects the fact that nobody is forced to eat fast food, or to eat everything that is served, or to eat huge portions several times a day. Why blame McDonald's when it only offers customers what they seem to want? People themselves are ultimately responsible for how they live, and this includes the nutritional choices they make. It is high time that individuals stop blaming others for everything that ails them.

Purpose

a. The writer wants to inform readers about the controversy surrounding fast-food outlets and their contribution to obesity in America.

b. The writer wants to persuade readers that the people who eat huge quantities of fast food are responsible for their weight problems.

4. Despite the high rates of obesity in the population, Americans idealize thinness, especially for women, and being overweight is often viewed in a negative light. In many other cultures, however, being fat is considered a sign of health and prosperity in men and beauty and sexual desirability in women. In some Hispanic cultures, for example, plumpness is the beauty ideal, and thinness is viewed as a sign of bad health and poverty. In many Pacific Island cultures, a man is successful if he can afford for his wife to become overweight. In many African cultures, too, being plump is interpreted as a symbol of sexual maturity, fertility, prosperity, strength, and wisdom. In Nigeria, young girls with high status actually spend two years in seclusion in "fattening huts," where they are supposed to eat and gain as much weight as possible so that they will be beautiful brides.

(*Sources of information:* Don Peck, "The Weight of the World," *Atlantic Monthly,* June 2003, p. 39; Clarke Johnson, University of Illinois at Chicago, "Notes for Dental Anthropology, Human Evolution, and Hominid Evolution," www.uic.edu/classes/osci/osci590/NOTES%20for%20Week%209.htm; and Lisa Henson, "Mirror, Mirror, On the Wall: Women and Body Image," FOR Families, www.cityofirvine.org/pdfs/cs/family/Mirror_Mirror.pdf.)

Purpose

a. The writer wants to inform readers about the way other cultures view plumpness in women.

b. The writer wants to persuade readers that being plump is better than being thin.

5. In the 1960 Olympics, the U.S. women's track-and-field runners seemed to be in deep trouble. They had come to Rome to earn a gold medal in the 4×100 meter relay, but a mishandled baton pass had left them trailing the lead. They needed a miracle to win—and they got it in six-foot-tall runner Wilma Rudolph. When her turn came, she breezed to the finish line three full steps ahead of her nearest rival, with the crowd cheering for the woman they called "the Gazelle." As a child, Rudolph had suffered from polio, and the disease had resulted in her left leg needing a brace. But Wilma Rudolph, who did indeed have the long legs of a gazelle, also had the heart of a lion. She was determined not just to walk without a limp but to be a runner. To that end, she began a program of rigorous training and exercise. By age twelve she was the fastest runner in junior high. Then, in high school, track coach Ed Temple became her mentor and helped guide her athletic career, inviting her to participate in summer track camps. By age sixteen, Rudolph was ready for the 1956 Olympics, where she helped her team win the bronze medal in the 4×100 meter relay. But it wasn't until 1960 that she truly showed the world what she could do, winning three gold medals. Rudolph had fought hard to become one of the greatest woman athletes of all time, but that fight didn't harden her toward the world. Always humble and gracious, she was remarkably generous. Rudolph dedicated her life and much of her earnings to helping young athletes achieve their dreams. She died in 1994 after becoming, in the words of Olympic historian Bud Greenspan, "the Jesse Owens of women's track and field."*

(*Source of information: Africana: The Encyclopedia of the African and American Experience,* Kwame Anthony Appiah and Henry Louis Gates, Jr., eds., p. 1640.)

Purpose

a. The writer wants to inform readers about the life of Wilma Rudolph and her triumph at the 1960 Olympics in Rome.

b. The writer wants to persuade readers that Wilma Rudolph was not only a fine athlete but a great human being.

*This is an allusion to another great runner who, at the 1936 Olympics in Berlin, revealed the lie of Adolf Hitler's racist politics by beating all the other runners, including the supposedly superior Germans.

Practice 15   ## Analyze Arguments

Directions: Read each passage. Circle the appropriate letter to identify the point of the writer's argument. Then use the blanks to answer
questions about the author's evidence.

1. The Governor Takes a Stand

Former Illinois governor George Ryan, a man with a conscience,
should be applauded for calling attention to the failure of capital
punishment as an instrument of justice. In the 1990s, more than
150 people were awaiting execution in Illinois. By 1996, six people
awaiting the death penalty had been proven innocent through a
reexamination of the evidence that had first proven them guilty.
Thus, even before Ryan took office, there was compelling proof that
the state had been on the verge of executing six innocent people.
Within a month of taking office in 1999, Governor Ryan was confronted by the case of Anthony Porter. Porter's defense revolved
around his competency to have committed the crime. While Porter's
mental fitness was being tested, a group of undergraduate journalism students at Northwestern University reinterviewed key witnesses in the case, all of whom recanted their original testimony
against Porter. The students then helped track down the real killer,
and Porter was freed.

Although the case made an impression on Governor Ryan, he
still allowed the execution of Andrew Kokoraleis. But the governor
was now a troubled man. The turning point came when the
Chicago Tribune published a five-part investigative series that
traced the history of capital convictions, including the mistakes
that had plagued those convictions. Ryan was appalled. A former
pharmacist, he claimed that had he made as many mistakes in his
job, he would have been out of business. By January of 2000, after
Steven Manning became the thirteenth death row prisoner to be
exonerated, Governor Ryan was ready to take action. On January
31, the governor made national news when he announced a mora-
torium on the use of the death penalty pending an investigation.
When the investigation was finished, a majority of the members
recommended that the death penalty be abolished. Because the
Illinois legislature failed to act on that recommendation, Ryan
granted blanket clemency for all 167 men on death row.

What is the point of the author's argument?

a. George Ryan did the right thing when he called for an investigation of the death penalty in Illinois.

b. George Ryan should be commended for bringing to public attention the problems with capital punishment.

c. A compassionate man, George Ryan believed that those who were mentally incompetent should never be given the death penalty.

In the context of the author's argument, what makes the date of 1996 relevant?

_____

_____

Why are the names of Anthony Porter and Steven Manning relevant?

_____

_____

2. A Call for Skepticism

In 2001, a Gallup poll found that half of all Americans believe in the ability of psychics to communicate with the dead. Forty percent believe in ghosts, haunted houses, demonic possession, and just about every other form of supernatural or paranormal activity. Now, the problem is not that people believe in such things. What's troubling is that many people believe in them _despite_ all evidence to the contrary. As an antidote to such gullibility, America needs more skeptics like Joe Nickell, author of _The Real-Life X-Files_. Nickell's brand of skepticism allows for the possibility of paranormal events but insists that those events only be given credence after close and critical scrutiny. If only more people would follow his lead.

Considered the country's most famous investigator of paranormal activity, Nickell has spent most of his life uncovering the fraud that always seems to be lurking behind the claims of ufologists, mediums, and psychics. While Nickell has respect for those who base their religious belief on faith, he despises the frauds who fake evidence in order to convince an all-too-willing public that paranormal events or extraterrestrial creatures are real. Nickell's mission in life is to reveal the trickery behind such claims.

For example, in 1987, the author of a book on Roswell released the so-called MJ-12 documents, which supposedly showed that a flying saucer had crashed near Roswell, New Mexico. According to the documents, President Harry Truman had authorized a secret cover-up of the saucer crash, and his successor, Dwight D. Eisenhower, was informed about the cover-up. Ever the skeptic, particularly where flying saucers are concerned, Nickell teamed up with forensic analyst John F. Fischer, and the two men proved that the MJ-12 documents were faked. The "documents" were nothing but crude paste-up forgeries created by affixing the photocopied signatures to real documents.

Nickell also analyzed a transcript of medium John Edwards's conversations with the dead when Edwards appeared on Larry King's talk show. According to Nickell, Edwards spent a good deal of time asking questions of those who sought out relatives or friends from beyond the grave. Edwards then used the questions to shape his responses about what the dead were supposedly saying. In that way, he was able to convince those asking for contact that he had actually contacted their deceased relatives and friends. Nickell also acted as a consultant for the television show *Dateline NBC* when it did a feature on Edwards. Nickell himself was briefly surprised when Edwards seemed to have special knowledge about the dead father of one of the cameramen. Only later did Nickell find out that Edwards had managed to have a private chat with the cameraman about the latter's father.

Despite such incidents, Nickell believes his investigations may one day lead him to a true miracle that cannot be explained away as fraud or trickery. But until that time comes, he continues to insist that skepticism is the only appropriate response to reports about aliens who come from other planets, mediums who can make contact with the dead, and psychics who can predict the future.

What is the point of the author's argument?

a. Despite all of his years as an investigator of the paranormal, Nickell is a true believer at heart.

b. More people should follow in the skeptical footsteps of paranormal investigator Joe Nickell.

c. Americans are among the most gullible people in the world.

Why are the MJ-12 documents relevant to the author's argument?

_____

_____

What does Nickell's analysis of the *Dateline NBC* transcript reveal, and why is it relevant to the author's argument?

_____

_____

Practice 16   ## Be on the Lookout for Errors in Arguments

Directions: If you detect an error in the author's argument, circle the appropriate letter to identify the error. Circle the letter *f* if there are no errors in reasoning.

1. In modern war, female soldiers are fighting, killing the enemy, and being killed, just like their male counterparts. As a matter of fact, about 15 percent of American troops are women, who now participate in every facet of war except infantry battles. However, it's time to admit that putting women into combat roles was a terrible mistake. Women are just not as physically strong as men, so they are at greater risk of being captured or killed. Do we really want to subject the American public to disturbing media images of American women being taken prisoner, tortured, and even executed by the enemy? Do we want to send American women into battle only to have them endure the trauma and humiliation of sexual assault when they are captured? And do we want to create orphans at home as well as overseas?

   (*Source of information:* Joe Mozingo, "Woman's Capture in Iraq Reopens Debate on Roles," *Miami Herald*, March 25, 2003, p. 1A.)

   a. slippery slope thinking

   b. hasty generalization

   c. confusing coincidence with cause and effect

   d. irrelevant reason

   e. overreliance on rhetorical questions

   f. no error

2. Despite the accident that destroyed the space shuttle *Columbia*, killing all the astronauts who were aboard, Americans should continue to support the manned space flight program. It is absolutely unthinkable that we would even consider abandoning space travel, for the space shuttle is important and certainly worthy of funding. It's true that seven brave men and women were lost in the *Columbia* disaster, but it would be a greater tragedy to permanently ground the shuttle fleet. Instead, we must ensure that NASA has what it needs to keep these spacecraft flying. We must remain committed to making the shuttle program vital again.

   a. circular argument

   b. hasty generalization

   c. confusing coincidence with cause and effect

d. irrelevant reason

e. overreliance on rhetorical questions

f. no error

3. Many Americans criticized Hollywood's decision to broadcast its Academy Awards ceremony while American troops had just begun fighting in the 2003 war with Iraq. These critics claimed that televising such frivolous entertainment while young soldiers were being wounded and killed in battle was disrespectful and distasteful. But Hollywood was justified in its decision to carry on as usual. American servicemen and women fight for the national security that permits events like the Academy Awards to take place. These brave people expect to do their jobs while American citizens live their lives as usual. The awards show also provided off-duty military personnel with a welcome and entertaining distraction from the stress of their responsibilities. Furthermore, the Academy Awards ceremony represents a long tradition in the history of entertainment, and we should not abandon it.

a. circular argument

b. hasty generalization

c. confusing coincidence with cause and effect

d. irrelevant reason

e. overreliance on rhetorical questions

f. no error

4. In an effort to overcome a historically tense relationship, the military and the media have decided to try embedding, or stationing, war correspondents within platoons of U.S. troops. But allowing these reporters to broadcast news of a battle even as the fight is raging will have dire consequences. Embedded reporting allows the enemy to intercept correspondents' communications and learn crucial information about troops' positions and movements. This compromises the safety of our soldiers. It also eliminates any element of surprise that our military forces might use to gain an advantage in combat. Now that the military has agreed to integrate journalists, the media will never tolerate their removal in future wars. As Vietnam War veteran William Hamilton put it, "The embedded-reportage genie is out of the bottle," and it will be impossible to stuff that genie back in.

(*Source of information:* William Hamilton, "War Reporting Can Backfire," *USA Today,* March 25, 2003, p. 16A.)

  a. circular argument

  b. slippery slope thinking

  c. confusing coincidence with cause and effect

  d. irrelevant reason

  e. overreliance on rhetorical questions

  f. no error

5. Surrogate mothers are women willing to bear children for couples unable to have a child of their own. Although surrogate mothers are sometimes family members who become pregnant to help those they love, others are strangers who agree to become pregnant, bear a child, and then give it up to the parents who hired them. When the surrogate mothers are not friends or family members, they usually receive a sum of money and are asked to sign a contract. Understandably many people find such business arrangements to be distasteful or inappropriate, and the use of surrogate mothers has been harshly criticized as harmful to one or all three of the parties involved: the surrogate mother, the infertile couple, and the child. Yet as the mother of a child born of a surrogate mother, I can reassure those who have objections. My husband and I are ecstatic and loving parents. Our child is healthy and happy and sees his biological mother on a regular basis. The surrogate mother, for her part, has used the money we gave her to get an education and improve the quality of her life. Those who criticize the practice of using surrogate mothers should come to visit and see for themselves what a blessing surrogate motherhood is to those of us who cannot create a child but who can give it a good and loving home. Without question, those critical of surrogate mothers and the couples who hire them would find their objections laid to rest.

  a. slippery slope thinking

  b. hasty generalization

  c. confusing coincidence with cause and effect

  d. irrelevant reason

  e. overreliance on rhetorical questions

  f. no error

6. Although they may hold their noses while doing so, university instructors should make courses in popular culture part of their curricula. We need to understand the enduring popularity of figures like

Madonna and Elvis. We need to know why the public tunes in to reality TV, where the main draw seems to be the participants' humiliation. And we certainly have to understand the widespread appeal of rappers like Nelly and Eminem. If we fail to do so, then we also fail to understand how young people view the world. As the Japanese sociologist Hidetoshi Kato has written, "The belief systems and behavior patterns of the younger generation in many societies today are strongly affected by the messages they prefer to receive . . . either directly or indirectly through the mass media." Kato's sentiments have been echoed by others like communications scholar Michael Real, who insists popular culture "spreads specific ideas" internationally. According to Real, if we don't understand those ideas, we can't comprehend the mindset of the young people we instruct.

a. circular argument

b. hasty generalization

c. confusing coincidence with cause and effect

d. irrelevant reason

e. overreliance on rhetorical questions

f. no error

7. Recently, a number of celebrities have casually mentioned in interviews that they or their friends have been helped by one or more miraculous drugs. One celebrity claimed, for example, to have come back from a crippling struggle with arthritis thanks to a new treatment. Another had a friend whose sight was saved by a brand-new medical miracle. Touching as these stories are, the public should know that much of the time the celebrities telling such moving tales have been highly paid for their services. In their ongoing efforts to boost drug sales, pharmaceutical companies have hit on the innovative idea of paying celebrities to talk about how their medical predicaments, or those of their friends, were solved by the use of a specific drug or treatment. In other words, the celebrities have been paid to make a commercial that isn't labeled as one, and the unsuspecting public thinks it's getting a totally objective endorsement of a particular product. In short, the grasping greed of drug companies has, when no one thought it was possible, encouraged them to become even more dishonest and manipulative than usual. Have you ever noticed how commercials touting new drugs list the possible side effects in the smallest print possible? And what about those celebrities who are acting as if they were doing a public service while in reality they

are cashing big checks for their services? Did they need more money so badly they were willing to abandon all sense of honesty and personal ethics? Apparently so, but then whoever claimed that Hollywood was a training ground for moral behavior?

a. circular argument

b. hasty generalization

c. confusing coincidence with cause and effect

d. irrelevant reason

e. overreliance on rhetorical questions

f. no error

8. As writer Michael Sokolove has pointed out in an apt metaphor, "Football is the S.U.V. of the college campus: aggressively big, resource guzzling, lots and lots of fun, and potentially destructive of everything around." Look, for example, at the lesson to be learned from the University of Alabama at Birmingham, which introduced football just ten years ago. As a consequence, the university is already in trouble. Trying to make football a campus draw, the university has gone into serious debt. The trustees are insisting that if the school can't reverse the deficit, it will have to be shut down. As if that weren't enough, a fifteen-year-old girl has accused several football players and the team mascot of rape. Many people think that having a winning football team can make a university thrive. But as the Alabama example shows, the arrival of football on campus has had exactly the opposite effect.

(*Source of quotation and information:* Michael Sokolove, "Football Is a Sucker's Game," *New York Times Magazine,* December 22, 2002, p. 37.)

a. circular argument

b. hasty generalization

c. confusing coincidence with cause and effect

d. irrelevant reason

e. overreliance on rhetorical questions

f. no error

9. If the current trend toward the control of the media by big business continues, we in the United States can bid democracy good-bye. To make informed decisions about both political leaders and political issues, we need to be well informed. Yet, step by step, big corporations are taking over our news sources. True, there once

was a time when Americans could rely on an independent press to monitor the activities of government and make an unbiased report to the American people. But that was decades ago. Now-adays, members of the media are simply mouthpieces for the corporations that pay their salaries.

   a. circular argument

   b. hasty generalization

   c. confusing coincidence with cause and effect

   d. irrelevant reason

   e. overreliance on rhetorical questions

   f. no error

10. Thanks to the efforts of feminists nationwide, opportunities for women have dramatically expanded in the last fifty years, and women have become a real force in fields like medicine, engi-neering, and business. They have swelled the ranks of factory workers and turned up wearing hard hats on construction sites. But as women have entered the workforce in ever greater num-bers, they have also abandoned their traditional role of stay-at-home mother. To keep working, women now have to turn their children over to babysitters and daycare centers. Is it any wonder, then, that during the same period we have seen an increase in children suffering from psychological ills like depression and attention-deficit disorder? Perhaps those women who have traded their aprons for briefcases and time cards should take a second look at the cost of their career choices.

   a. circular argument

   b. hasty generalization

   c. confusing coincidence with cause and effect

   d. irrelevant reason

   e. overreliance on rhetorical questions

   f. no error

Practice 17

Watch for Allusions

Directions: Read each passage and look at the italicized allusion. Then read the explanation of that allusion. When you finish, explain the point of the allusion on the blank lines provided.

1. During the debate, the Republican candidate advocated tax cuts for the wealthy, and he criticized his Democratic opponent for his *Robin Hood* taxation policies. In turn, the Democratic candidate accused his rival of budget proposals that would only help the rich get richer and the poor get poorer.

   > Robin Hood was a legendary outlaw and people's hero who lived in England's Sherwood Forest. Noted for his bravery and his skill in archery, Robin Hood is said to have robbed rich people and then distributed the loot among poor peasants.

   What is the point of the author's allusion?

   _____

   _____

2. Today, women all over America are dieting and exercising in an attempt to look like thin supermodels. But not so long ago, fuller-figured women were seen as both beautiful and sexy. Consider the *Rubenesque* Marilyn Monroe, for instance, who wore a size 12. In her day, she was widely considered one of the most beautiful women in America.

   > Peter Rubens was a seventeenth-century Flemish artist now famous for painting many plump, attractive women.

   What is the point of the author's allusion?

   _____

   _____

3. That preschool teacher definitely has the patience of *Job*. Even when the twenty children in her class are crying, screaming, running around, making messes, and fighting, she manages to remain calm and unruffled.

Job was a biblical character who suffered greatly when God tested his faith and loyalty. God permitted Satan to heap misfortune on Job, but he remained patient and steadfast in his devotion to God nonetheless. In the end, God rewarded Job with happiness and prosperity.

What is the point of the author's allusion?

_____

_____

4. Mothers who receive welfare are in a *Catch-22* situation. The state pays for childcare so welfare moms can work. But when they're working and off welfare, they can't afford childcare.

Catch-22 was the title of a 1961 novel by Joseph Heller. The phrase "catch-22" is a military term that refers to contradictory regulations. In the story, a combat pilot cannot get out of serving in World War II. His doctor explains that although the pilot is clearly insane to keep flying missions that endanger his life, he would not be considered insane if he displayed the presence of mind to ask his doctor for a discharge, which is the only way for him to get out. Thus, the phrase has come to mean a frustrating, no-win situation that trips you up no matter which way you turn.

What is the point of the author's allusion?

_____

_____

5. At first, she loved her new job and went to work eager to learn. But her tasks soon became frustratingly routine, and her supervisor refused to let her take on new challenges. Before long, she felt like *Sisyphus* and had to force herself to get up in the morning to face another long and boring day.

Sisyphus was a figure in Greek mythology condemned by the gods to push a heavy rock up a hill only to see it tumble down over and over again.

What is the point of the author's allusion?

_____

_____

6. Researchers are excited about their discovery of a new vaccine against cancer. In announcing the news that they had created the vaccine, one cancer researcher said that finding a vaccine has always been the *Holy Grail* of medical research.

> According to legend, the Holy Grail is the cup used by Jesus at the Last Supper. It was said to have disappeared when the world became too sinful for such a sacred relic. The quest for the Grail occupied many of King Arthur's knights, who were determined to find it.

What is the point of the author's allusion?

_____

_____

7. Some Americans have argued that the terrorist attacks of September 11, 2001, were our modern *Pearl Harbor*. The attacks took us by surprise, and the devastation and loss of life not only sparked our determination to strike back but also aroused our suspicion of people with certain religious and ethnic backgrounds.

> Pearl Harbor, a U.S. naval station in Hawaii, was attacked without warning by the Japanese Air Force in December 1941. The attack, which caused a great loss of American lives, led to the United States' entry into World War II and the forced removal of many Japanese Americans to detention camps.

What is the point of the author's allusion?

_____

_____

8. Comedienne Whoopi Goldberg says that Mavis, the character she played on her 2003 television sitcom, was a liberal black female *Archie Bunker*. Goldberg hoped to make people laugh while also

delivering biting, cutting-edge commentaries about society and politics.

> Archie Bunker was a character in the TV sitcom *All in the Family*. He was an uneducated, narrow-minded, outspoken blue-collar worker who was openly intolerant of viewpoints that differed from his own.

What is the point of the author's allusion?

_____

_____

9. According to environmentalists, the senator is a *Benedict Arnold*. During his campaign, he promised to work hard to strengthen regulations that would protect the quality of our air and water. However, he has not fulfilled his promises; as a matter of fact, he has actually voted to weaken current anti-pollution laws.

> Benedict Arnold was a U.S. Army officer during the American Revolutionary War. He became a traitor to his country when he secretly plotted to surrender the fort at West Point to the British in exchange for money.

What is the point of the author's allusion?

_____

_____

10. All over the country, schools have had to rewrite their dress codes. To prevent young girls from coming to class looking like *Britney Spears* wannabes, school officials have had to outlaw shirts that expose the stomach and mandate a minimum length for shorts and skirts.

> Britney Spears, a pop music performer who is popular with adolescents, is noted for her provocative style of dress.

What is the point of the author's allusion?

_____

_____

Should you or your instructor feel the need for additional practice with any one of the reading skills covered in Parts I and II of this book, additional exercises are included in the manual and on the Web at http://users.dhp.com/~laflemm.

Part III

Making a Match Between the Reader and the Text

What follows are four units of readings, each one revolving around a specific theme. While it's true that these readings are here to help you practice being a flexible reader, they were also chosen to make you think. Once you understand what the author's message is, you should take the next step and form your own opinion. Assignments at the end of each reading will help you determine your personal point of view.

Unit 1 The Mysteries of Memory

The human memory has long been the object of study. For centuries researchers have posed questions: Why do some events and experiences stay with us while others disappear from memory practically moments after they happen? And just how accurate is the human memory? Can we trust what it tells us? The authors in the following unit all agree that human memory is a complex mechanism. No one really knows for sure how it works. Because memory is such a mystery, we should perhaps be suspicious of its contents. As some of the following readings suggest, it's often hard to tell if what we remember is what really happened.

Reading 1   # The Nature of Memory

GETTING FOCUSED

Theories about the workings of memory have been around for years. At one time, for example, it was thought that the human memory acted like a camera that took mental snapshots of events and then stored them in the brain for later retrieval. But that theory, or model, of memory—like several others—has come and gone. In its place stands the information-processing model explained in the following reading.

Textbook Features and Readers' Strategies

Feature: *The headings introduce the topics of the sections.*

Strategy: Pre-read the headings and turn them into questions like "What is the power of chunking?"

Feature: *In addition to headings, questions also help break up the text.*

Strategy: When you finish the chapter section introduced by a question, see how well you can answer that question. If your mind goes blank, reread the chapter section.

Feature: *The authors use marginal annotations of all kinds to help readers understand key ideas and terms.*

Strategy: Read all of the marginal annotations before you actually read the text from beginning to end. Reread the annotations when you reach the passages they help explain.

Feature: *The authors supply several visual aids.*

Strategy: Study the visual aids before you begin reading. Reread them when you get to the passages they illustrate, only this time look at them *after* you have read the text.

Feature: *Key terms are printed in boldface type.*

Strategy: Pre-read all of the terms and their definitions. When you read the text from beginning to end, jot terms and definitions in the margins.

Feature: *The writing is straightforward and clear but densely packed with information.*

Strategy: Take your time reading. Mark particularly difficult passages with the letters *RR* (for "reread") or some other symbol. Go back to those passages once you finish the entire excerpt and read them again. Then check your comprehension by paraphrasing.

Evaluating Your Background Knowledge

The authors of this reading are relying on your knowledge of these words and terms. Look over this list carefully to make sure you know everything on it. *Note:* The number in parentheses indicates the paragraph where the word can be found while an asterisk accompanies the word's first appearance in the reading.

comprehensive (3): complete

encoded (4):   put into a form that makes information capable of being held in memory

perception (4):   image, view, understanding

neural (5):   related to the nervous system

integrated (5):   unified, combined

retrieval (6):   the process of recalling information stored in memory

sensory (7):   related to sight, smell, sound, and touch

auditory (8):   related to hearing

discrete (14):   individual, separate

elaborative rehearsal (16): processing new information by repeating it or relating it to information already stored in memory

adaptive (18):   able to make changes

semantic coding (21): storing experiences according to their general meaning

1   Memory is a funny thing. You might be able to remember the name of your first-grade teacher, but not the name of someone you met just five minutes ago. Mathematician John Griffith estimated that in an average lifetime, a person stores roughly five hundred times as much information as can be found in all the volumes of the *Encyclopaedia Britannica* (M. Hunt, 1982). Keep in mind, however, that although we retain a great deal of information, we also lose a great deal (Bjork & Vanhuele, 1992).

2   Memory plays a critical role in your life. Without memory, you would not know how to shut off your alarm, take a shower, get

dressed, recognize objects, or communicate. You would be unaware of your own likes and dislikes. You would have no idea of who you are (Craik et al., 1999). The impressive capacity of human memory depends on the operation of a complex mental system (Schacter, 1999). . . .

information processing model
Information is processed in three stages: sensory memory, short-term memory, and long-term memory.

3   **Information Processing**   The **information-processing model** is probably the most influential and comprehensive* model of memory. It suggests that for information to be firmly implanted in memory, it must pass through three stages of mental processing: sensory memory, short-term memory, and long-term memory (see Figure 1).

4   In **sensory memory,** information from the senses—sights or sounds, for example—is held in sensory registers very briefly, often for less than one second. Information in the sensory registers may be attended to, analyzed, and encoded* as a meaningful pattern; this is the process of *perception.** If the information in sensory memory is perceived, it can enter *short-term memory.* If nothing further is done, the information will disappear in less than twenty seconds. But if the information in short-term memory is further processed, it may be encoded into *long-term memory,* where it may remain indefinitely.

sensory memory
A type of memory that is very brief, but lasts long enough to connect one impression to the next.

5   The act of reading illustrates all three stages of memory processing. As you read any sentence in this book, for example, light energy reflected from the page reaches your eyes, where it is converted to neural* activity and registered in your sensory memory. If you pay attention to these visual stimuli, your perception of the patterns of light can be held in short-term memory. This stage of memory holds the early parts of the sentence so that they can be integrated* and understood as you read the rest of the sentence. As you read, you are constantly recognizing words by matching your perceptions of them with the patterns and meanings you have stored in long-term memory. Thus, all three stages are necessary for you to understand a sentence.

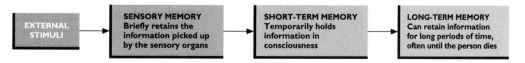

Figure 1
Three Stages of Memory
This traditional information-processing model describes memory as consisting of three storage systems.

Storing New Memories

6   The model of memory we've been discussing gives us a way to think about the three basic memory processes of encoding, storage, and retrieval.* We code information in order to store it, and we can retrieve only information that has been stored. Obviously, the storage of information is critical to memory. According to the information-processing model, sensory memory, short-term memory, and long-term memory each provide a different type of storage. Let's take a closer look at these three memory systems in order to better understand how they work—and sometimes fail.

Sensory Memory

7   To recognize incoming stimuli, the brain must analyze and compare them with what is already stored in long-term memory. Although this process is very quick, it still takes time. The major function of sensory* memory is to hold information long enough for it to be processed further. This "holding" function is the job of the **sensory registers,** which act as temporary storage bins. There is a separate register for each of the five senses. Every

sensory registers
Memory systems that briefly hold incoming information.

> **Sensory Memory at Work**
>
> In a darkened room, ask a friend to hold a small flashlight and move it very slowly in a circle. You will see a single point of light moving in a circle. If it appears to have a "tail," like a comet, that is your sensory memory of the light before it fades. Now ask your friend to speed up the movement. This time, you should see a complete circle of light, because as the light moves, its impression on your sensory memory does not have time to fade before the circle is completed. A similar process allows us to see still images "move" when we watch a film or video.

register is capable of storing an almost complete representation of a sensory stimulus (J. B. Best, 1999). However, the sensory registers hold this representation for only a very brief period of time, often less than one second.

8   Sensory memory helps us experience a constant flow of information, even if that flow is interrupted. To appreciate this fact, move your head and eyes slowly from left to right. Although it seems to you that your eyes are moving smoothly, like a movie camera scanning a scene, this is not what happens. Your eyes fixate at one point for about one-fourth of a second and then rapidly jump to a new position. You perceive smooth motion because you hold the scene in your visual sensory register until your eyes fixate again. Similarly, when you listen to someone speak, your auditory* sensory register allows you to experience a smooth flow of information, even though there are actually short silences between or within words.

9 The fact that sensory memories fade quickly if they are not processed further is actually an adaptive characteristic of this memory system (Baddeley, 1998). You simply cannot deal with all of the sights, sounds, odors, tastes, and touch sensations that come to your sense organs at any given moment. Using **selective attention,** you focus your mental resources on only part of the stimuli around you, thus controlling what information is processed further in short-term memory.

selective attention
The process of focusing mental resources on only part of the stimulus field.

Short-Term, or Working, Memory

10 The sensory registers allow your memory system to develop a representation of a stimulus. However, they do not allow the more thorough analysis needed if the information is going to be used in some way. That function is accomplished by **short-term memory (STM),** the part of your memory system that stores limited amounts of information for up to about eighteen seconds. When you check *TV Guide* for the channel number of a show and then switch to that channel, you are using short-term memory.

short-term memory (STM) A stage of memory in which information normally lasts less than twenty seconds. Also called *working memory.*

11 Many researchers refer to short-term memory as working memory, because it helps you to do much of your mental work, from punching in a phone number to solving a math problem (Baddeley, 1992). Suppose you are buying something for 83 cents. You go through your change and pick out two quarters, two dimes, two nickels, and three pennies. To do this you must remember the price, retrieve the rules of addition from long-term memory, *and* keep a running count of how much change you have so far. Now try to recall how many windows there are on the front of the house or apartment where you grew up. To answer this question, you will probably form a mental image of the building. Here, too, you are using a working-memory process that allows you to keep that image in your mind while you count the windows.

12 **Encoding in Short-Term Memory** The encoding of information in short-term memory is much more elaborate and varied than encoding in the sensory registers (Brandimonte, Hitch, & Bishop, 1992). Acoustic coding (by sound) seems to dominate short-term memory. This conclusion comes from research on the mistakes people make when encoding information in short-term memory. These mistakes tend to involve the substitution of similar sounds. For instance, Robert Conrad (1964) showed people strings of letters and asked them to repeat the letters immediately. Among their most common mistakes was the replacement of the correct letter with another that sounded like it. For example, the correct letter *C* was replaced with a

D, P, or *T.* The participants made these mistakes even though the letters were presented visually, without any sound. Studies in several cultures have also shown that items are more difficult to remember if they sound similar. For example, native English speakers perform more poorly when they must remember a string of letters like *ECVTGB* (which all have similar sounds) than when asked to remember one like *KRLDQS* (which have distinct sounds).

13   Although encoding in short-term memory is usually acoustic, it is not *always* acoustic. Information in short-term memory can be also coded visually, semantically, and even kinesthetically, in terms of physical movements (J. B. Best, 1999). In one study, deaf people were shown a list of words and then asked to immediately write down all they could remember (Shand, 1982). When these participants made errors, they wrote words that are expressed through similar *hand movements* in American Sign Language, rather than words that *sounded* similar to the correct words. Apparently, these individuals had encoded the words on the basis of the movements they would use when signing them.

14   **Storage Capacity of Short-Term Memory**   How much information can you hold in short-term memory? You can easily determine the answer by conducting the simple experiment shown in Figure 2 (Howard, 1983). Your **immediate memory span** is the maximum number of items you can recall perfectly after one presentation. If your memory span is like most people's, you can repeat six or seven

immediate memory span The maximum number of items a person can recall perfectly after one presentation of the items.

```
9 2 5
8 6 4 2
3 7 6 5 4
6 2 7 4 1 8
0 4 0 1 4 7 3
1 9 2 2 3 5 3 0
4 8 6 8 5 4 3 3 2
2 5 3 1 9 7 1 7 6 8
8 5 1 2 9 6 1 9 4 5 0
9 1 8 5 4 6 9 4 2 9 3 7
```

Figure 2
The Capacity of Short-Term Memory
Here is a test of your immediate, or short-term, memory span. Ask someone to read to you the numbers in the top row at the rate of about one per second; then try to repeat them back in the same order. Then try the next row, and the one after that, until you make a mistake. Your immediate memory span is the maximum number of items you can repeat back perfectly.
Source: Howard (1983).

items from the test in this figure. You should come up with about the same result whether you use digits, letters, words, or virtually any type of unit (Hayes, 1952; I. Pollack, 1953). George Miller (1956) noticed that many studies using a variety of tasks showed the same limit on the ability to process information. This "magic number," which is seven plus or minus two, appears to be the immediate memory span or capacity of short-term memory, at least in laboratory settings. It is generally considered to be somewhat less in more naturalistic settings (Martindale, 1991). The "magic number" refers to meaningful *groupings* of information, called **chunks,** not to a certain number of discrete* elements.

chunks Stimuli that are perceived as units or meaningful groupings of information.

15   To see the difference between discrete elements and chunks, read the following letters to a friend, pausing at each dash: *FB-IAO-LM-TVI-BMB-MW.* The chances are very good that your friend will not be able to repeat this string of letters perfectly. Why? There are fifteen letters, which exceeds most people's immediate memory span. Now, give your friend the test again, but group the letters like this: *FBI-AOL-MTV-IBM-BMW.* Your friend will probably repeat the string easily (Bower, 1975). Although the same fifteen letters are involved, they will be processed as only five meaningful chunks of information.

16   **The Power of Chunking**   Chunks of information can be quite complex. If you heard someone say, "The boy in the red shirt kicked his mother in the shin," you could probably repeat the sentence easily. Yet, it contains twelve words and forty-three letters. How can you repeat the sentence so effortlessly? The answer is that you are able to build bigger and bigger chunks of information (Ericsson & Staszewski, 1989). In this case, you might represent "the boy in the red shirt" as one chunk of information rather than as six words or nineteen letters. Similarly, "kicked his mother" and "in the shin" represent separate chunks of information. You can also create chunks by using elaborative rehearsal.* To do this, you would find a set of rules or associations in long-term memory that you could use to group several items together. Thus, you might represent "the boy in the red shirt" as a single visual image.

17   Learning to use bigger and bigger chunks of information can greatly benefit short-term memory. This effect can easily be seen in children. Their short-term memories improve partly because they become able to hold as many as seven chunks in memory, but also because they get better at grouping information into chunks (Servan-Schreiber & Anderson, 1990). Adults also can greatly increase the capacity of their short-term memory by using more appropriate chunking. For example, after extensive training, one college student increased his immediate memory span from seven to eighty digits (Neisser, 2000b). So although the capacity of short-term memory is more or less constant (from five to nine chunks of meaningful information), the size of those chunks can vary tremendously.

18   **Duration of Short-Term Memory** Why don't you remember every phone number you ever dialed or every conversation you ever had? The answer is that you usually forget information in short-term memory quickly. Although this adaptive* feature of short-term memory gets rid of a lot of useless information, it can be inconvenient. You may have discovered this if you ever looked up a phone number, got distracted before you could call it, and then forgot the number.

19   How long does information remain in short-term memory if you don't keep rehearsing it? John Brown (1958) and Lloyd and Margaret Peterson (1959) devised the **Brown-Peterson procedure** to measure the duration of short-term memory when no rehearsal is allowed. In this procedure, participants are presented with a group of three letters, such as *GRB*. They then count backward by threes from some number until they get a signal. Counting prevents the participants from rehearsing the letters. At the signal, they stop counting and try to recall the letters. By varying the number of seconds spent counting backward, the experimenter can determine how much forgetting takes place over time. As you can see in Figure 3, information in short-term memory is

Brown-Peterson procedure A method for determining how long unrehearsed information remains in short-term memory.

Figure 3
Forgetting in Short-Term Memory
This graph shows the percentage of nonsense syllables recalled after various intervals during which rehearsal was prevented. Notice that virtually complete forgetting occurred after a delay of eighteen seconds.

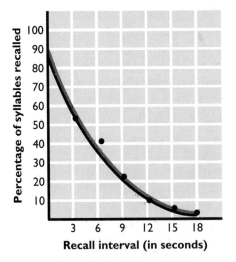

Source: Data from L. R. Peterson & Peterson (1959).

forgotten gradually until, after only eighteen seconds, participants can remember almost nothing. Evidence from other such experiments also suggests that *unrehearsed* information can be held in short-term memory for no more than about eighteen seconds. However, if the information is rehearsed or processed further in some other way, it may be encoded into long-term memory.

Long-Term Memory

20   When people talk about memory, they are usually referring to long-term memory. **Long-term memory (LTM)** is the part of the memory system whose encoding and storage capabilities can produce memories that last a lifetime.

long-term memory (LTM) The stage of memory for which the capacity to store new information is believed to be unlimited.

21   **Encoding in Long-Term Memory**   Some information is encoded into long-term memory automatically, without any conscious attempt to memorize it (N. R. Ellis, 1991). However, placement of information into long-term memory is often the result of more elaborate and conscious processing that usually involves *semantic coding.** Semantic encoding often leaves out details in favor of the more general, underlying meaning of the information.

22   The notion that semantic encoding dominates in LTM was demonstrated in a classic study by Jacqueline Sachs (1967). Her participants first listened to tape recordings of people reading from books. Then Sachs showed them sets of sentences with the same meaning and asked whether each exact sentence had been read on the tape. Participants did very well when tested *immediately,* using mainly short-term memory. After only twenty-seven seconds, though, they could not be sure which of two sentences they had heard. For example, they could not remember whether they had heard "He sent a letter about it to Galileo, the great Italian scientist" or "A letter about it was sent to Galileo, the great Italian scientist." Why did this happen? It occurred because the delay was long enough that the participants had to recall the information from long-term memory, where they had encoded the *general meaning* of what they had heard, but not the exact wording.

23   Counterfeiters depend on the fact that people encode the general meaning of visual stimuli rather than specific details. For example, look at Figure 4, and find the correct drawing of a U.S penny (Nickerson & Adams, 1979). Most people from the United States are unsuccessful at this task. People from Great Britain do poorly at recognizing their country's coins, too (G. V. Jones, 1990).

(A)   **(B)**   **(C)**   **(D)**   **(E)**

Figure 4
Encoding into Long-Term Memory
Which is the correct image of a U.S. penny?
Source: Nickerson & Adams (1979).

24   **Storage Capacity of Long-Term Memory**   The capacity of long-term memory is extremely large. Indeed, many psychologists believe that it is literally unlimited (Matlin, 1998). There is no way to prove this, but we do know that people store vast quantities of information in long-term memory that can be remembered remarkably well after long periods of time. For example, people are amazingly accurate at recognizing the faces of their high school classmates after having not seen them for over twenty-five years (Bruck, Cavanagh, & Ceci, 1991). They also do surprisingly well on tests of a foreign language or high school algebra fifty years after having formally studied these subjects (Bahrick et al., 1994; Bahrick & Hall, 1991). And college students are fairly accurate in remembering their high school grades—especially if they were good grades (Bahrick, Hall, & Berger, 1996).

25   But long-term memories are also subject to distortion. In one study illustrating this point, students were asked to describe where they were and what they were doing at the moment they heard about the verdict in the O. J. Simpson murder trial (Schmolck, Buffalo, & Squire, 2000). The students reported their recollections three times, first just three days after the verdict, and then again after fifteen and thirty-two months. At the final reporting, almost all the students claimed they could still remember accurately where they were and what they were doing, but more than 70 percent of their memories were distorted and/or inaccurate. For example, three days after the verdict, one student said he heard about it while in a campus lounge with many other students around him. Thirty-two months later, this same student recalled hearing the news in the living room of his home with his father and sister. Most of the students whose memories had been substantially distorted over time were unaware that this distortion had occurred; they were very confident that the reports were accurate. Later, we will see that such overconfidence can also appear in courtroom testimony by eyewitnesses to crime.

Storing New Memories			
Storage System	**Function**	**Capacity**	**Duration**
Sensory memory	Briefly holds representations of stimuli from each sense for furthur processing	Large: absorbs all sensory input from a particular stimulus	Less than 1 second
Short-term, or working, memory	Holds information in awareness while it is being processed	Five to nine distinct items or chunks of information	About 18 seconds
Long-term memory	Stores new information indefinitely	Unlimited	Unlimited

Distinguishing Between Short-Term and Long-Term Memory

26   Some psychologists argue that short-term memory and long-term memory have different features and obey different laws (N. Cowan, 1988). Evidence that information is transferred from short-term memory to a distinct storage system comes primarily from experiments on recall.

27   You can conduct your own recall experiment. Look at the following list of words for thirty seconds, and then look away and write down as many of the words as you can, in any order: *desk, chalk, pencil, chair, paperclip, book, eraser, folder, briefcase, essays.* Which words you recall depends in part on their serial position, or where the words are in the list. The *serial-position curve* in Figure 5 shows this effect. From this curve you can see the chances of recalling words appearing in each position in a list. For the first two or three words in a list,

Figure 5

A Serial-Position Curve

The probability of recalling an item is plotted here as a function of its serial position in a list of items. Generally, the first several items and the last several items are most likely to be recalled.

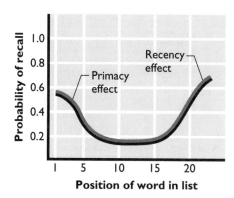

primacy effect
A phenomenon whereby recall for the first two or three terms in a list is particularly good.

recency effect
A phenomenon whereby recall for the last few items in a list is particularly good.

28

recall tends to be very good. This phenomenon is called the **primacy effect**. The probability of recall decreases for words in the middle of the list and then rises dramatically for the last few words. The ease of recalling words near the end of the list is called the **recency effect**. The primacy effect may reflect the rehearsal that puts early words into long-term memory. The recency effect may occur because the last few words are still in short-term memory when you try to recall the list (Glanzer & Cunitz, 1996; Koppenaal & Glanzer, 1990; see Figure 6).

K. Anders Ericsson and Walter Kintsch (1995) proposed a different way of thinking about the relationship between short-term and long-term memory. Studying people who display unusually good memory abilities, they suggested the operation of a "long-term, working memory." By this they mean that people who are skilled at remembering a list of items may be especially capable of rapidly transferring information from working (or short-term) memory into long-term memory. Once the transfer occurs, networks of related information already in long-term memory are activated to help the person remember the items. Many people with excellent memories

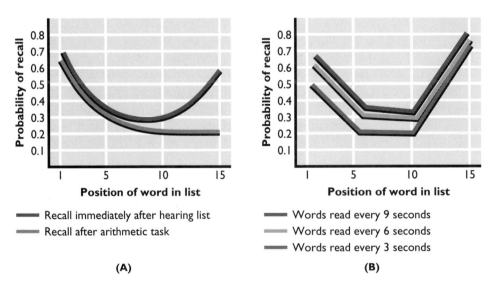

(A)

Recall immediately after hearing list
Recall after arithmetic task

(B)

Words read every 9 seconds
Words read every 6 seconds
Words read every 3 seconds

Figure 6
Separating Short-Term from Long-Term Memory
The results of two studies by Murray Glanzer and Anita Cunitz support the idea that short- and long-term memory are distinct systems. Part A shows that doing arithmetic before trying to recall a list of words destroys the recency effect but does not alter the primacy effect. Part B shows that presenting words at a faster rate—which keeps people from rehearsing the early words enough to put them into long-term memory—reduces the primacy effect but does not change the recency effect.
Source: Part A: data from Glanzer & Cunitz (1966); part B: data from Koppendal & Glanzer (1990).

appear to operate this way. In one study, researchers tested a waiter who was famous for remembering up to twenty dinner orders without writing anything down. He didn't do as well as that under laboratory conditions, but he was still able to remember five complex dinner orders almost to perfection. College students who tried the same task got about 20 percent of the orders wrong (Ericsson & Polson, 1988).

Adapted from Douglas Bernstein and Peggy W. Nash, *Essentials of Psychology*, pp. 180–189.

CHECKING YOUR COMPREHENSION

Directions: Circle the letter of the correct answer.

1. Which of the following statements expresses the overall main idea of the entire reading?

   a. Although chunking information takes time, learning bigger and bigger chunks of information can enlarge the capacity of short-term memory.

   b. The capacity of long-term memory is extremely large, and memories that are stored long-term may last forever.

   c. Long-term memories are not always accurate.

   d. The information-processing model of remembering suggests that information passes through three stages of mental processing.

2. In paragraph 5, the topic sentence is

   a. the first sentence.

   b. the second sentence.

   c. the third sentence.

3. In paragraph 12, the topic sentence is

   a. the first sentence.

   b. the second sentence.

   c. the third sentence.

4. In paragraph 13, the study about the deaf is used to support which main idea?

   a. Encoding in short-term memory is always by sound.

   b. Encoding in short-term memory is not always by sound.

   c. The deaf have better short-term memories than the hearing.

   d. Visual encoding is the best way to store information in short-term memory.

5. Which statement most effectively paraphrases the definition of "immediate memory span" in paragraph 14?

   a. Your immediate memory span is the number of items you are trying to absorb at one time.

   b. The term "immediate memory span" refers to the time needed to accurately absorb new visual and auditory information.

   c. The phrase "immediate memory span" refers to the greatest number of items you can correctly remember after seeing or hearing them just once.

   d. The term "immediate memory span" refers to the number of multisyllabic words you can recall after a one-minute presentation.

6. Which statement most effectively sums up the main idea of paragraph 17?

   a. Children are better at chunking information than adults are.

   b. College students, in particular, should make an effort to chunk new information.

   c. Although the number of chunks in short-term memory is fairly fixed, the size of the chunks can vary.

   d. Increasing the size of information chunks is one way to improve the capacity of short-term memory.

7. What's the implied main idea of the section titled "Duration of Short-Term Memory" (paragraphs 18–19)?

   a. The Brown-Peterson procedure enabled researchers to determine what causes forgetfulness.

   b. Rehearsal determines whether or not information in short-term memory makes its way into long-term memory.

   c. Unrehearsed information stays in long-term memory much longer than information that has been repeatedly rehearsed.

8. Which statement most effectively summarizes the main idea of the section titled "Encoding in Long-Term Memory" (paragraphs 21–23)?

   a. Even without any kind of rehearsal, much of what we see and hear readily makes its way into long-term memory.

   b. We use semantic coding when we store information according to sound.

   c. New information is most likely to enter long-term memory if we make use of semantic coding.

   d. The inability of most people to remember what a penny looks like illustrates how most of us rely on semantic coding to store familiar information.

9. What's the implied main idea of the section titled "Storage Capacity of Long-Term Memory" (paragraphs 24–25)?

   a. Long-term memory has a great deal of storage space, but the memories stored there are not necessarily accurate.

   b. When information makes its way to long-term memory, it's there forever.

   c. The capacity of long-term memory may be unlimited, particularly where faces are concerned.

   d. Most people remember the faces of their high school class-mates even if they haven't seen one another for years.

10. The reading is organized by which patterns?

    a. cause and effect; definition

    b. definition; comparison and contrast

    c. definition; cause and effect; time order

    d. definition; cause and effect; time order; classification

DEEPENING YOUR UNDERSTANDING

Directions: Answer the following questions by circling the letter of the correct response or filling in the blanks where required.

1. How would you describe the authors' tone? _____

2. What would you say is the author's purpose?

   a. to describe the information-processing model of memory

   b. to convince readers that the information-processing model of memory is the best description of human memory

3. What kind of language do the authors rely on?

    a. connotative or emotionally charged language

    b. denotative or neutral language lacking in emotion

    c. a mixture of connotative and denotative language

4. Do you think the authors rely

    a. mainly on fact?

    b. mainly on opinion?

    c. on a mixture of fact and opinion?

5. If asked to remember whose face appears on a one dollar bill, a five, a ten, and a twenty, most people can't remember. This illustrates what point made in the reading?

    a. We usually forget information in short-term memory.

    b. Chunking can increase the capacity of short-term memory.

    c. Semantic coding leaves out details in favor of more general meaning.

    d. The capacity of long-term memory is extremely large.

6. In paragraph 25, the authors say, "we will see that such overconfidence [in the accuracy of memories] can also appear in courtroom testimony by eyewitnesses to crime." You will be reading about eyewitness testimony later in this unit. But just having read this excerpt on remembering, how do you think the authors would answer this question: Is eyewitness testimony completely

trustworthy? _____ Please explain your answer.

_____

_____

7. Using what you learned from the reading, see if you can chunk these words: *infancy, winter, red, spring, childhood, white, autumn, blue, summer, adolescence, adulthood* so they'd be easier to remember.

_____

_____

8. Based on what you have read, circle the words in the following list that you would be most likely to forget after looking at the list for thirty seconds: *fork, knife, table, cup, saucer, bowl, spoon, whisk, napkin, plate, salt, pepper*

   _____

   Explain why you would be likely to forget the words you circled.

   _____

   _____

9. Many people believe that a good memory is a special gift possessed by a lucky few. How do you think the authors would respond to that claim?

   _____

   _____

10. Imagine that you need to remember the names of the eight people sitting at your conference table. As each one is introduced, what

    will you do?_____

    What is that process called? _____

AIRING YOUR OPINIONS

Do you think you will be able to put what you have read to practical use? In other words, having read this selection, do you think you will

remember more of what you read or heard? _____
Why or why not?

_____

_____

Reading 2

Getting Information Into and Out of Long-Term Memory

GETTING FOCUSED

The previous reading gave you a fairly detailed picture of how information makes its way into long-term memory. The authors of the following reading continue that discussion by offering practical suggestions to make sure that new information enters long-term memory despite various obstacles.

Textbook Features and Readers' Strategies

Feature:	*Numerous topic headings divide up the text.*
Strategy:	Pre-read those headings and turn them into questions, for example, What are "mnemonic devices"? Then read to find the answers.
Feature:	*Marginal annotations highlight the key points and terms.*
Strategy:	Preview the annotations before you start reading. While you read, compare the textual explanation to the marginal one. Sometimes, one or the other adds an extra detail.
Feature:	*The authors supply graphs and diagrams.*
Strategy:	Look over the graphs and the diagrams before you start to read. Reread both when you reach the text they illustrate. Check to see if you understand how each one fleshes out the text.
Feature:	*Stories and anecdotes illustrate key points.*
Strategy:	When you come across a story or anecdote to illustrate an idea, you can read a little more quickly. Just make sure that you know *what* each story illustrates.

Evaluating Your Background Knowledge

The authors of this reading are relying on your knowledge of these words and terms. Look over this list carefully to make sure you know everything on it. *Note:* The number in parentheses indicates the paragraph where the word can be found while an asterisk accompanies the word's first appearance in the reading.

randomly (1):	without plan
scrutinize (4):	study carefully

Evaluating Your Background Knowledge (continued)

passively (7):   without effort or activity

phenomenon (11): occurrence, event, happening

accessible (12):   available, capable of being retrieved

literal (16):   realistic, happening in reality

retention (24):   act of holding or keeping

---

1   Sherlock Holmes considered the brain to be like the attic of a house, in which we store all the things we know. The fictional detective, who was a master of memory, emphasized that to be able to find the information we need, we must stock our brain attic with great care. What Holmes referred to as the "brain attic" is what psychologists today call long-term memory. Research has shown that Holmes was right in recommending that we stock the attic carefully. Unless information is carefully coded and filed, it will be impossible to retrieve the information when we need it. The task would be like trying to find a book in a large library where the volumes are arranged randomly* and the card catalogue is disorganized.

Encoding

encoding Linking new information to already learned concepts and categories.

2   We transfer information from short-term memory to long-term memory through a process called **encoding**. Encoding involves linking new information to concepts and categories that we have already learned. It is something like filing things in a cross-referenced file system—for example, indexing library books by title, author, and subject headings.

3   Most of the time, we encode information automatically, without giving much attention to the mental filing system that we are using. The key to encoding material successfully in long-term memory, however, is to think about the meaning of the material and attempt to understand it (Craik & Lockhart, 1972). If you are taught a new formula in a physics class, simply repeating the formula to yourself over and over will not be a very good way of fixing it in your memory. A more effective approach will be to ask yourself what the formula really means and how it relates to other principles that you've already learned. In one series of experiments that illustrates the

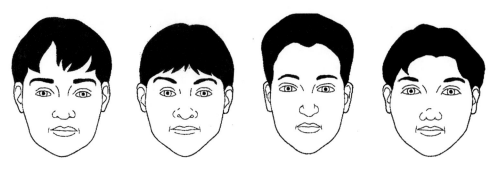

Figure 7

One group of subjects was asked to look at faces like these and decide what gender each face represented. A second group of subjects was asked to decide how "honest" each face was. When tested at a later session, the subjects who had rated the faces for "honesty" were better able to recognize the faces they had seen, apparently because they had thought more deeply about the "meaning" of the faces' features.

importance of focusing on meaning, Fergus Craik and Endel Tulving (1975) presented college students with long lists of words, such as "bear," "vest," "apple," and "string." After each word was presented, the subject was asked a question about it. Some of the questions directed the subject's attention to the *meaning* of the word (for example, "Is it a wild animal?"); other questions directed attention to the *sound* of the word (for example, "Does it rhyme with 'chair'?"). In later memory tests, the students were much more successful at remembering the words on which they had had their attention focused on meaning.

4   The principle that encoding is most effective when we think about the meaning of the material applies even to our memory for people's faces. The more closely and thoughtfully we scrutinize* a person's features, the better we will remember the face. In several studies, subjects were shown pictures of faces and asked to make judgments either of the person's personality traits (such as the person's honesty) or of the person's gender (see Figure 7). The personality judgments required the subjects to examine the faces more carefully and to think about them at a deeper level. Later the subjects were tested for their recognition of the faces they had seen. The result: subjects recognized the faces best when they had focused on personality traits—and, as a result, had given more thought to the "meaning" of the faces' features (Bloom & Mudd, 1991; Bower & Karlin, 1974).

5   The value of thinking deeply about material helps to explain the effectiveness of several memory-improvement techniques. You can make good use of these techniques in mastering course material and studying for tests:

6   **Space Your Study Sessions**   Studying is usually more effective when you spread it out over several sessions instead of doing it all at once in a single, concentrated block of time (Dempster, 1988). If you read the same passage over and over on a single occasion, you are not likely to think about the passage very deeply on the second, third, and subsequent run-throughs. Instead, the rereading is likely to be a rather thoughtless, mechanical exercise. But if you read the passage once today and then come back to it tomorrow and again the next day, you are likely to pay more attention to its meaning the second and third times around. The result is a deeper processing of the material, more effective encoding, and, ultimately, better learning (Krug, Davis, & Glover, 1990).

7   **Read and Listen Actively**   As you read a textbook or listen to a lecture, don't read or listen passively.* Instead, write down questions about the material in the margins of your lecture notes or textbook. If a textbook section is headed "Encoding," you might ask: "What role does encoding play in memory?" "What sort of encoding is most effective?" "Why does the spacing of study sessions lead to more effective encoding?" Generating questions for yourself—and then trying to answer them—helps guarantee that you will organize the material in a way that is meaningful to you and, therefore, a way that will help you to remember the material.

8   **Use Mnemonic Devices to Give Material "Meaning"**   Techniques designed to help memorize material are called *mnemonic* (pronounced "ne-*mahn*-ic") *devices.* Sometimes you are called on to memorize material, such as vocabulary lists in a foreign language, that is not easily connected to your existing store of knowledge. To give strange words a memorable meaning, you can try the *keyword method*, a mnemonic device developed by Richard Atkinson (1975). First, make up a keyword—an English word that sounds like the foreign word you need to remember. If you're trying to learn that "duck" in Spanish is *pato* (pronounced "pot-o"), your keyword might be "pot." Second, form a mental image that links the object with the keyword— for example, visualize a duck with a pot over his head (see Figure 8). Now when you're called on to translate "duck," you can retrieve your mental image, observe the pot that the duck is wearing, and remember that the word is *pato*. Although it is not always easy to come up with effective keywords and images (Hall, 1988), the method can be quite effective (Pressley, 1991).

Figure 8
The keyword method for learning vocabulary words in a foreign language. The Spanish word for duck is pato *(pronounced pot-o)—so your keyword could be "pot." Now visualize a duck with a pot over its head. The next time you're asked to translate "duck," simply retrieve your mental image, and you'll remember* pato.

Retrieval

9   Regardless of the method used to get material into long-term memory, the next problem is **retrieval**—locating the information in long-term memory and bringing it back into consciousness. What is the capital of Iowa? It's a good bet that you know the answer—it's likely to be somewhere in your long-term memory—but you can't get it out at the moment. Can you remember the name and face of the pediatrician you used to visit? That information, too, is probably in your long-term memory. The question is, can you retrieve it?

retrieval Locating information in long-term memory and recalling it to consciousness.

10   The retrieval of information from long-term memory is easiest if the information was encoded effectively in the first place. But to retrieve information successfully, we also need reminders, or retrieval cues, that we can associate with the material being retrieved. For example, people can remember the words of a song more easily when they hear the melody, and they can remember the melody more easily when they read or hear the words. The words and the melody became connected when the person first heard the song, and each serves as a retrieval cue for the other (Crowder, Serafine, & Repp, 1990).

11   The importance of retrieval cues is illustrated by the phenomenon* of *context-dependent memory*—the tendency for people's memories to be best when they recall material in the same locale or in the same physical or mental state they were in when they first learned it. For example, scuba divers were asked to memorize lists of words either on shore or ten feet underwater. The divers were later able to recall more words when they were tested in their original learning environment than when they were tested in the other environment (Godden & Baddeley, 1975).

12   Similarly, memories acquired when a particular odor was present— say, the musty odor of grandma's basement—are most accessible* when the odor is encountered again (Schab, 1990). In such cases, the locale or context appears to be closely associated with the memory and can therefore serve as a retrieval cue. Returning to the same state makes this cue highly available, increasing the chances of recalling the rest of the original memory. Criminal investigators make use of this principle when they bring witnesses back to the scene of the crime in the hope of jogging their memories.

13   Among the most frustrating experiences connected with memory retrieval are the cases in which we feel that we can *almost* remember a word that we are searching for . . . but not quite. "I *know* his name," you say to yourself. "It's something like Montego or Morocco or Menudo—but I can't come up with it." When you finally manage to get the name in mind—it was Mancuso—you feel tremendous relief. This feeling of being almost-but-not-quite able to remember a word has been aptly named the **tip-of-the-tongue phenomenon** (Brown & McNeill, 1966). Just as you did when you were trying to remember Mancuso's name, people who experience the tip-of-the-tongue phenomenon often come up with words that sound like the one they are groping for, starting with the same letter and containing the same number of syllables (Brown, 1991).

tip-of-the-tongue phenomenon The feeling of being almost-but-not-quite able to remember.

14   Research on the tip-of-the-tongue phenomenon has helped to show that words that are filed in long-term memory are indexed not only by their meaning but also by their sound. Your stumbling attempts to come up with "Mancuso" showed that you were in the right mental "file drawer" but were unable to find the right "file card." Our sound-filing system is especially helpful in enabling us to recognize and understand words spoken by other people. When we hear people say something that sounds more or less like the word they intended—like "I saw a bassoon at the zoo"—we can quickly figure out what they mean.

Remembering as a Reconstructive Process

15   Sherlock Holmes's image of the "brain attic" seems to imply that the pieces of information filed away in long-term memory—like the old clothes, books, and furniture stored in an attic—are fixed entities, unchanged by the passage of time. But retrieval is not simply

a matter of "finding" some piece of information that is filed away. Instead, psychologists have come to view remembering as a reconstructive process that is affected by our knowledge of the world. Remembering a specific event is often more like "rebuilding" the event than it is like replaying a mental videotape of what actually happened.

16   The process of reconstruction begins when we initially transfer material into long-term memory. We usually encode information in terms of its meaning for us, rather than as a literal* account of what occurred. When I (Zick) got up one December morning, I called the weather line and got the recorded report for the Boston area. A couple of hours later, I jotted down what I recalled the recorded voice saying:

> Today will be cloudy and mild, with possibility of showers this afternoon. Highs in mid-60's.

Then I called the number again—the recorded message hadn't changed yet—and wrote down the forecast word for word. Here it is:

> Cloudy and mild today with a few periods of rain. It'll be windy today. Temperatures approaching the record of 63 set in 1984.

As is typical, I had filed only the gist of the report in my memory store. All I really wanted to know was how warmly to dress and whether to carry an umbrella. So I missed some of the details, such as the possible record-setting temperature, which may have been more important to the weather reporter than to me. Unless we're rehearsing our lines in a play or trying to memorize a particularly significant phrase, we encode the meaning of material, not its literal content.

17   As time goes by, our memories of past events are further shaped by other information that we have about ourselves, others, and the world. The general bodies of knowledge that we have about particular people (including ourselves), things, and events are called *schemas,* and these schemas inevitably shape our memories. Your memory of

the first time you rode a bicycle may be shaped not only by what you saw and felt at that time but also by your schema of how a bicycle works, your general picture of what you were like at that age, and stories your parents have told about you as a child. In recalling an event, you are likely to tie it into the context of your life at the time, rather than remembering every detail as it was. As Elizabeth Loftus puts it, "When we remember, we pull pieces of the past out of some mysterious region in the brain—jagged, jigsaw pieces that we sort and shift, arrange and rearrange until they fit into a pattern that makes sense" (Loftus & Ketcham, 1991, p. 67).

18   Memories are often reshaped by later information. For example, your memory of a first meeting with a person is likely to be colored by whether that person later became a good friend or a bitter enemy (Barclay, 1986). In one study that illustrated such shaping of memories by subsequent events, subjects read a paragraph about a woman named Carol Harris. The paragraph included the information that "Carol Harris was a problem child from birth. She was wild, stubborn, and violent." A week later the subjects were asked whether the passage had included the sentence "She was deaf, dumb, and blind." In fact, the paragraph included no such statement, and only about 5 percent of the subjects answered yes to the question. But another group of subjects was told that the paragraph they had read a week earlier was actually about Helen Keller (who, as most people know, was indeed blind and deaf). About 50 percent of the subjects in this group reported that the paragraph *had* included the sentence "She was deaf, dumb, and blind." Although these subjects were trying to report accurately on what they had read, the later information had influenced their memories (Dooling & Christiaansen, 1977).

19   Once we have encoded things in long-term memory, why do we ever forget them? To answer this question, we need to begin with a brief look at how psychologists have studied forgetting.

The Forgetting Curve

20   Forgetting was first explored systematically by a turn-of-the-century German psychologist named Hermann Ebbinghaus. Using himself as his only subject, Ebbinghaus spent thousands of hours memorizing nonsense syllables (such as "KEJ," "GOK," and "PUM") and then measuring his memory performance. He used nonsense syllables because he wanted to focus on those aspects of learning and memory that did *not* involve meaning—what is sometimes called rote learning.

21

One of Ebbinghaus's (1885/1913) basic findings was that the greatest memory loss occurs soon after learning and that the rate of loss declines as time passes. This decelerating rate of forgetting is summarized in what is known as the **forgetting curve** (see Figure 9). Many subsequent studies have confirmed this finding. When remembering nonsense syllables, meaningful words, and even events in their lives, people show rapid initial forgetting of newly learned information and slower forgetting later on (Anderson, 1990; Thompson, 1982).

Recall, Recognition, and Relearning

22

How can we tell whether people retain or have forgotten something they have learned? A common approach is to teach subjects something and then observe whether they remember it over the course of time. Much of this research has involved **verbal learning**—the retention in memory of words, syllables, and other verbal material. Investigators studying verbal learning have used three measures of memory: recall, recognition, and relearning.

verbal learning Retention in memory of words, syllables, and other verbal material.

23

In **recall**, the subject must repeat or reproduce something previously learned, with the help of only the barest cues. "Which psychologist first identified the forgetting curve?" is a question that calls for recall. In **recognition**, the subject must only pick out from a list something that the subject has encountered before. "Was the psychologist who first identified the forgetting curve Ebbinghaus, Freud, or Skinner?" is a question that calls for recognition. As you might expect, people's recognition of words, faces, or events tends to be considerably better than their recall. In many cases the person has the information stored in memory but is unable to retrieve it. But if the person encounters this information as part of a list, as in a recognition task, the retrieval problem is solved.

recall A measure of retention in which an individual must recount or reproduce something previously learned, with the help of only the barest clues.

recognition A measure of retention in which an individual must pick from a list something previously encountered.

24

In **relearning**, the measure of retention* that Ebbinghaus used in his pioneering research, subjects are asked to relearn material that they learned previously. The researcher compares the length of time required to master the previously learned material with the time needed to master it originally. If it takes you an hour to memorize a poem today but only 45 minutes to memorize the same poem a year from now, you "save" 25 percent of the original learning time when you relearn the poem.

relearning A measure of retention in which the time an individual needs to relearn material is compared with the time the individual originally needed to learn the material.

25

Of the three measures, relearning generally shows the greatest amount of retention over the longest period of time. In many instances, people who have once learned something cannot recall or even recognize the material at a later time, yet they are able to relearn the material more quickly than if they had never learned it in the first place. This

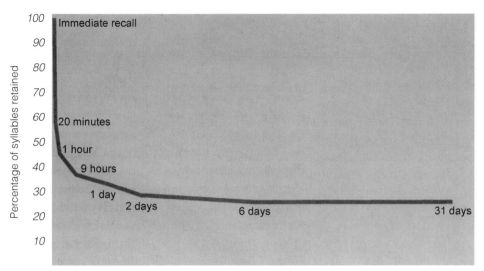

Figure 9

Ebbinghaus's forgetting curve. When nonsense syllables are memorized, most forgetting takes place within nine hours of the memorization (the rate of forgetting is especially high during the first hour). After that, forgetting continues, but at a much slower rate.

Source: Adapted from Ebbinghaus (1885).

ability to relearn material quickly can be of great practical value later in life—when, for example, one needs to relearn a computer word-processing program in order to move to a desired job.

Retrieval Failure

26   As noted earlier, some information, such as a telephone number, may be forgotten almost as soon as it is perceived. Once such information drops out of short-term memory, it seems to be lost to us forever. When we talk about forgetting things, however, we are usually talking about information that we once knew—that was part of our long-term memory store—but can no longer bring to mind. Psychologists used to believe that information in long-term memory would "decay" over time if it

Unfinished Business

In a famous study of memory, Bluma Zeigarnik (1927) asked her subjects to perform several simple tasks. She allowed them to complete some of the tasks but she interrupted others. When they were tested several hours later, the subjects recalled more of the incomplete tasks than the completed ones. This tendency to recall incomplete tasks is now called the "Zeigarnik effect." We often make a point of remembering things that are still unfinished so that we can go back and finish them. Once the task is completed, there may be less need to remember it. As swimsuit designer Anne Cole reports, "After we show the line, I don't remember what was in it" (Beyette, 1991).

was never used or that it would fade as the result of interference from new material. But recent research suggests that this is not typically the case. In fact, long-term memories seem to remain in indefinitely long—and perhaps permanent—storage, embedded in chemical codes in the brain that scientists are just beginning to understand. The main reason that we forget things is not that the memories have decayed or disappeared but rather that we cannot retrieve them from the long-term memory store. This phenomenon is called **retrieval failure**.

retrieval failure
Forgetting that results from the inability to locate material in long-term memory.

27   Retrieval failure is illustrated most clearly in those cases in which we are utterly unable to remember something until some retrieval cue brings it to mind. In studies by Endel Tulving (1974), subjects first memorized lists of words. When they were asked to recall the words some time later, they seemed to have forgotten many items. But when they were given cues to jog their memories—such as the category to which the word belonged ("four-footed animal") or words that rhymed with the word to be recalled ("it rhymes with *chair*")—they remembered much of the "forgotten" material.

28   You have undoubtedly experienced retrieval failure on many occasions in your own life. Suppose a friend mentions a day several months ago when you joined a group of people in the cafeteria for a cup of coffee. You have absolutely no recollection of the event. It's not that the event has evaporated from your memory store but that you are unable to retrieve it. As soon as your friend reminds you that it was raining, that it was the day that Joel showed up with his arm in a cast, and that the group was discussing a particular movie, the "forgotten" incident comes back to you.

Interference

29   In presenting his advice about memory, Sherlock Holmes added that it is a mistake to try to cram too much material into one's "brain attic." "Depend upon it," he told his friend Dr. Watson, "that there comes a time when for every addition of knowledge you forget something you knew before" (Doyle, 1927, p. 21). Since Holmes's time, researchers have confirmed that his observation holds true, at least in certain circumstances. One of the reasons that we sometimes forget things is that one bit of learning is interfered with by another.

retroactive interference
Interference with the ability to recall previously learned material that is caused by recently learned material.

30   When newly learned information hinders the recall or recognition of information that was learned previously, it is called **retroactive interference** (see Figure 10A). In a language class, a student may do well on the first few vocabulary tests, but as the number of vocabulary items increases through the semester, recently learned items may begin

to interfere with memory for items learned earlier. Almost anything can be an interfering activity. This may help to explain the finding that subjects who go to sleep after learning new material tend to retain more of the material than subjects who remain awake (Ekstrand, 1967). When you are asleep, fewer new inputs can interfere with what

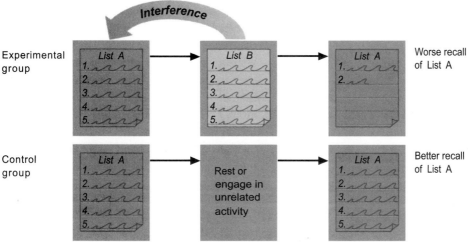

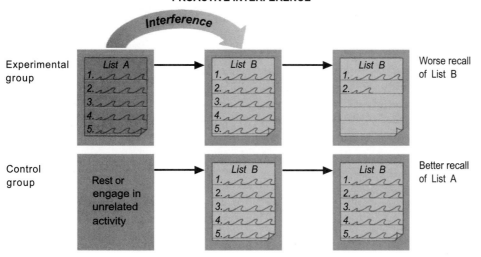

Figure 10

Design of experiments on the effects of interference on verbal learning. In retroactive interference, later learning (memorizing List B) interferes with earlier learning (recalling List A). In proactive interference, earlier learning (memorizing List A) interferes with later learning (recalling List B).

you have learned. For years, students have used this idea to justify abandoning their books and going to sleep the night before a big exam. Keep in mind, though, that sleep works to reduce interference only when the material has been learned well in the first place.

31

proactive interference Interference with the ability to remember recently learned material that is caused by previously learned material.

When material learned earlier interferes with the retention of something learned more recently, it is called **proactive interference** (see Figure 10B). For example, students who have learned the French words for certain objects sometimes have trouble learning the Spanish words for the same objects because the French versions keep popping into their heads. Perhaps you have experienced some of these familiar instances of proactive interference:

- You move to a new apartment and often find yourself looking in "old" places for your silverware, tools, towels, and other items.

- You switch from driving a stick-shift car to one with an automatic transmission and find yourself reaching for a clutch pedal that isn't there.

- Your high school teacher keeps calling you by the name of your older brother or sister, whom the teacher had in class a few years earlier.

Forgetting and the Life Span

32   I'm no math genius, and the last time I took an algebra course was more than thirty years ago. But last year, when my son Elihu entered the eighth grade and started studying algebra, I was pleasantly surprised to discover that I still remembered how to solve equations and could even help Elihu with his homework. How could I possibly have remembered algebra for all these years? It's not because I kept practicing it. Although I took four years of math in high school, I have managed to stay clear of x's and y's for most of my adult life. But my experience fits a pattern that has been identified in recent research: when knowledge is initially acquired over a period of several years, it can be maintained for decades—and even for a lifetime—without further rehearsals (Bahrick & Hall, 1991).

> **College Memories**
>
> Years from now, what will you remember about your college days? David Pillomer and his colleagues (1988) asked women who had graduated 2, 12, or 22 years earlier to list the first few things that came to mind about college. Nearly half of these memories were about incidents that had occurred in September of the first year. Events associated with major life transitions, such as beginning college, seem to be especially memorable. Most of the memories were about incidents—whether in the dormitory, in the classroom, or during extracurricular activities—that had elicited strong emotional reactions. Surprisingly, only 6 percent of the memories concerned romance.

33   In a striking demonstration of such lifetime retention, Harry Bahrick and Lynda Hall (1991) gave algebra tests to more than a thousand people who had taken their last algebra course anywhere from a few months to seventy years earlier. The researchers concluded that if the subject had taken only a single high school algebra course and no subsequent math courses, the subject's knowledge of algebra years later was no better than it would have been if he or she had not taken algebra at all. But those subjects who had taken three or more advanced math courses (as I had in high school) maintained their knowledge as long as a half-century later—and this was true even if they had had little or no contact with algebra in the intervening years.

34   It appears that something learned during a short period of time and not rehearsed afterward—whether it is the rules of a card game or the names of the people you met while on vacation—is likely to be lost over the years (Squire, 1989). "Use it or lose it" is the general rule. But if the same material is acquired and used over a period that extends over several years, it is likely to last for a lifetime. This principle has been found to apply not only to people's knowledge of mathematics but also to people's retention of foreign language vocabulary (Bahrick, 1984; Bahrick & Phelps, 1987).

35   The principle has important educational implications. In Bahrick's view, if educators want students to learn material in a form that will remain accessible for many years, they should teach it over a period of several years and provide frequent opportunities for review. Full-year courses will typically lead to greater retention over the years than single-semester or single-quarter courses, even when the total amounts of class time and study time are the same. And cumulative examinations after several years, as well as continuing education and refresher courses, will help to ensure that material that we once knew will not soon be forgotten.

Adapted from Zick Rubin, Letitia Anne Peplau, and Peter Salovey, *Psychology,* pp. 149–160.

CHECKING YOUR COMPREHENSION

Directions: Circle the letter of the correct answer.

1. Which of the following statements most effectively summarizes the *overall* main idea of the entire reading?

   a. If we don't make a conscious effort to create links between what we know and what we are learning, the chances are good that we will forget rather than remember.

   b. Although linking new information to old is a good way to enhance remembering, the quality of the experience is what really aids retrieval of memories.

   c. Long-term memory has a limited storage capacity; when we reach the limits of long-term memory, we forget new information no matter how hard we try to hold on to it.

   d. Our memories are always being reshaped by new information.

2. Which statement best paraphrases the "key" to encoding (paragraph 3)?

   a. New information can be successfully encoded if we repeat the information aloud.

   b. Focusing on the meaning of new information is what makes encoding a successful strategy.

   c. Silently reciting the information we want to remember is the key to encoding it.

   d. Visualization is the key to encoding new information, as long as the associated images are highly detailed.

3. The material on memory-improvement techniques (paragraphs 5–8) is there to illustrate which main idea?

   a. Most college students have trouble remembering new information because they don't apply the right memory techniques.

   b. Anyone who makes an effort can improve his or her ability to remember.

   c. Effective memory-improvement techniques take into account the importance of encoding new material.

   d. Active listening and reading are the twin keys to encoding material in order to remember it over time.

4. Which statement best sums up the implied main idea of the section titled "Retrieval" (paragraphs 9–14)?

   a. Retrieval of memories is easiest when we are in circumstances similar to those present when the actual events first occurred.

   b. Retrieval cues are essential to remembering.

   c. The tip-of-the-tongue phenomenon affects us all.

   d. Odors are among the most common retrieval cues.

5. In paragraph 10, the reference to melody is a supporting detail for which main idea?

   a. People who hear a few bars of a song can often call up the words.

   b. The effective encoding of information is the key to a good memory.

   c. Retrieval cues are essential to remembering.

6. In paragraph 12, the supporting detail about criminal investigators is there to illustrate which main idea from paragraph 11?

   a. Criminal investigators are well versed in the principles of remembering.

   b. Retrieving information in long-term memory depends on using odors as retrieval cues.

   c. Human memory works most effectively when people are asked to recall information under conditions similar to those present when they first learned it.

   d. Scuba divers have better memories underwater than they do on land.

7. What's the main idea of the section titled "The Forgetting Curve" (paragraphs 20–21)?

   a. German psychologist Hermann Ebbinghaus made himself the subject of his research on remembering.

   b. One of Hermann Ebbinghaus's most important findings was that the rate of forgetting decreases over time.

   c. To do his research, German psychologist Hermann Ebbinghaus used nonsense syllables that had no meaning attached to them.

   d. All of Hermann Ebbinghaus's findings have been confirmed by modern research on memory.

8. What's the main idea of the section titled "Retrieval Failure" (paragraphs 26–28)?

   a. We forget not because memories decay or disappear, but because we cannot find a way to retrieve them from long-term memory.

   b. Psychologists once believed that we forgot because new information crowded out the old.

   c. At one time or another, we have all experienced retrieval failure.

   d. Recent research suggests that we forget because with the passage of time, the traces of old memories weaken or decay until we can no longer retrieve them at will.

9. What's the implied main idea of the section titled "Interference" (paragraphs 29–31)?

   a. Retroactive interference occurs when new material interferes with the recall of old.

   b. When material learned earlier interferes with remembering new material, that process is called *proactive interference*.

   c. Two kinds of interference, *retroactive* and *proactive,* can hinder the recall of information.

10. What's the main idea of the section titled "Forgetting and the Life Span" (paragraphs 32–35)?

    a. Our educational system would benefit if administrators would pay attention to the current research on long-term remembering.

    b. People who took several advanced math courses retained their knowledge for more than half a century mainly because they were able to use the right retrieval cues.

    c. Information acquired over a brief period of time—less than a month—can be retained for a lifetime.

    d. Information acquired and reviewed over an extended period of time can be remembered for a lifetime.

DEEPENING YOUR UNDERSTANDING

Directions: Answer the following questions by circling the letter of the correct response or filling in the blanks where required.

1. How would you describe the authors' tone? _____

2. What would you say is the authors' purpose?

   a. to tell readers how we go about retrieving information from long-term memory

   b. to persuade readers that new theories of memory are much better researched than earlier ones

3. When Sherlock Holmes used the phrase "brain attic" (paragraph 1),

   what figure of speech was he using? _____

4. According to the reading, Holmes was both right and wrong in his comparison between memories stored in the brain and objects stored in an attic.

   What did Holmes get right? _____

   What did he get wrong? _____

5. In this reading, the authors discuss *encoding* (paragraphs 2–4), a process that aids long-term remembering. This term is already familiar from reading 1 (pp. 79–91, paragraphs 21–23). Reread both discussions of encoding. Then answer the following question: Which statement best synthesizes or connects the two readings?

   a. The authors say the exact same thing in different words.

   b. The authors' descriptions are similar, but the second reading explains the term in more detail.

   c. The authors discuss encoding from two different perspectives.

6. Which statement more effectively synthesizes, or connects, the previous reading and this one? *Note:* To answer, you will probably need to skim both readings.

   a. Both readings describe how we remember and why we forget.

   b. Both readings focus on how information gets stored, but reading 2 puts more emphasis on the retrieval of memories.

   c. Both readings focus on how we remember long-term, but reading 2 puts more emphasis on the faulty nature of memory.

7. Imagine you complained to the authors that you had a terrible memory and couldn't remember anything you read in your textbooks. How do you think they would respond?

   a. They would tell you that you needed to get a tutor, who would quiz you on a regular basis.

   b. They would tell you to be more attentive to how you encode new information.

   c. They would tell you to apply the principle of context-dependent remembering.

   d. They would tell you to avoid interference.

   Please explain your answer

   _____

   _____

8. Imagine that you were studying for a final exam. Based on what you have learned from the reading, where would be the best place to learn the information you need to know for the final?

   a. in your bedroom sitting at your desk

   b. in the room where you will take your exam

   c. at your kitchen table

   d. at the library

   Please explain your answer.

   _____

   _____

9. Memory researchers say "one of the most difficult kinds of amnesia to overcome involves the inability of the patient to integrate new information into previously acquired knowledge." In other words, someone with this kind of amnesia has lost the ability to perform what function of memory discussed in readings 1 and 2?

   _____

10. Imagine that your instructor has just given a lecture on the Fourth Amendment, which protects Americans from unlawful search and seizure. It was a long lecture and packed with information. Based on what you learned about Ebbinghaus's research and the "forgetting curve," should you review your lecture notes right after class, or right before the next class a week later?

    _____

    Please use Ebbinghaus's research to explain your answer.

    _____

    _____

AIRING YOUR OPINIONS

1. Read the authors' description of how educators should teach in order to apply the principles of remembering (paragraph 35). Then explain how your high school or college would fare if evaluated by the authors.

    _____

    _____

2. Based on what you now know about remembering, which type of test relies more heavily on your ability to remember long-

    term: multiple choice or fill in the blank? _____

    Please explain your answer.

    _____

    _____

Reading 3   # Can Repressed Memories Be Recovered?

GETTING FOCUSED

The following reading from a psychology textbook focuses on the theory that memories of a childhood trauma can be repressed for years and then, with the right treatment, be accurately recalled. Throughout the 1990s, stories about the recovery of repressed memories were much written about and hotly debated. In several cases, recovered memories were used as evidence in jury trials. Yet, as the title of this reading suggests, it's not completely clear that such memories *can* be recovered.

Textbook Features and Readers' Strategies

Feature:	*The title poses a question.*
Strategy:	Any time a title poses a question, you need to read for the answer because there's a good chance that the answer is the main idea of the entire reading.
Feature:	*Like many textbooks, this one uses questions as headings to focus the reader's attention.*
Strategy:	Pre-read all the questions. Then read to answer the questions posed in the headings.
Feature:	*The writers of this excerpt occasionally use number transitions (first, second, and so on) to identify and separate supporting details.*
Strategy:	Note the points following those transitions. Make sure you understand each one because they are likely to be important.
Feature:	*The reading pointedly tries to address both sides of the issue under discussion.*
Strategy:	Identify each of the sides in the margins and jot down arguments for both. When you finish reading, ask yourself if both sides received equal treatment.
Feature:	*The reading emphasizes the results of research.*
Strategy:	Each time the authors offer a research result, paraphrase the findings in your own words.

Evaluating Your Background Knowledge

The authors of this reading are relying on your knowledge of these words and terms. Look this list over carefully to make sure you know everything on it. *Note:* The number in parentheses indicates the paragraph where the word can be found while an asterisk accompanies the word's first appearance in the reading.

inadvertently (7): without meaning to; unintentionally

repression (10): the act of forgetting unpleasant or frightening events

cognitive (10): related to thought

objective (11): without bias; neutral

empirical (12): based on factual evidence or scientific study

intuition (13): the art of knowing without any physical evidence or proof

controlled experiments (13): experiments performed under circumstances that can be recreated, allowing the tests to be repeated and verified

circumstantial (13): depending on surrounding events

1   While looking into her young daughter's eyes one day in 1989, Eileen Franklin-Lipsker suddenly had a vivid memory. She remembered seeing her father kill her childhood friend more than twenty years earlier. On the basis of her testimony about this memory, her father, George Franklin, Sr., was sent to prison for murder (E. F. Loftus & Ketcham, 1994).

What Am I Being Asked to Believe or Accept?

2   The prosecution in the Franklin case successfully argued that Eileen had recovered a *repressed memory*. Similar arguments in other cases tried in the early 1990s also resulted in imprisonment as now-adult children claimed to have recovered childhood memories of physical or sexual abuse at the hands of their parents. The juries in these trials accepted the assertion that all memory of shocking events can be repressed, or pushed into an inaccessible corner of the mind where, for decades, subconscious processes keep it out of awareness, yet potentially subject to recall (I. E. Hyman, 2000). And juries are not the only believers. A few years ago a large American news organization reported that the United States had illegally used nerve gas

during the war in Vietnam. This story was based, in part, on a Vietnam veteran's account of recovered memories of having been subjected to a nerve gas attack.

Is There Evidence Available to Support the Claim?

3 Proponents of the repressed memory argument point to several lines of evidence to support their claims. First, they argue that a substantial amount of mental activity occurs outside of awareness (Kihlstrom, 1999). Second, research on implicit memory shows that our behavior can be influenced by information of which we are unaware (Schacter, Chiu, & Ochsner, 1993). Third, retrieval cues can help people recall memories that had previously been inaccessible to conscious awareness (Andrews et al., 2000; Landsdale & Laming, 1995). For example, carefully documented cases report that these cues have helped soldiers remember for the first time the circumstances under which they had been wounded many years before (Karon & Widener, 1997). Fourth, research on *motivated forgetting* suggests that people may be more likely to forget unpleasant events than pleasant ones. In one study, a psychologist kept a detailed record of his daily life over a six-year period. When he later tried to recall these experiences, he remembered more than half of the positive events but only one-third of the negative ones (Waagenaar, 1986). In another study, 38 percent of women who, as children, had been brought to a hospital because of sexual abuse did not recall—or at least did not report—the incident as adults (L. M. Williams, 1994).

Can That Evidence Be Interpreted Another Way?

4 Those who are skeptical about repressed memories do not deny that subconscious memory and retrieval processes exist (Kihlstrom, 1999). They also recognize that, sadly, child abuse and other traumas are all too common. But these facts do not eliminate the possibility that any given "recovered" memory may actually be a distorted, or constructed, memory (Clancy et al., 2000). Our recall of past events is affected by what happened at the time, what we knew beforehand, and everything we experienced since. The people who "remembered" nonexistent books in an office constructed that memory based on what prior knowledge led them to *assume* was there.

5 False memories—distortions of actual events and the recall of events that didn't actually happen—can be just as vivid as real, accurate

memories, and people can be just as confident in them (Pezdek, Finger, & Hodge, 1997; Roediger & McDermott, 2000). In one case study, for example, a teenager named Chris was given descriptions of four incidents from his childhood and asked to write about each of them every day for five days (E. F. Loftus, 1997a). One of these incidents—being lost in a shopping mall at age five—never really happened. Yet Chris eventually "remembered" this event, and he even added many details about the mall and the stranger whose hand he was supposedly found holding. He also rated this (false) memory as being more vivid than two of the other three (real) incidents he wrote about. A more recent study found similar results in about half of seventy-seven child participants (Porter, Yuille, & Lebman, 1999). Experiments, too, show that children who are repeatedly asked about a nonexistent trauma (getting a hand caught in a mousetrap) eventually develop a vivid and unshakable false memory of experiencing it (Ceci et al., 1994).

6   Some people appear more likely than others to develop false memories. For example, two studies have found that women who have suffered physical or sexual abuse are more likely to falsely remember words on a recall test. This tendency appears strongest among abused women who show signs of posttraumatic stress disorder (Bremner, Shobe, & Kihlstrom, 2000). Another study found that susceptibility to false memory in the word-recall task was greater in women who reported recovered memories of sexual abuse than in nonabused women or those who had always remembered the abuse they suffered (Clancy et al., 2000).

7   Why would anyone remember a trauma that did not actually occur? Elizabeth Loftus (1997a) suggests that for one thing, popular books such as *The Courage to Heal* (Bass & Davis, 1994) and *Secret Survivors* (Blume, 1998) may lead people to believe that anyone who experiences guilt, depression, low self-esteem, overemotionality, or any of a long list of other problems is harboring repressed memories of abuse. According to Loftus, this message is reinforced by some therapists, particularly those who specialize in using guided imagination, hypnosis, and other methods to "help" clients recover repressed memories (Polusny & Follette, 1996; Poole et al., 1995). In so doing, these therapists may inadvertently* influence people to construct false memories (Olio, 1994). As one client described her therapy, "I was rapidly losing the ability to differentiate between my imagination and my real memory" (E. F. Loftus & Ketcham, 1994, p. 25). To such therapists, a client's failure to recover memories of

abuse, or refusal to accept that they exist, is evidence of "denial" (E. F. Loftus, 1997a).

8   The possibility that recovered memories might actually be false memories has led to dismissed charges or not-guilty verdicts for defendants in some repressed memory cases. In other cases, previously convicted defendants have been released. (George Franklin's conviction was overturned, but only after he spent five years in prison.) Concern over the potential damage resulting from false memories has prompted the establishment of the False Memory Syndrome Foundation, a support group for families affected by abuse accusations stemming from allegedly repressed memories. More than 100 of these families (including George Franklin) have filed lawsuits against hospitals and therapists (False Memory Foundation, 1997). One recent suit led to a $2 million judgment against a Minnesota therapist whose client discovered that her "recovered" memories of childhood were false; a similar case in Illinois resulted in a $10.6 million settlement and the suspension of the license of the psychiatrist who had "found" his patient's lost memories.

What Evidence Would Help to Evaluate the Alternatives?

9   Evaluating reports of recovered memories would be easier if we had more information about how common it is for people to forget traumatic memories *and* how accurate their memories of such events are, if and when they recall them. So far, we know that some people apparently forget intense emotional experiences, but that most have vivid and long-lasting memories of them (H. G. Pope et al., 1998; Strongman & Kemp, 1991). Especially valuable is research like the sexual abuse survey mentioned earlier in which women were interviewed long after documented incidents of sexual abuse had occurred. Further research of this kind will yield better estimates of the prevalence of repressed memories, and might also offer clues as to the kinds of people and events most likely to be associated with this kind of forgetting.

10   It would also be valuable to know more about the processes through which repression* might occur. Is there a mechanism that specifically pushes traumatic memories out of awareness, then keeps them at a subconscious level for long periods? Thus far, cognitive* psychologists have not found evidence for such a mechanism (E. F. Loftus, 1997a; H. G. Pope et al., 1998).

What Conclusions Are Most Reasonable?

11   An objective* reading of the research evidence supports the view that recovery of traumatic memories is at least possible. But the implantation of false memories is also possible and has been demonstrated experimentally.

12   The intense conflict between organizations such as the False Memory Syndrome Foundation and people who believe in recovered memories reflects a fundamental disagreement about evidence. To many therapists who deal daily with victims of sexual abuse and other traumas, clients' reports constitute stronger "proof" of recovered memories than do the results of laboratory experiments. Those reports are viewed with considerably more skepticism by psychologists who engage in, or rely on, empirical* research on the processes of memory and forgetting (K. S. Pope, in press).

13   In short, whether one believes a claim of recovered memory may be determined by the relative weight one assigns to evidence based on personal experiences and intuition* versus evidence that comes from controlled experiments.* Still, the apparent ease with which false memories can be created should lead judges, juries, and the general public to exercise great caution before accepting unverified memories of traumatic events as the truth. At the same time, we should not uncritically reject the claims of people who appear to have recovered memories (Nadel & Jacobs, 1998). Perhaps the wisest course is to use all the scientific and circumstantial* evidence available to carefully and critically examine claims of recovered memories while keeping in mind the possibility that constructive memory processes *might* have influenced them. This careful, scientific approach is vital if we are to protect the rights of those who report recovered memories, as well as those who face accusations arising from them.

Douglas A. Bernstein and Peggy W. Nash, *Essentials of Psychology*, pp. 199–202.

CHECKING YOUR COMPREHENSION

Directions: Circle the letter of the correct answer.

1. Which statement best paraphrases the main idea of the entire reading?

   a. The belief in the recovery of repressed memories has resulted in the unjust imprisonment of countless innocent people.

b. Although there is some evidence suggesting that the recovery of repressed memories is possible, there is more evidence suggesting that the memories recovered can be false ones.

c. Throughout the nineties, therapists went overboard in their efforts to recover repressed memories; often they ended up implanting memories rather than recovering them.

d. At least four different lines of evidence prove that traumatic memories of childhood abuse can be recovered through therapy.

2. In paragraph 3, the reference to the psychologist who kept a detailed record of his life for six years is a minor detail used to support which major detail?

a. We are not always aware of our thoughts.

b. Specific cues can help people recall memories they had forgotten.

c. Behavior can be influenced by information we aren't even aware of.

d. We are more likely to forget unhappy events than happy ones.

3. In paragraph 4, the topic sentence is

a. sentence 1.

b. sentence 2.

c. sentence 3.

d. sentence 4.

4. In paragraph 5, the studies cited all serve to support which main idea?

a. The vividness of a memory is an indication of its accuracy.

b. Children are prone to distort past events.

c. If children are repeatedly asked about a trauma, they are likely to remember it.

d. The fact that memories are vivid and realistic does not mean they are accurate.

5. In paragraph 7, how does the author answer the following question: "Why would anyone remember a trauma that did not actually occur?"

   a. People, particularly those who are depressed, are inclined to have distorted memories of past events.

   b. The success of best-selling books about recovered memories of abuse made some people think they could make money from "recalling" a traumatic event.

   c. Therapists told people suffering from depression that their problems had to be caused by a repressed memory.

   d. Popular books about recovered traumatic memories tend to encourage the idea that feelings of anxiety, depression, or worthlessness stem from repressed memories of abuse.

6. From what the authors say in paragraph 7, you can infer that researcher Elizabeth Loftus believes the therapists involved

   a. were consciously trying to manipulate their patients.

   b. may have unconsciously encouraged their patients to dredge up distorted memories.

   c. told their patients exactly what to say.

7. In paragraph 8, the author mentions that more than one hundred families have filed lawsuits against hospitals and therapists. Based on this fact, you could infer that

   a. the people filing the lawsuits blame the doctors who treated the patients more than they blame those who reported the recovered traumatic events.

   b. the people filing lawsuits believe that they will be able to get more money from therapists and hospitals than they will from the patients who made the claims.

   c. lawyers have been encouraging families involved in recovered memory cases to file lawsuits.

8. In paragraph 8, the authors cite a number of cases involving "recovered memories." From the cases they cite, what is the implied main idea?

   a. In cases involving "recovered memories," juries tend to believe that the recovered memory is accurate.

   b. Claims of recovered memories are not holding up in the courts.

   c. Juries were too quick to release those who had gone to jail because of evidence from recovered memories.

   d. Recovered memories of childhood traumas are all false or distorted memories.

9. What inference can readers correctly draw in paragraph 9?

   a. Evaluating the claims of recovered memories is simply impossible.

   b. As of yet, we just don't know enough to effectively and fairly evaluate the claims for recovered memories.

   c. It's simply not possible for people to "recover" long-forgotten memories of abuse.

10. Which statement most effectively paraphrases the authors' position on believing claims about recovered memories (paragraphs 12–13)?

   a. If claims based on recovered memories cannot be tested through controlled experiments, then we should probably ignore them.

   b. It is a tragic mistake to dismiss claims about recovered memories because the majority have been proven true.

   c. We need to listen carefully to claims about recovered memories of abuse, but we also need to subject them to close scrutiny.

   d. Above all, we need to protect the rights of those accused of abusive behavior on the basis of recovered memories.

DEEPENING YOUR UNDERSTANDING

Directions: Answer the following questions by circling the letter of the correct response or filling in the blanks where required.

1. How would you describe the authors' tone? _____

2. What would you say is the authors' purpose?

   a. to inform readers about the use of recovered memories in court cases

b. to persuade readers that we need to be cautious about accepting, without question or scrutiny, stories of recovered memories

3. With which of the following statements do you agree?

   a. The authors treat both sides of the controversy equally.

   b. The authors try to treat both sides of the controversy fairly, but they include more evidence supporting the notion that recovered memories should be accepted as true.

   c. The authors try to treat both sides of the controversy fairly, but they include more evidence that inclines readers to discredit the accuracy of recovered memories.

4. In paragraph 7, the authors describe therapists who believe "a client's failure to recover memories of abuse, or refusal to accept that they exist, is evidence of 'denial.'" Which statement most accurately resembles the therapists' position?

   a. If you say no, you better really mean it or you won't be believed.

   b. Never say no without questioning your motives.

   c. If you say no, you must really mean yes.

   What's the problem with that position?

   _____

   _____

5. In paragraph 13, the authors write that "whether one believes a claim of recovered memory may be determined by the relative weight one assigns to evidence based on personal experiences and intuition versus evidence that comes from controlled experiments." What two kinds of evidence are being contrasted in that statement?

   a. insight versus polls

   b. feelings versus opinions

   c. personal testimony versus scientific research

   d. personal testimony versus expert opinion

6. In your own words, summarize the reasons used to argue the idea that recovered memories are accurate.

_____

_____

_____

_____

7. The previous reading discussed retrieval cues at length. In this reading, why are retrieval cues essential to believing in the recovery of repressed memories?

_____

_____

8. Summarize the argument used to challenge the idea that recovered memories are bound to be accurate.

_____

_____

_____

9. In paragraph 11, the authors say that an "objective reading of the research evidence supports the view that recovery of traumatic memories is at least possible." Where in the reading do the authors supply that "objective reading of the research?"

_____

10. According to the authors, children repeatedly asked about a nonexistent traumatic event began believing that one had occurred. Does this information

a. confirm what you learned about remembering in paragraphs 17 and 18 of reading 2 (pp. 102–103)?

b. contradict what you learned about remembering in reading 2?

c. have nothing to do with what you learned about remembering in reading 2?

Please explain your answer.

_____

_____

AIRING YOUR OPINIONS

1. Imagine you are interviewing the authors for a research paper, and you ask them if they think repressed memories should be used in criminal trials. Based on the reading, what do you think they will say?

_____

_____

2. Do you think recovered memories should be used as legal evidence in a trial?

_____

_____

Please explain your answer.

_____

_____

Reading 4   # Can Eyewitness Testimony Be Trusted?

GETTING FOCUSED

The authors of this reading know full well that juries are deeply impressed by eyewitness testimony. For that reason in particular, they offer a note of caution: Because the testimony of eyewitnesses depends on the accuracy of their memories, it may not be quite as trustworthy as some people think.

Textbook Features and Readers' Strategies

Feature: *Toward the end of the reading there is a summary of key points.*

Strategy: Pre-read the list of key points before you start reading the excerpt.

Feature: *The authors use topical headings to break up the text.*

Strategy: Pre-read the headings and turn the topic into questions such as, "Are cases of mistaken identity common?" and "Why do they occur?" Then read to answer these questions.

Feature: *The authors rely heavily on topic sentences to communicate their message.*

Strategy: After you read the opening sentence of each paragraph, look to see if the authors continue to develop that point. If they do, underline key words in the opening sentence or paraphrase it in the margins. Of course, if the authors don't maintain the explanation or argument begun in the opening sentence, then you need to look elsewhere for the topic sentence.

Feature: *Researcher Elizabeth Loftus turns up repeatedly in this reading just as she did in the previous one.*

Strategy: When a researcher is repeatedly mentioned in one reading and then turns up again in another reading on the same topic, that person is of particular importance to the field. You need to pay close attention to anything attributed to the frequently referenced person.

Evaluating Your Background Knowledge

The authors of this reading are relying on your knowledge of these words and terms. Look over this list carefully to make sure you know everything on it. *Note:* The number in parentheses indicates the paragraph where the word can be found while an asterisk accompanies the word's first appearance in the reading.

paradox (2):   a seeming contradiction that actually makes sense once you understand the situation

malleability (3):   having the ability to be easily shaped or manipulated

simulated (9):   imitated, mock or pretended

credence (9):   credit, belief

discriminating (11): thoughtful, aware of differences

1   The testimony of eyewitnesses about events that they saw and heard is central to our system of justice. The trial scenes on the popular television series *L.A. Law* illustrate some of the varieties of eyewitness testimony. A patient who is suing his doctor for malpractice testifies about the advice and treatment his doctor gave him; in her own defense, the doctor gives a rather different account of the same events. Participants in a business deal that went sour give contrasting testimony about who said what to whom. A victim of a mugging is asked whether her assailant is sitting in the courtroom and, if he is, to point him out.

2   Eyewitness testimony presents a paradox* (Brown, 1986). On the one hand, psychologists—as well as many judges and lawyers (Brigham & Wolfskeil, 1983)—are skeptical of eyewitness testimony. Research has shown that such testimony is often inaccurate, reflecting the imperfections of human perception and memory. On the other hand, jurors who listen to eyewitness testimony, particularly when it is given with an air of confidence, tend to believe it uncritically. If eyewitness testimony is unreliable, why are people so ready to believe it?

The Malleability* of Memory

3   Underlying the law's heavy reliance on eyewitness testimony is the wide acceptance of the "videotape" model of memory—the notion that in order to report on a past event, a person simply "replays" a permanently stored mental tape of what happened. But memory rarely works this way. When we remember an event, we don't recover a fully formed mental picture. Rather, we reconstruct the event out of mental bits and pieces, making associations with events that may have occurred at other times and places and even incorporating details that we have imagined rather than experienced. The result is that memory is highly malleable: it can be shaped and sometimes distorted by other events and experiences.

4   Eyewitnesses' recollections can be dramatically influenced by the suggestive questions that investigators and lawyers may put to the witnesses before the trial. In a study of such effects, Elizabeth Loftus and J. C. Palmer (1974) showed students a short film depicting a traffic accident. Some of the student witnesses were later asked, "About how fast were the cars going when they hit each other?" For other witnesses, the verb "hit" was replaced with "smashed," "collided," "bumped," or "contacted." The witnesses' estimates of speed proved to be strongly influenced by the particular verb used. Those questioned with "contacted" gave the lowest speed estimates (30.8 miles per hour

on the average), while those questioned with "smashed" gave the highest speed estimates (40.8 miles per hour). The questioner's assumption that the cars either barely "contacted" or really "smashed" each other apparently became incorporated into the witnesses' memories of the event. At a later session the subjects were also asked whether they had seen any broken glass at the accident scene. There had not in fact been any glass in the film. But witnesses who had previously been questioned with the suggestive word "smash" were much more likely to remember having seen glass than were those who had been questioned with the more neutral word "hit."

5   This sort of reconstruction can affect real trials. Before witnesses take the stand, they are typically questioned about the event by investigators and lawyers, some of whom inevitably convey their own views about the event. Even though a witness may try to be accurate, the interpretations suggested by the investigators' and lawyers' questions may become incorporated into the witness's memory.

6   Eyewitnesses are often called on to identify a person—in many instances, the person who robbed or assaulted them. Many witnesses make such identifications confidently, pointing their fingers at the defendant and testifying without hesitation, "That's the one." Unfortunately, such identifications can be unreliable. In hundreds of cases, eyewitness testimony has led to the conviction of a person later found to be innocent (Brandon & Davies, 1973). In the early 1980s, for example, Lowell Geter, an African American engineer with no criminal record, was convicted by a jury and sentenced to life in prison for the armed robbery of a Kentucky Fried Chicken store in a small Texas town. The only evidence against Geter was the testimony of five white employees of the store, each of whom had picked Geter's picture out of a set of photos shown to them by the police. Geter remained in prison for months, until the real robber came to light and was identified by four of the original witnesses (Wrightsman, 1987).

7   Like the white eyewitnesses who misidentified Lowell Geter, people are especially prone to error when they try to identify a person of a race different from their own. Perhaps because white people have less contact with blacks than with other whites, they tend to be poorer at making accurate distinctions among the faces of blacks than among the faces of whites. The same difficulty besets black people when they attempt to identify a white culprit (Brigham & Malpass, 1985).

8   In cases of violent crimes there is an additional reason why identifications can be unreliable. Crime victims often pay more attention to the weapon that threatens them—the gun or knife in the assailant's

hand—than to the attacker's face. In one study, students were shown a series of slides depicting an armed robbery in a fast-food restaurant (Loftus, Loftus, & Messo, 1987). Through the use of equipment that recorded eye movements, the researchers were able to measure what parts of the slides the subjects were inspecting at every moment. It was found that the subjects spent a large amount of time looking at the robber's gun. These subjects were less attentive to the robber's appearance and were less able to identify him later than were subjects in a control group who viewed a robbery in which there was no weapon.

The Believability of Eyewitness Testimony

9 Despite the unreliability of eyewitness testimony, jurors typically find such testimony to be extremely convincing. In one study, 68 percent of the student-jurors in a simulated* murder trial voted to convict the defendant on the basis of a single eyewitness report even when the evidence indicated that the eyewitness had 20/400 vision, was not wearing his glasses, and therefore could not possibly have seen the face of the murderer. When there was no eyewitness, only 18 percent of the jurors voted for conviction (Loftus, 1979). Jurors seem to pay too little attention to the conditions under which the original event was witnessed and to give too much credence* to a witness's apparent confidence (Lindsay, Wells, & O'Connor, 1989). In fact, a witness's air of confidence is *not* a good indicator of accuracy (Wells & Murray, 1984).

10 Why are jurors so easily swayed by eyewitness testimony? For one thing, most of us believe that we are good at recognizing faces—after all, we successfully recognize our friends and acquaintances all the time. What we may fail to appreciate is how much harder it is to identify a stranger than it is to recognize someone whose features we know well (Brown, 1986). In addition, we tend to underestimate the difficulty of accurately encoding people's features under highly stressful conditions, such as those of a robbery or an assault. As a result, when a witness takes the stand and says with conviction, "That's the man—I could never forget that face!" most jurors are strongly inclined to believe the witness.

11 To combat the tendency of jurors to be overly influenced by eyewitness testimony, some psychologists have begun to testify in trials as expert witnesses (see Loftus & Ketcham, 1991). These psychologists do not comment directly on the evidence in the case, but they do

inform the jury about the limitations of perception and memory that may affect eyewitness testimony. Some judges refuse to allow such psychological briefings on the ground that jurors can evaluate eyewitness testimony for themselves, without being told by "experts" how they should think. Recent research suggests, however, that expert testimony can help jurors to be more discriminating* in their evaluation of eyewitness testimony (Cutler, Penrod, & Dexter, 1989).

Hypnosis and Eyewitnesses

12   In California, in 1976, a school bus was forced off the road, and the schoolchildren were held captive. The bus driver managed to escape but couldn't remember anything about the kidnapper. The driver was then placed under hypnosis and asked to search his memory for details concerning the crime. Under hypnosis, the driver was able to remember almost the complete number of the license plate of the kidnapper's van. This information enabled police to track down the kidnapper and release the children. The same technique has led to the solution of several other dramatic cases.

13   Because of such successes, most major police departments use hypnosis to elicit information from witnesses in certain cases. But hypnosis does not appear to enhance memory as a general matter. For every case in which hypnosis has elicited truthful and useful information there have been others in which the information has proved to be inaccurate. In one case, a woman had disappeared. Hoping to learn what had become of her, police investigators hypnotized her young son. The boy was able to recount an event that until then he had apparently repressed: he had seen his father murder his mother. The father was charged with first-degree murder, tried, and convicted. Long after the trial, the woman turned up alive in another state. The "memory" elicited from the boy was based in fantasy, not reality.

14   If anything, hypnosis may make people's reports *less* rather than more reliable (Smith, 1983). Hypnosis heightens people's moti-

Summary

1. Eyewitness testimony in trials is not as reliable as is commonly believed. People's memories of events can often be influenced by subsequent events and experiences, such as the suggestive ways in which they are questioned about the event.
2. Mistaken identification is common in criminal cases. Misidentification is particularly likely when the suspect is of a different race than the eyewitness, and when a weapon has been involved in the crime.
3. Jurors typically find eyewitness testimony to be highly believable—even when it is inaccurate—especially if the witnesses speak with confidence.
4. Although hypnosis is often used to "improve" the memories of eyewitnesses, hypnotized eyewitnesses may actually reconstruct details that did not occur.

vation to act in ways suggested to them by the hypnotist. Under hypnosis, therefore, people may be highly motivated to retrieve memories of the crime they witnessed. But this motivation, as often as not, leads people to reconstruct details that did not actually occur (Orne & others, 1984).

15   In light of such research, the use of testimony from eyewitnesses who have been hypnotized has become controversial. Martin Orne (1979) has suggested that hypnosis may profitably be used to gain leads in a case—which the police can then check out—but such recollections should not be admitted as evidence in a trial. In recent years, some states have banned testimony from eyewitnesses who have been hypnotized. In other states the courts will admit such evidence only if precautions are taken to minimize the chance of the hypnotist's biasing the witness's memories. Few would deny that hypnosis can be a valuable investigative tool, but it is a tool that should be used with great caution.

Zick Rubin, Letitia Peplau, and Peter Salovey. *Psychology,* pp. 171–173.

CHECKING YOUR COMPREHENSION

Directions: Circle the letter of the correct answer.

1. Which statement best summarizes the implied main idea of the entire reading?

   a. Although psychologists know that eyewitness testimony can be inaccurate, juries tend to accept it without question.

   b. Unless hypnosis is involved, eyewitness testimony is now generally discredited as a source of evidence in criminal cases.

   c. The ability of human memory to be influenced makes eyewitness testimony less reliable than juries seem to think.

   d. In crimes involving different races, eyewitness testimony is useless as evidence.

2. Which statement comes closest to paraphrasing the authors' description of how memory really works (paragraph 3)?

   a. When we remember, we call up a detailed and exact picture of an event or experience; in other words, the human memory works like a video of past events.

   b. When we remember, we see a picture of what happened in the past; only the sound is missing.

    c. When we remember, we recreate the original experience from bits and pieces of memories, and we often add memories of experiences from other times and places.

3. In paragraph 4, research done by Elizabeth Loftus and J. C. Palmer supports which main idea?

    a. The words an eyewitness uses play an important role in convincing a jury.

    b. The word *smashed* has more negative connotations than the word *contacted*.

    c. The questions eyewitnesses ask can affect their testimony.

    d. Eyewitness testimony can be affected by the questions put to the witness.

4. In paragraph 6, which of the following words or phrases is a transition introducing the topic sentence?

    a. often

    b. in many instances

    c. in hundreds of cases

    d. unfortunately

5. Lowell Geter's experience (paragraph 6) is used to support which main idea?

    a. In eyewitness testimony, racism almost always plays a role.

    b. The more confident the eyewitness, the more accurate the testimony.

    c. A confident eyewitness is no guarantee of accuracy.

    d. Eyewitness testimony is only reliable when the witness is also the victim of the crime.

6. In paragraph 8, the research involving a fast-food restaurant supports what main idea?

    a. Victims of violent crimes are the most reliable eyewitnesses.

    b. In violent crimes, the victims focus more on the weapon than on the criminal's appearance.

    c. People in groups make particularly unreliable eyewitnesses.

    d. New technology that can record eye movements has thoroughly discredited eyewitness testimony.

7. In paragraph 10, the authors ask: "Why are jurors so easily swayed by eyewitness testimony?" Which of the following statements offers the most complete answer?

   a. Jurors are often eager to come to a verdict to please the judge and are therefore overly willing to believe a confident eyewitness who displays no doubt.

   b. Jurors are often fooled when an eyewitness displays great confidence.

   c. Jurors don't realize that the human memory can be inaccurate particularly if the events being recalled are frightening or stressful.

   d. Jurors don't realize how hard it is to remember faces, particularly the faces of strangers and are, therefore, inclined to believe a confident witness.

8. In paragraph 11, the topic sentence is

   a. sentence 1.

   b. sentence 2.

   c. sentence 3.

   d. sentence 4.

9. What point do the authors make about the heading of paragraphs 12–15, "Hypnosis and Eyewitnesses."

   a. Eyewitness testimony has been extremely important in solving crimes like the 1976 kidnapping of a school bus filled with children.

   b. Hypnosis has proven to be utterly useless in the recovering of forgotten memories.

   c. Hypnosis can be useful in criminal investigations, but memories induced by hypnosis should not be used as evidence.

   d. Memories recalled under hypnosis are always inaccurate.

10. Which of the following patterns organizes the reading?

   a. comparison and contrast

   b. time order

   c. cause and effect

   d. classification

DEEPENING YOUR UNDERSTANDING

Directions: Answer the following questions by circling the letter of the correct response or filling in the blanks where required.

1. How would you describe the tone of the reading?_____

2. What would you say is the author's purpose?

   a. to inform readers about the use and misuse of eyewitness testimony

   b. to persuade readers that eyewitness testimony is not necessarily accurate

3. In your own words, why does eyewitness testimony present a paradox?

   _____

   _____

4. The authors reject the comparison of human memory to a videotape. Based on this reading and the two previous ones, which metaphor or simile might they find more appropriate?

   a. In the act of remembering, the human mind acts like a computer that hits the right key to call up past experience.

   b. In the act of remembering, the human mind puts the past together like the pieces of a puzzle.

   c. To remember the past, all we need is to locate the key to that room in our minds where the past is kept, some say, forever.

5. The word *malleable* was originally used to describe substances that could be hammered or stretched into various shapes. When the authors use the heading "The Malleability of Memory," what are they implying about remembering?

   _____

   _____

6. Read the following statement (paragraph 4): "Eyewitnesses' recollections can be dramatically influenced by the suggestive ques-

tions that investigators and lawyers may put to the witnesses before the trial." Is that statement

   a. a fact?

   b. an opinion?

   c. a blend of both?

7. According to research described in paragraph 4, those questioned using the word *contacted* responded differently from those questioned using the word *smashed*. What was the difference between the two groups, and why do you think the change in words made a difference?

_____

_____

8. In paragraph 8, the authors use research to prove their point. What point do they want to prove?

_____

Do you think the research mentioned effectively proves their point? Why or why not?

_____

_____

9. In paragraph 11, the authors point out that some judges don't allow psychologists to brief jurors on the potential problems with eyewitness testimony. In your opinion, do the authors think those judges are correct in wanting to eliminate the psychological briefing?

_____

Please explain your answer.

_____

_____

10. Based on what the authors say in paragraph 15, do you think they believe that hypnotism should or should not be used as an investigative tool? Please explain your answer.

_____

_____

AIRING YOUR OPINIONS

1. Based on what you have read, should hypnosis play any role in

criminal investigations? _____

If your answer is "no," please explain why. If you answered "yes," please explain how hypnosis should be used.

_____

_____

2. Imagine you are a juror in a murder trial and have just listened to some compelling and confident eyewitness testimony. How do you think you would react?

_____

_____

Reading 5   # Invasion of the Mind Snatchers

GETTING FOCUSED

The belief in UFOs has been around for decades. But as the writer of the following article points out, the 1980s, with their emphasis on feelings over reason and spirit over logic, was a particularly ripe time for UFO sightings, making books about alien abduction extremely popular. Readers were fascinated by the writers' detailed accounts of the aliens who captured and mistreated them. Then and now, however, skeptics have questioned the reliability of those memories.

Textbook Features and Readers' Strategies

Feature:	*The reading is from a popular magazine, not a textbook.*
Strategy:	Be prepared to draw more inferences.
Feature:	*The word* confabulation *is given heavy emphasis. It is introduced in italics and repeated several times.*
Strategy:	Once the author defines *confabulation,* write the definition in the margins.
Feature:	*The author uses two books as illustrations.*
Strategy:	Each time a reference to either the books or their authors appears, ask yourself what point it illustrates.

Evaluating Your Background Knowledge

The author of this reading is relying on your knowledge of these words and terms. Look over this list carefully to make sure you know everything on it. *Note:* The number in parentheses indicates the paragraph where the word can be found while an asterisk accompanies the word's first appearance in the reading.

extra-terrestrial (1): a being not from Earth; also *extraterrestrial*

ET (2): the adorable alien who starred in Steven Spielberg's movie of the same name

tabloid (3): newspaper known more for sensationalism than the news

uncannily (7): in a peculiar or unsettling fashion

buffs (8): fans

cracking good (9): British expression meaning "very good"

occult (10): dealing with the supernatural

1   The triangular, bug-eyed face of the alien stares from the cover of Whitley Strieber's *Communion,* a "true story" of extra-terrestrial* abduction that topped best-seller lists for more than a year.

2   No lovable ET* here. Former horror-novelist Strieber tells in gruesome detail precisely how "the visitors" operated on his brain and raped him with enormous, scaly objects.

3   In the New Age climate of the 1980s, *Communion* and other best-sellers such as Bud Hopkins's *Intruders* have given alien abduction accounts a credibility that extends beyond tabloid* headlines to the mainstream world of the morning talk shows and shopping-mall bookstores.

4   Readers may be impressed by Strieber's eyewitness account, or by the apparently scientific tone of Hopkins's work, which centers on interviews with hypnotized "abductees." But most psychologists agree that such tales spring not from the alien world of extraterrestrials but from the dark interior world of the human psyche.

5   The simplest psychological mechanism fueling UFO accounts is confabulation, something we all do in storing our vast array of memories. Think of those events you remember as if they happened yesterday—that perfect summer, that train ride when you were five years old. They may well be confabulations, tapestries stitched together from actual experience, the stories of others who were there, events that have happened since, and perhaps a dash of wishful thinking. People who have experienced something together— even a recent event—may have strikingly different memories due to confabulation.

6   And while confabulation is normal, psychologists recognize that some of us are fantasy-prone personalities, people who are highly suggestible and can confabulate in vivid detail. Given the right cues— and existing knowledge of "alien abductions"—their imaginations may soar.

7   But Hopkins and other investigators use hypnosis to help people recall their abductions. Isn't memory uncannily* accurate under hypnosis?

8   Unfortunately for UFO buffs,* no. Countless experiments have shown that, while hypnosis may elicit remarkably detailed accounts, they are no more accurate than normal memories. Indeed, suggestible people may produce notably less accurate accounts under hypnosis. In psychologist Robert Baker's experiments, hypnotized subjects recalled details of objects in the laboratory that were not there and remembered imaginary events that Baker had discussed just before hypnotizing them.

9   Baker, professor of psychology at the University of Kentucky, doesn't say "abductees" are lying. Rather, they may read something that reminds them of an experience they believe they've had. Once they contact a UFO investigator, the attention makes them feel important. "And the more the volunteer is observed and interrogated, the greater the motivation to come up with a cracking good* story," he says. An

abductee who has been written about once, for example, seems remarkably prone to being abducted again. Each successive story becomes more elaborate.

10   Baker points out that individuals who believe hypnotism unearths deeper truths come to believe the tale more completely each time they retell it. Moreover, people who are not consciously lying will, like Whitley Strieber, easily pass a polygraph test. Baker points out that in *Communion,* Strieber shows the classic symptoms of a fantasy-prone individual: "He is easily hypnotized; he is amnesiac; he has vivid memories of his early life; body immobility and rigidity; a religious background; a very active fantasy life; he is a writer of occult* and highly imaginative novels."

CHECKING YOUR COMPREHENSION

Directions: Circle the letter of the correct answer.

1. The topic of the reading is

   a. UFO accounts.

   b. Whitley Strieber's abduction account.

   c. Bud Hopkins's interview with UFO abductees.

   d. The psychological origins of UFO accounts.

2. Which statement best expresses the overall main idea of the reading?

   a. Bud Hopkins's *Intruders* was a bestseller because his interviews with abductees were remarkably believable and fed the public's interest in UFOs.

   b. Whitley Strieber's *Communion* was a bestseller because of the gruesome details he provided.

   c. Despite the popularity of Strieber's and Hopkins's books, psychologists believe that the stories the writers tell were more about human psychology than about alien abduction.

   d. Psychologists generally believe that the accounts by Hopkins and Strieber were fueled by the authors' greedy desire to make money by writing a bestseller.

3. The main idea of the entire reading is stated in

   a. paragraph 1.

   b. paragraph 2.

   c. paragraph 3.

   d. paragraph 4.

4. Which of the following statements best defines the word *confabulation*?

   a. A confabulation is a delusional story told by someone suffering from a mental illness.

   b. A confabulation is a true story that is not readily believed because it contradicts everyday experience.

   c. A confabulation is a story that is woven together out of bits and pieces of actual experiences.

   d. A confabulation is the story of a group's experience of a single event.

5. Which statement more effectively paraphrases the topic sentence in paragraph 5?

   a. The human mind's tendency toward *confabulation* may well be the source of alien abduction accounts.

   b. Accounts of alien abductions are the result of a mental disturbance called *confabulation*.

   c. Some of our best and most favorite memories never really happened; they are the product of *confabulation*.

6. Reference to the research of psychologist Robert Baker (paragraph 8) is a supporting detail that serves to develop which of the following ideas?

   a. Under hypnosis, most subjects give remarkably detailed accounts of their experiences.

   b. The stories of UFO abductees can be verified by hypnosis.

   c. The human memory is no more accurate under hypnosis than it is under ordinary circumstances.

   d. Skeptics who refuse to believe the accounts of UFO abductees are often silenced by the detailed accounts hypnotized abductees give of their experiences.

7. What's the implied main idea of paragraph 9?

   a. Baker doesn't believe that abductees are lying; rather, he is convinced that they are delusional.

   b. Baker believes that a thirst for attention is a major source of UFO abduction stories.

   c. Baker believes that UFO abduction stories are lies that get repeated so often, the alleged abductee starts to believe them.

   d. Baker believes that UFO abduction stories are more common than most realize but that doesn't mean they are true.

8. Based on what the author says in paragraph 6, you can infer

   a. that only delusional people engage in confabulation.

   b. that we all engage in confabulation, but some do so more than others.

   c. that all of our memories are false.

9. Paragraphs 4 through 6 illustrate which patterns at work?

   a. cause and effect; definition

   b. definition; comparison and contrast

   c. time order; definition

   d. comparison and contrast; time order

10. Paragraph 9 implies that

   a. under cross-examination, alien abductees slip up and reveal that they are lying.

   b. the more alien abductees talk about their experience, the clearer it becomes that they are delusional.

   c. the more alien abductees talk about the experience, the more they believe in it.

DEEPENING YOUR UNDERSTANDING

Directions: Answer the following questions by circling the letter of the correct response or filling in the blanks where required.

1. How would you describe the author's tone?

2. What would you say is the author's purpose?

   a. to inform readers about the different accounts of UFO abductions

   b. to persuade readers that accounts of UFO abductions are more fantasy than reality

3. Would you say that the author's personal bias is

   a. not reflected in the reading?

   b. inclined in favor of those who believe they were abducted by aliens?

   c. inclined against those who believe they were abducted by aliens?

   Please explain your answer.

   _____

   _____

4. The author argues that memories induced under hypnosis are

   _____

   What evidence does she use in support of that claim?

   _____

   What question or questions should you ask about that evidence?

   _____

   _____

5. In paragraph 5, what metaphor does the author use to describe the workings of human memory?

   _____

6. Would you say that this author's account of how memory works (paragraph 5) is similar to or different from the descriptions in the two previous readings? _Note:_ Feel free to review the previous readings to answer the question.

Please explain how they are similar or different.

_____

_____

7. In paragraph 8, the author tells us that in "Robert Baker's experiments, hypnotized subjects recalled . . . imaginary events that Baker had discussed just before hypnotizing them." Does this statement

   a. contradict what you have learned about remembering from the previous readings?

   b. confirm what you have learned about remembering from the previous readings?

   Please explain how Baker's statement confirms or contradicts what you learned from the previous readings.

   _____

   _____

8. Look at this statement from paragraph 4: "Most psychologists agree that such tales spring not from the alien world of extra-terrestrials but from the dark interior world of the human psyche." Is the author communicating an opinion or a fact?

   _____

9. Do you think that a confirmed believer in UFOs would agree or disagree with the claim that "the simplest psychological mechanism fueling UFO accounts is confabulation"(paragraph 5)? Why or why not?

   _____

10. According to the authors of readings 3, 4, and 5, what and how we remember can be influenced by several factors. What are those factors?

   _____

   _____

   _____

1. According to the author, readers of *Communion* and *Intruders* were impressed because the abduction accounts were so detailed. Based on what you learned about the workings of memory in readings 1 and 2, are the remembered details a clear indicator that the accounts must be accurate? Please explain your answer.

   _____

   _____

2. In discussion or on paper, explain why you do or do not believe in UFOs.

Unit II Media Watch

The media—newspapers, television, and radio—have an incredible amount of influence on almost everyone. They report on the world around us and give us information about current events and trends. We rely on the media to tell us what we need to know in order to make informed decisions about how we should best live our lives. That's why the notion of a "media watch" is extremely important. If members of the media do not do their job, we suffer for it. In other words, we need to keep an eye on the media to make sure that they live up to our expectations and keep us well informed. Unfortunately, most of the writers in this unit of readings are convinced that the current media are, in different ways, not doing their jobs as well as they should.

Journalists Under Fire

GETTING FOCUSED

The author of this reading believes that the public has high expectations of journalists. He also suggests that currently those expectations are not being met. Read to see if you can find out why.

Textbook Features and Readers' Strategies

Feature: *The title describes an existing situation or state of affairs.*

Strategy: When the title of a reading indicates that a particular situation or state of affairs exists, start your reading with a question in mind, such as "Why are journalists under fire?" or "Why are journalists being criticized?"

Feature: *The author uses italics and boxes to highlight key points.*

Strategy: Anytime an author goes to the trouble of highlighting text, whether through boldface, italics, colored ink, or icons, you should pre-read that material before you actually start reading the text from beginning to end.

Evaluating Your Background Knowledge

The author of this reading is relying on your knowledge of these words and terms. Look over this list carefully to make sure you know everything on it. *Note:* The number in parentheses indicates the paragraph where the word can be found while an asterisk accompanies the word's first appearance in the reading.

cavalcade (6):   parade

ire (8):   rage

Watergate scandal of the early 1970s (10): On June 17, 1972, five men were arrested for burglarizing the offices of the Democratic National Committee, located in the Watergate Hotel apartment complex. After eighteen months of denials on the part of the White House that the president had played no role in the affair, President Richard M. Nixon was publicly named as a coconspirator in the break-in. On August 8, 1974, President Nixon announced his resignation. The Watergate scandal, covered by two young journalists, Bob Woodward and Carl Bernstein, is considered by many to be a highpoint of investigative reporting.

Evaluating Your Background Knowledge (continued)

chasm (14):   divide

boon (29):   favor

slippery slope (33): The phrase is used to describe the kind of thinking that suggests one event or series of events is bound to produce another train of similar but much worse events. For example: If we discourage children from playing aggressively competitive games in grammar school, pretty soon there won't be any competitive sports in high school or college either.

News

1   When Americans discuss issues such as sex, violence, and stereotyping in the mass media, they almost always separate their discussions of entertainment from news. That's not because they believe that news people are doing such a good job. On the contrary, it's because they have been taught to expect more from journalists than from the creators of action films, TV sitcoms, and fashion magazines.

2   Judging by the curriculum students traditionally learn in journalism school, these expectations are not unreasonable. For more than one hundred years, news people have told themselves and society at large that they are professionals who help keep democracy alive by keeping their readers informed about what their elected representatives are doing or not doing to make the world better.

3   Historians and sociologists point out that the actual way newspapers, radio, and television create news never quite matches this ideal. Editors have long known that one of their primary goals is to attract audiences for advertisers. Experience has told them that sensational events and human interest stories draw the most attention. They have long known the difficulty of writing catchy stories that require a lot of explanation of history or politics.

4   Despite decades of criticism that the reality of the American press has not lived up to the ideal, some contemporary observers of the American scene say that journalism has not improved and may be getting substantially worse. They point to a number of recent developments:

5   ■ *Critics argue that many local newspapers have adopted eye-catching graphics, a human interest perspective, shorter stories, and a news-you-can-use*

philosophy. Newspaper executives hope that this change will help their papers stay relevant to the large numbers of busy readers.

6 ■ *Television journalism, they argue, has become increasingly sensational. Local TV news programs are immersed in a strange mixture of action stories and happy talk among its anchors.* Desperate to attract audiences that now have many more media choices than they did a couple of decades ago, local news directors have in many cases given up trying to seriously cover the governmental and political system. Instead, local news shows have become a cavalcade* of murders, robberies, rapes, fires, and car accidents punctuated by weather, sports, and human interest stories.

7   Network television news directors, these critics say, are not that far behind their local counterparts. Although not yet as obviously sensational as the local news programs, network news broadcasts and their newsmagazine programs increasingly emphasize major court trials, political scandals, human interest tales, and news-you-can-use stories (often relating to health or money). Particularly pushed out of the picture is international news (when not related to U.S. military involvement) and the careful discussion of political ideas.

8 ■ *Critics reserve special ire* for the coverage of government and politics by the print and electronic press.* Scholarly research supports what many observers say they have noticed: during the past few decades, journalists have increasingly covered political campaigns and even day-to-day activities of government mostly as if they were football games, not serious debates over beliefs and policies.

9   They argue, for example, that the coverage most Americans received about topics as profound as the Clinton administration's health care initiative of the mid-1990s and the presidential election of 1996 actually told them very little about the varying viewpoints behind these campaigns. Instead, the stories emphasized strategies for winning, the power brokers who were involved in helping, and what political polls suggested about the outcome.

10   The critics note that part of the reason for this focus on strategy over ideas may be that suspicion of politicians became part of the journalist's trade after the Watergate scandal of the early 1970s* and other examples of government corruption. Another reason may be the belief that equating politics with sport gives politics a touch of sensationalism that can make it more interesting to their audiences.

11 ■ *Critics of the news believe that the charge of inappropriate coverage of politics applies generally to American reporting at the turn of the twenty-first*

century. Many also argue, though, that U.S. society is seeing a growing, and potentially dangerous, divide in the journalism industry. The divide is between the so-called popular press and elite press. The popular press includes most daily newspapers, newsmagazines, and broadcast news operations. The elite press includes a small number of prestigious newspapers (particularly the *New York Times, Washington Post,* and *Wall Street Journal*), National Public Radio news, and perhaps a few policy-oriented magazines such as *Foreign Affairs, New Republic,* and *American Spectator.*

12   The audiences and content of these two kinds of news operations have always been different, the critics concede. The elite press has always catered to high-income decision makers in business and government, whereas the popular press has gone after the rest of the population. Still, the critics contend, until not too long ago much of the popular press pretty well mirrored the issues that elite outlets discussed. Viewers of network and even local news were likely to learn about many of the same national and international news events as readers of the New York Times or Wall Street Journal.

13   However, during the past decade or so the formerly more prestigious end of the popular press (network news, for example) has gravitated to the sensational, the human interest, and the usable, whereas the elite press has continued its stress on the national and international trends that occupy business executives and government officials. The result, they argue, is that a person watching the Today Show for two hours gets a very different view of what is going on from someone reading the *New York Times* that same morning or listening to National Public Radio. The basic newscast may have two or three of the same stories, but the rest of the coverage reflects very different worlds. Moreover, these worlds are extended into new media, as both prestige and popular media construct Web sites and encourage their target audiences to follow them.

14   The reason this chasm* is dangerous, some observers contend, is that the news business is reinforcing and extending a gap between the elites in the society and most others about what are the most important issues facing society. Historically, one of the ideals of journalism has been the notion that news encourages democracy by giving the people access to issues they need to discuss publicly with their leaders. Increasingly, the critics say, the news that "regular" people get is so different from the news that elites receive that they have little to share and discuss.

15   Ironically, critics point out, the one aspect of news that elites and others do seem to share a lot is the continual portrayal of government actions as reflecting a power struggle rather than a desire to help the

nation. This portrayal, they argue, seems to be having a corrosive effect on the citizenry. Critics note that recent scholarly research suggests that it may be encouraging a "spiral of cynicism" among Americans about their political system.

16   In response to these comments, it's hard to find observers of the American scene—even journalists—who think news organizations do a great job. Even the staunchest defenders of the news business stress that journalists are too often manipulated by political figures. They blame both politicians and journalists for stories that often reflect the agenda of those in power.

17   At the same time, defenders of the news business stress that the state of journalism is not nearly as dire as some critics make it out to be. Sure, local and network news has gotten more sensational, they might say. That's to be expected given the competition for viewership. It pays to remember, though, that sensationalism and tawdriness has always been a part of the American news business. At the same time, people who care to find quality reporting probably have more choices than ever. It is only during the past two decades that satellite distribution technology has made it cost-effective for the *New York Times* and *Wall Street Journal* to truly become national papers. Moreover, National Public Radio is available free all over the country. A person who wants access to "elite" news doesn't have to look far to find it.

18   People who stand up for the press add that it is not journalists' fault that they deemphasize ideas in favor of politicians' strategies. They insist that politics does, in fact, work this way. The press, they say, is reflecting this reality, not creating it.

Commercialism

19   If you ask media critics what forces lie behind the problems they have with news and entertainment, sooner or later—probably sooner—you'll hear about the role **commercialism** plays in shaping the kinds of material available to the American people and the way in which it is available.

20   *Commercialism* refers to a situation in which the buying and selling of goods and services is a highly promoted value. Many people say that the United States is a nation in which commercialism runs rampant. Everywhere we turn, we see a sales pitch.

21   Its defenders insist that Americans would never have the high standard of living that they now have, nor the products that they take for granted, were it not for industrial competition that commercialism has encouraged. Detractors of commercialism question this notion of

progress. They insist that many problems come along with making commercialism a central tenet of American society. A number of their objections have to do with what they consider the unfortunate effects of commercialism on the mass media and their audiences.

22   ■ *Critics of commercialism point out that advertisers have a large say in the basic structure of American media—the personalities of media outlets that exist and the audiences they go after.* The reason is that advertisers are extremely important to the survival of many U.S. media. Media executives must take the needs of potential advertisers into account when they make decisions about whom to reach and with what sorts of material.

23   Are women twenty-five to fifty-four a viable audience for a fashion magazine, or would advertisers be happier with younger demographics? If so, what kinds of columns and covers would best attract younger readers? If you multiply these sorts of questions and their answers thousands of times, you will understand that when people read a magazine, watch a TV show, get on many Web sites, or use any other ad-sponsored medium, they are entering a world that was created as a result of close cooperation between advertisers and media firms. Foes of commercialism contend that because marketers foster an American media system that matches their needs, they reinforce a view that society is merely a huge marketplace.

24   ■ *Critics also argue that commercialism fosters an atmosphere of censorship in much of the American media.* The First Amendment does not protect media practitioners from advertisers, they note. In fact, because of their importance in funding the media, advertisers actually have a lot more power than government agencies have over the content of media in the United States.

25   What advertisers get from that power, say the critics, are media vehicles that create a friendly environment for them among the audiences they target. The rules are typically clear. TV executives are aware, for example, that some major advertisers won't fund content that involves too much violence, or gays and lesbians. Newspaper editors understand that investigating local real-estate brokers (the sponsors who support the papers' real-estate sections) is not a healthy activity. Magazines know that they will lose lucrative tobacco accounts if they publish articles about the hazards of cigarette smoking. A number of incidents of advertiser anger happen every year. They clearly show what is at stake if media executives don't create environments that are friendly to marketers in general and to individual advertisers in particular.

26   ■ *Critics of commercialism believe, too, that the preoccupation of media with advertising and marketing often leads them to exploit children.* You can find

examples of media for children that do not carry ads. In general, though, children aged two through twelve are often treated like other consumers. Ad people know that children influence parental spending and, as they get older, have their own purchasing power from gifts and allowances.

27   Media critics contend that advertising to children is ethically unacceptable. They cite scholarly research that the youngest children (under age four or five) often don't have the skills to be critical of advertisers' claims. As for the older kids, the critics contend that by getting children hyped for toys, foods, and other products that their parents must approve, the advertisers may be encouraging family arguments. In fact, marketers and media firms that invite children into a separate channel to advertise to them are quietly setting themselves up in opposition to the children's parents—a situation that, the critics argue, is morally highly questionable.

28   Defenders of advertising have developed a number of responses to these critiques.

29   ■ One response has been to emphasize that advertisers' influence has been a boon* rather than a hindrance to diversity within the U.S. media structure. Take a look at the range of media outlets available under commercial sponsorships. There are thousands of magazines, thousands of radio stations, more than a hundred cable channels, and so many other ways for people to get information, education, news, and entertainment.

30   This sort of abundance would not exist without advertisers. People wouldn't have enough money to pay for all the magazines, newspapers, and TV channels that come to their homes. And the government not only would be unlikely to pay for all of that, it would bring questions of control that would be much worse than what you see with advertisers.

31   ■ When it comes to the area of content censorship, defenders of advertising argue that advertisers have a perfect right to decide where to put their money. It's natural, they add, not to want to place ads on material that would embarrass the sponsor or its audience. They also contend that if a media outlet cannot satisfy one advertiser, another will often take its place.

32   ■ The topic of advertising to children is a touchy subject with many advertisers. Defenders of the practice emphasize that by the age of five children do understand what advertising is and are often suspicious of it. Advocates contend that sponsors, media firms, and the government have developed rules that insulate children from exploitation. Ultimately, though, they

fall back on a basic principle that has for decades guided their policy about advertising to kids. If companies stopped advertising toward children under pressure, they state, that action will open the door to eliminate advertising in other kinds of material (say, the news) or for particular products or in particular media.

33   Critics of advertising reject this slippery-slope* argument. The debate goes on.

Joseph Turow. *Media Today: An Introduction to Mass Communication*, pp. 423–428.

CHECKING YOUR COMPREHENSION

Directions: Circle the letter of the correct answer.

1. Which statement most effectively sums up the overall point of the reading?

   a. For years, the American press has had its critics, but those critical of the press insist that the situation is getting worse rather than better.

   b. Journalists have been under fire for decades, but the current crop of critics seems unnecessarily negative and pessimistic about the free press.

   c. The American press corps is not aggressive enough when it comes to pursuing a story that requires a lot of legwork.

   d. Journalists are the people who keep democracy alive.

2. Which statement most effectively paraphrases the main idea of paragraph 6?

   a. Local news programs are much too focused on sensational events like robbery, rape, and murder.

   b. Local and network news programs are equally bad when it comes to the coverage of international news.

   c. Although the network news programs are somewhat better than the local news programs, both are spending too much airtime on crime and human interest stories.

3. Which statement most effectively paraphrases the main idea of paragraph 7?

a. Network news programs do little more than entertain viewers.

b. Although they are an improvement over local news programs, network news programs don't do a good job informing the public.

c. Network and local news programs completely ignore international news.

4. Which patterns organize paragraphs 6 and 7?

a. cause and effect; definition

b. comparison and contrast; cause and effect

c. classification; comparison and contrast

d. time order; classification

5. Which pattern organizes paragraphs 11, 12, and 13?

a. cause and effect

b. definition

c. comparison and contrast

d. time order

6. In paragraph 10, the Watergate scandal is used to explain why

a. the Clinton administration's health care plan of the mid-1990s failed to get approved.

b. scholarly researchers are critical of journalists' hostility toward the government.

c. journalists focus more on campaign strategies than campaign issues.

d. International news does not get much media coverage.

7. *Commercialism* is a key definition in this reading. Which statement most effectively paraphrases the author's definition in paragraph 20?

a. Commercialism is a state of affairs in which making and spending money is considered extremely important.

b. Commercialism encourages the unnecessary purchase of high-end luxury items.

    c. Commercialism refers to the belief that everyone and everything has a price tag.

8. Which statement better paraphrases the response of those who defend commercialism (paragraph 21)?

    a. The desire to buy and sell is an essential part of human nature and is therefore unavoidable.

    b. Americans can thank commercialism for their standard of living and the number of products at their disposal.

    c. The United States was founded on commercialism.

9. In paragraph 25, the author doesn't specifically explain why newspaper editors "understand that investigating local real-estate brokers . . . is not a healthy activity." He expects readers to infer that

    a. local real-estate brokers will personally boycott the paper.

    b. local real-estate brokers will tell their clients not to read any paper that criticizes the brokers' behavior.

    c. local real-estate brokers will withdraw their advertising, and the paper will lose money.

10. Paragraphs 6, 7, 9, and 12 all include transitional devices that signal

    a. addition.

    b. contrast.

    c. order in time.

    d. cause and effect.

DEEPENING YOUR UNDERSTANDING

Directions: Answer the following questions by circling the letter of the correct response or filling in the blanks where required.

1. What would you say is the author's purpose?

    a. to outline the current controversy surrounding journalists and the news

    b. to persuade readers to take a side in the controversy surrounding journalists in the news

2. How would you describe the author's tone?

    a. skeptical

    b. critical

    c. neutral

    d. angry

3. Do you think the author

    a. agrees with journalism's critics?

    b. agrees with journalism's defenders?

    c. gives no indication of his personal bias?

Please explain your answer.

_____

_____

4. What developments do journalism's critics mention to support their opinion that journalism is getting worse?

    (1) _____

    (2) _____

    (3) _____

    (4) _____

5. Some observers insist that the division between the popular and the elite press is dangerous. How do they support this opinion?

_____

_____

6. Critics of journalism claim that commercialism has distorted the content of the news. Defenders of commercialism in journalism insist that thanks to the commercial incentive, we have many more news outlets than we would ever have had without the incentive to sell products. How do you think the critics of commercialism would respond to that claim?

_____

_____

7. Some schools have started including televised news programs in their curricula, complete with ads from the companies that sponsor the programs. What do you think the critics described in paragraphs 26–27 would have to say about these school news programs?

_____

_____

8. In paragraph 3, the author mentions "historians and sociologists." Later on, in paragraph 27, the author says media critics "cite scholarly research," indicating that children under four or five "don't have the skills to be critical of advertisers' claims." How would a critical reader respond to that statement?

_____

_____

9. In paragraph 32, the author notes: "Defenders of the practice [advertising to children] emphasize that by the age of five children do understand what advertising is and are often suspicious of it." Does this claim make sense to you or not?

_____ Please explain your answer.

_____

_____

10. Paraphrase the slippery slope argument the author refers to in the last sentence of the reading.

_____

_____

AIRING YOUR OPINIONS

1. Who in the reading do you think offers the best arguments, those in favor of journalism as it is currently practiced (the pros) or those opposed (the cons)? Explain your answer.

_____

_____

2. What do you think of the slippery slope argument offered at the end of the reading? Does it make good sense in this case, or is it

nonsense? _____ Please explain your answer.

_____

_____

Reading 2   # Ethical Issues in Journalism

GETTING FOCUSED

The author of this reading airs his concerns about the way journalists report—and sometimes create—the news. After reading it, you will probably look at the news and how it is presented with a much more critical eye. While you read, compare and contrast this reading with the previous one. Do you think the two authors share a similar point of view? If not, where do they differ?

Textbook Features and Readers' Strategies

Feature:	*The title uses the plural word* issues.
Strategy:	Titles with plural words like *issues, problems,* or *concerns* all but shout out to readers that the author is going to make several different points rather than focusing on just one. In this case, each time you see the word *issue* or one of its synonyms, check to see if a new ethical concern is being introduced. If it is, paraphrase the issue in the margins.
Feature:	*The author poses numerous questions throughout.*

Textbook Features and Readers' Strategies (continued)

Strategy: In general, never ignore questions posed by the author. Even rhetorical questions can tell you a lot about an author's point of view. But when an author does what this one does—includes a list of bulleted questions— you need to look over the questions before you begin your reading. Then you can look for the answers while you read. When you find an answer, jot the question in the margin. Then use lines or arrows to indicate the location of the answer.

Feature: *The author uses case studies to illustrate particular ethical concerns.*

Strategy: Make sure you can explain how each case study illustrates a larger ethical issue.

Feature: *The writing is heavy on stories, reports, and case studies.*

Strategy: When a piece of writing is as rich in narratives as this one, it's tempting to just read for the story. Don't do it. The stories and case studies are there for a reason. After every example, story, or case study, ask yourself what ethical issue or problem each one illustrates.

Evaluating Your Background Knowledge

The author of this reading is relying on your knowledge of these words and terms. Look over this list carefully to make sure you know everything on it. *Note:* The number in parentheses indicates the paragraph where the word can be found while an asterisk accompanies the word's first appearance in the reading.

postmodern (1): For the author, this is the period from 1965 until the present (other writers often identify 1945 as the beginning of postmodernism). But whatever the dates, postmodernism signals a period of very rapid social and political change that undermines or challenges more traditional points of view.

cognitive dissonance (1): Psychology term that describes a conflict between belief and action, or between principle and reality

"If it bleeds, it leads" (2): Reference to media critics' claim that television networks often pick their most violent stories to start off the news as a way of gaining the audience's attention

proximity (3): closeness

Evaluating Your Background Knowledge (continued)

Ed Murrow (9):   Edward R. Murrow became the nation's most famous journalist during World War II when he broadcast on radio from Europe, often with gunfire and bombs dropping in the background. He was and is considered one of the most respected journalists ever to be in the profession. Allusions to Murrow are often used to suggest a high standard of journalistic integrity.

laissez-faire attitude (12): Originally, laissez-faire was an economics term referring to a hands-off or unregulated economy; now used to describe any situation that lacks all external controls

Émile Durkheim (1858–1917) (12): social scientist known for his study of social values

Arthur Schopenhauer (1788–1860) (12): German philosopher who believed that following the dictates of the human will leads to misery

voyeurism (24):   a fascination with viewing the sensational or the sexual from a distance

cronyism (37):   taking care of one's friends first

symbiotic (44):   closely associated but not necessarily beneficial

Postmodern Ethical Concerns

1   As our culture moved into the postmodern era, additional ethical concerns surfaced. Some of these may have been around for a while, but they seem more easily recognized now because they reflect postmodern* characteristics, particularly in terms of stressing victimization and in the cognitive dissonance* created by some current journalistic practices.

2   It often seems that the most important philosophy for most news operations is "If it bleeds, it leads."* This phrase reflects the news selection policy of many television stations and some newspapers. An examination of the types of stories appearing on evening newscasts on many local television stations reveals much emphasis on crime news. Some news operations seem obsessed with reporting crime news. A local television newscast that does not lead with a crime story of some sort is a rare find; often the crime story has few or no implications for the audience. For example, on one particular Friday night, one

television station in the South apparently ran short of brutal killings and rapes. The station settled on a story about a 7-year-old boy who was accidentally shot in the leg with a BB by two older boys who were harassing him. The camera zoomed in to show the bruise on the boy's leg. Interviews were conducted all around. The investigating police officer called the incident "a shame." The two older boys said they only wanted to scare the boy, and didn't mean to shoot him. The little boy's mother said the two older boys were nothing but bullies. A local television critic called this approach to news "junior high journalism."

3   Is this a news story? . . . The boy was obviously distressed by the incident, as was his mother. And he was lucky that the BB did not strike an eye, but this sort of interaction among the young, although not desirable, is fairly routine. Does the story meet the tests of audience, impact, proximity,* timeliness, prominence, or unusualness? Probably not, yet it was the lead story on the evening newscast. Weren't there other, more important things going on in the area—a major metropolitan area, the fifteenth largest in the nation? Was there important news at the national or international level? Was it less important than the "bully" story?

4   If the emphasis on reporting crime news weren't enough, some stations appear to have reporters (or news executives) who would really rather be cops. "Crimestoppers" segments are popular with many broadcast news operations. The notion here is that the station can use its personnel to reenact, or dramatize, an unsolved crime. In doing so, it is hoped that some member of the audience will remember having seen the incident and phone police, providing important information that may lead to a resolution of the case. It should be noted that while newspapers often splash crime news on their front pages, they are much less inclined to let this type of news dominate. Crime news of all sorts can be found in newspapers, but usually it is tucked inside, and often presented in capsule form.

5   When crime news is emphasized by news organizations, it almost certainly reinforces the postmodern *trend toward victimization*. Mass communication researchers have studied the degree to which television "cultivates" a particular view of crime in viewers. We know that viewers who watch a lot of television consider themselves to be likely victims of crime or wrongdoing to a greater extent than is probable in the real world. Viewers often live in the "TV world" of violent crime. This is not to say that crime is not a problem in contemporary America; it is. But not everyone is guaranteed victim status. Is it any wonder so many trivial lawsuits are filed over things like spilled coffee

or hurt feelings? How can the public place the various aspects of life in any sort of context when television news, particularly, reports that the most important news of the day is related to crime. Agenda-setting, indeed!

6   Another disturbing contemporary journalistic practice is an increasing tendency of news organizations (and personalities) to become *involved with the stories* they are reporting. There is some evidence of this in the "Crimestoppers" news approach. But there is additional evidence. Here, too, television news organizations seem to be more deeply involved than newspapers or magazines, but there are instances where the print media are also becoming involved.

7   Twice in a period of a year (in February 1996 and in January 1997), "media organizations have paid to fly relatives to retrieve youths at the center of attention-getting disappearance cases." In the 1996 incident, "five Tampa Bay and three Orlando TV stations," as well as the two local Tampa Bay newspapers, "split the cost of an $8,314 Learjet charter to pick up a 17-year-old in New York, where she had been discovered after a five-week disappearance that made national headlines." In the 1997 incident, another television station flew a father to Virginia to reunite him with his 7-year-old daughter who had been taken by her mother in violation of a custody agreement. As a result, the station had an exclusive story because a camera crew accompanied the father on the plane.

8   These incidents—and they are only two among many—clearly demonstrate the willingness of news organizations to participate in a story. Has the line between reporting the news and making the news been crossed? Indeed it has. Yet this sort of action, in postmodern America, is not causing the cognitive dissonance it should. Few seem to care that news is being redefined by those who most benefit from its redefinition. Can the audience tell the difference between *spontaneous coverage* and *choreographed coverage*? Are media in the business of reporting the news, or serving as charities for those who are sitting on a hot story but are in financial need? The inconsistencies here are clear. News no longer has to meet a set of clear standards. News is simply what news organizations say it is, and they often say it is what benefits them economically. Cognitive dissonance alarms should be going off in the heads not only of the audience but also of those involved in the news process. However, most just shrug their shoulders and, in postmodern fashion, ignore the inconsistencies between what should be done and what is being done.

9   CBS newsman Ed Murrow,* in his 1958 speech, was "frightened by the imbalance, the constant striving to reach the largest audience for everything; by the absence of a sustained study of the state of the nation." Although postmodernism was a barely developed concept in 1958, it is clear that Murrow was troubled by the inconsistencies, by the cognitive dissonance, resulting from news practices in his day. One shudders to think how Murrow would react to news practices today.

10   Anyone can be a journalist. No examinations are required to enter the field; no licenses must be obtained. No oversight board monitors the work and behavior of journalists. Economic influences, that is, the desire to garner high ratings and more revenue, have made the field wide open to some who wouldn't have even been considered in pre-postmodern times. For example, in the early summer of 1997, the Fox News Channel hired rapper Chuck D to provide news and commentary. Chuck D has made his living as a rap music artist. What qualifies him to provide news and commentary to a cable news operation? Chuck D himself provided the answer: "I'm a thirty-six-year-old black man. . . . I've graduated from college, I'm a taxpayer and I can put sentences together. Why shouldn't I do commentary?" Precisely! Chuck D's response is an excellent example of postmodern reasoning and symbolic of all that's wrong with TV news these days. He sees no conflict between his life experiences as an entertainer and his future work as a journalist. Chuck D, whose real name is Carlton Ridenhour, said he wants to bring something different to the news. "I want to alert younger viewers to the news and knock the older people in the head."

11   What were Fox news executives thinking when they hired Ridenhour? Were they aware of any inconsistencies between the job he had and the job he was seeking? Were they aware that he may have had an agenda of some sort and how this agenda might impact on the important job of providing accurate and meaningful news reports? Were their cognitive processes undisturbed as they considered a person with no credentials for an important news job? In postmodern America, these questions are never asked and therefore never answered.

12   This *laissez-faire attitude* * regarding the news and those who present it has important ethical implications. Does such action as has been taken by various news organizations reflect poor ethics or merely poor judgment? Durkheim* reminds us that we should determine the moral ideal or standard that governs a planned action and explain how

society benefits from the action. What moral ideal or standard governs participation in a news story? What ideal or standard allows the employment of an entertainer as a journalist? In point of fact, there are others, nonentertainers, who have jumped from their particular fields to journalism. It is routine for an individual who has been in politics or government to quit that job and become a journalist. President Clinton's adviser George Stephanopoulos quit his White House job and went to work for ABC. New York Congresswoman Susan Molinari resigned her House seat to become a weekend news anchor for CBS. Is this more acceptable than giving a news job to an entertainer? Do these individuals have any sort of political agenda they will be advancing in the performance of their news jobs? Schopenhauer* urged giving mature and repeated consideration to any plan before carrying it out. He warned that without such serious consideration, the "greedful will" will triumph and your action will lack balance and appropriateness. Has the greedful will overtaken American news organizations in postmodern America?

13   There is no need to belabor the point beyond the degree to which we have already gone. However, additional questions need to be asked and answered, and ethical positions need to be examined. Consider these items:

- Why do reporters insist on telling us what they *think*, rather than what they have *seen*?

- Just because a story has good visuals, does that make it good news?

- How do media "frame" their stories? That is, from what perspective is a story, particularly one involving conflict, told?

- What impact does the newsroom culture have on the selection and preparation of news stories?

- Are codes of ethics developed by the various news organizations actually practiced in newsrooms, or merely posted?

14   Do these and similar issues clearly involve ethics? The answer depends on one's definition of ethics, but if there is substantial agreement that ethics involves making judgments between appropriate and inappropriate behavior, then the answer, of course, is yes. More than forty years ago, Ed Murrow observed that media needed to be reminded that "the fact that your voice is amplified to the degree where it reaches from one end of the country to the other does not confer upon you greater wisdom or understanding than you possessed when your voice reached only from one end of the bar to the other."

Case Studies

15   Use the following case studies to stimulate your thinking about some of the ethical issues facing journalists.

Case Study #1. Supporting Professional Football

16   Tampa Bay, Florida, was awarded a professional football franchise in 1976. The team was purchased by Malcolm Glazer in 1994, shortly after the death of original owner Hugh Culverhouse. The team was no more productive under Glazer than it had been under Culverhouse. At one point in 1995, Glazer appeared to be on the verge of selling or moving the team. If sold, the team would likely move to another city; Baltimore and St. Louis were among the top choices. If not sold, the team might be moved anyway. The potential sale and possible move of the Bucs generated much local attention. Some fans wanted them to stay; others were willing to help them pack.

17   As events developed, it appeared that the Glazer family, composed of Malcolm and his sons, Bryan and Joel, were willing to make a long-term commitment to keeping the Bucs in Tampa Bay if the community would provide the team with a new stadium. There was nothing really wrong with the stadium the team was currently using. It just wasn't new. It did not have luxurious "suites" from which the rich and famous could view the game, and for which privilege they would pay top dollar. In fact, the stadium was acceptable enough to the NFL for the area to be awarded Super Bowl XXV. A problem developed, however, when neither the Tampa City Council nor the Hillsborough County Commission was willing to raise taxes to support the construction of a new stadium. It was decided that the issue would be put before area voters in the form of a referendum, a penny on the dollar sales tax. One half-cent would go toward the construction of a new stadium; the other half-cent could go to a fund for schools and to finance improvements in police and fire protection.

18   As might be expected, the community was divided over whether this referendum ought to be passed. Some objected to "rich" sports owners leaning on taxpayers for facilities that would make the owners even richer. Others felt the civic pride of having a professional football team justified additional taxes. Still others noted that the stadium tax should not be combined with a school and community services tax; these were, in their view, separate issues.

19   Tampa Bay area television stations and newspapers followed this story closely. There were daily updates on where things stood with regard to the proposed referendum as well as the proposed sale of

the team. Local media took sides in the battle in mid-October, just a few weeks before the referendum. Seven local television stations aired a program titled "Home Field Advantage." The program featured local sports anchors, local politicians, and representatives of the football team in a spirited discussion asking viewers "to pony up for a new stadium for the Tampa Bay Buccaneers before the team is lured out of town." All the stations promoted the program heavily. The *St. Petersburg Times* gave stadium backers a special low rate for a full-page advertisement promoting the broadcast. The broadcast was carried live and at no charge by the participating stations. There was no place for non-cable viewers to go if they wanted to see something else during that time period. The program effectively blanketed the coverage area. Cable subscribers, of course, had other alternatives. One local sports anchor, when questioned about his participation in the event, said he was simply trying to inform the people about an important issue. "This was no different than going on a telethon," he said.

20   There is no way to determine the precise impact the program had on the attitudes of Bay area residents. Nevertheless, the referendum passed by a small margin a few weeks later.

21   **Key Questions**   Is there an ethical difference between television stations providing free time for fund-raising telethons (like Jerry Lewis's Labor Day MDA telethon) and providing free time for supporters of a local sports franchise to argue for public funding of a new stadium? Were Tampa Bay sports anchors acting ethically when they appeared on behalf of the local professional football team? Does a reporter's responsibility to objectivity include those individuals who report on sports?

Case Study #2. Chopper Journalism

22   Daniel Jones was apparently a troubled man. The forty-year-old maintenance worker from Long Beach, California, was HIV-positive and was angry about the way he had been treated by his health maintenance organization (HMO). He felt that there was too much bureaucratic red tape and that HMOs emphasized making money rather than caring for the ill.

23   On April 30, 1998, Jones stopped his pickup truck on a busy Los Angeles expressway overpass and spread a banner out on the ground so that the news helicopters could see it. The banner read: HMOS ARE IN IT FOR THE MONEY!! LIVE FREE, LOVE SAFE OR DIE. By this time, of course, the always vigilant choppers were hovering overhead, and traffic was clogged. Jones returned to his truck and set the vehicle

afire. He then placed his chin on the barrel of a shotgun and pulled the trigger. The television newscopters captured it all for live broadcast as *breaking news.*

24   Suicides like the one involving Jones are common and seem to be increasingly presented as a staple of the news. It is probably true that this was a news story of some sort. As Larry Perret of KCBS-TV noted, "This was a legitimate news story. You got a guy on the freeway closing two of L.A.'s most populated interchanges." True, but the cameras were not focused on the traffic but on a man who was about to do violence to himself. Is this news or voyeurism?*

25   These types of stories are usually ratings winners. Los Angeles is a competitive news market. News is expensive to cover. The lease on a news helicopter can cost upwards of $1 million. Kerry Brock of New York City's Media Studies Center suggested that "if you're a television station and don't have a helicopter, you're not in the game." Nevertheless, criticism of the coverage of the Jones suicide was immediate. Television stations were inundated with phone calls, most complaining about the graphic nature of the broadcast. Of particular concern to some was the fact that the incident was broadcast in midafternoon, "just in time to greet kids returning home from school. Two stations actually cut away from children's programming to get in on the action." Cable's MSNBC also carried live video from the scene.

26   Derwin Johnson of the Columbia Graduate School of Journalism was bothered by the incident. "It's a classic case of technology running the beast instead of a clear editorial process. I don't think there was any reason to go live with this." Although Los Angeles television news directors expressed their regret at showing the graphic violence of the incident—they noted that they had not anticipated its outcome— many stations "stayed on the story for an hour during which time they could have discerned that the man was obviously disturbed and that a catastrophe might have been in the offing." Radio Television News Directors Association president Barbara Cochran said she believed the industry needs to develop some guidelines for live coverage of potentially explosive situations. However, Howard Rosenberg of the *Los Angeles Times* observed that "the media don't tend to learn from mistakes like this."

27   **Key Questions**   What ethical responsibilities do television stations have in carrying live broadcasts of breaking news? Are television stations under any ethical obligation to moderate or modify their news programming because children might be in the audience? What

is the ethical motivation for live coverage of potentially explosive situations? Are there unethical motivations that might stimulate such coverage? . . .

Case Study #3. A Glass Not So Transparent

28   Stephen Glass was hot—at least several well-known magazines thought so. The twenty-five-year-old journalist had talent. His stories were compelling, and his work was published in *Rolling Stone, George, Harper's,* and the *New York Times Magazine.* The editors of the *New Republic,* a magazine of political opinion, were particularly delighted because Glass was on the publication's staff and made regular contributions to the magazine. As one editor observed, Glass "could get into rooms other reporters couldn't get into, and come away with quotes and anecdotes the others couldn't get."

29   Yes, it was clear that Steve Glass had talent, but, as his editors unhappily discovered, his particular talent was in making things up. "Glass concocted story after story and slipped them all past his editors and fact checkers." He often supported his stories with forged notes and interview transcripts.

30   How clever was he? Pretty clever, actually. He invented a computer association called the National Assembly of Hackers and a special interest group called the Association for the Advancement of Sound Water Policy. He invented the town of "Werty, Iowa," and even created a fake Web site for Jukt Micronics, a nonexistent computer software company. Perhaps fact checkers should have gotten a little suspicious when they read of a George Bush cult group called The First Church of George Herbert Walker Christ, but they didn't. An examination of the forty-one stories Glass had written for the *New Republic* revealed that almost two-thirds of them were at least partly fabricated; six were apparently entirely made up.

31   How could this happen? Two explanations were offered. One suggested that staff turnover at the *New Republic*—four editors in four years and the departure of several skilled staff writers—was to blame. Too little time and effort were assigned to fact checking. The other explanation suggested that journalism is a youth-happy industry and that many reporters land high-profile jobs before they have fully grasped the fundamentals of their craft. Glass rose quickly at the *New Republic,* from an intern in 1995 to assistant editor and then to associate editor. However, it is also possible that Glass was simply a pathological liar. Glass disappeared for a time following his firing at the *New Republic,* but reportedly surfaced again in the spring of 1998

when he took final exams at the Georgetown Law School, where he had been attending evening classes.

32 **Key Questions**   What responsibilities do newspapers and magazines have in checking the factual accuracy of stories they print? How can young journalists be encouraged to act ethically in the performance of their duties? . . .

Case Study #4. Conflict of Interest

33 CBS's Walter Cronkite said no; CNN's Bernard Kalb said no; NPR's Daniel Schoor said no. But David Brinkley, formerly of NBC and ABC, said yes! The question put to each of these journalists was whether they would be willing to endorse a product in a commercial message.

34 David Brinkley had a brilliant journalistic career, one that spanned fifty years. He is probably best known for his Sunday ABC morning program *This Week with David Brinkley,* which began in 1981. Prior to that, he was part of NBC's Huntley-Brinkley evening news team. His face is recognized by millions, and he is easily one of the most respected newsmen of our era. Shortly after his retirement from ABC in October 1997, Brinkley agreed to appear in several commercials for Archer Daniels Midland (ADM), an Illinois-based food processing company. ADM was one of the sponsors of Brinkley's Sunday ABC program. In 1996, ADM paid $100 million in price-fixing fines and had, at the time, charges pending against two company executives for trying to fix the world market in lysine, a food additive. Three company executives were later convicted on the price-fixing charges, each facing up to three years in prison.

35 Criticism of Brinkley's action came quickly. His appearance in the commercials, some critics said, "created the possibility that the audience might think he still worked on his former program." Joan Konner, former dean of the Columbia School of Journalism, felt the switch in roles was improper. "I think it's awful," she said. "Lines should be distinct and they are not distinct in this case."

36 Brinkley is not alone in his role as reporter-turned-pitchman. Linda Ellerbee, formerly of NBC, did an ad for Maxwell House coffee. Former CBS morning host Kathleen Sullivan appeared on behalf of Weight Watchers. Other former journalists who moved to the ad world include Deborah Norville, Mary Alice Williams, and Richard Valeriani. Even Chet Huntley, Brinkley's old evening news partner, was a spokesperson for American Airlines after retiring from NBC.

Still, Brinkley is viewed as something of a role model, a dedicated journalist with over a half-century of faithful reporting.

37   Not everyone is bothered by Brinkley's actions. Marshall Loeb, editor of the *Columbia Journalism Review*, noted that there is a significant difference between an active and a retired journalist, and that he was not much bothered by Brinkley's actions. Other critics, however, charged the entire news industry with a kind of cronyism.* Many journalists appear to be models of journalistic integrity and independence, yet pocket "hefty fees for friendly lectures to corporate lobby groups."

38   **Key Questions**   Since Brinkley was retired and was no longer a practicing journalist, was it really unethical for him to earn a little extra money by appearing on behalf of an advertiser? Are all reporters, retired or not, ethically bound to disclose their connections to those individuals or organizations on which they report? Is it possible for a media employee, journalist or not, to avoid unethical practices in an industry so dominated by economic concerns? . . .

Case Study #5. The Stars Shine in Magazines

39   Americans have a large appetite for celebrity news. Viewers consume television talk and newsmagazine shows with relish. Newspapers often run celebrity news on their front pages. Now, it seems, magazines, too, are succumbing to the celebrity culture in ways that may not be obvious to their readers. Pop singer Madonna is a good case in point.

40   Madonna proved that she was indeed a "material girl" by insisting that she have control of the material, specifically material *Rolling Stone* proposed to use in its thirtieth anniversary special issue. The material in question included a cover photo, layout, story photos, and the copyright to the photos.

41   Did *Rolling Stone* turn over editorial control of the piece to the pop diva? Yes, mostly. It said no to layout approval but agreed to everything else. Madonna appeared with singers Tina Turner and Courtney Love on the cover of the Fall 1997 issue of *Rolling Stone*.

42   An unusual practice, you might wonder? Not really. These days more and more celebrities are asking for control of how magazines present information about them. Magazines say they have no choice. The magazine market is competitive. Many magazines must compete with television newsmagazine programs. In order to get the cooperation of many celebrities, magazines are caving in to their demands.

43   Actually, the relationship between celebrities and magazines has always been symbiotic.* Celebrities need the magazines for publicity;

magazines need celebrities for sales. But now, many feel, the situation is out of control. *Details* magazine editor Michael Caruso feels that the balance of power has shifted. Things that were previously forbidden are now being negotiated. Some publicists even go so far as to give magazines a list of questions that a reporter may and may not ask their clients. Others specify the makeup, clothing, even the camera angles to be used.

44   One solution to this problem is to eliminate the reporter altogether and have the stars essentially interview themselves. In *US* magazine, for example, actor Mel Gibson prepared an article titled "The Unbelievable Truth about Mel Gibson. By Mel Gibson."

45   Some observers wonder what happened to journalistic integrity and editorial control. They seem to have been caught between the economic interests of the magazines and the publicity needs of the celebrities.

46   **Key Questions**   Can a magazine or newspaper allow the subject of a story to control the story's content and still maintain journalistic integrity? Are the celebrities themselves acting unethically when they try to influence editorial content?

Larry T. Leslie, *Mass Communication Ethics*, pp. 185–194.

CHECKING YOUR COMPREHENSION

Directions: Circle the letter of the correct answer.

1. Which statement most effectively sums up the main idea of the entire reading?

   a. Journalists today think nothing of shaping their stories to suit public interests, and if that means adding a few spicy details of their own, most journalists don't worry about the ethics of tampering with the news.

   b. It's now acceptable for a journalist to endorse a product as long as he or she has been retired for a number of years; furthermore, any journalist, whether retired or not, is free to accept fees for lectures even if they are lecturing to groups who regularly make the news.

    c. Although it's fashionable to decry the current ethical practices of journalists, particularly television journalists, a look at past journalistic behavior suggests there isn't much difference between journalism as practiced today and in the past.

    d. Many of today's journalists seem to have shaky or nonexistent ethical standards about what is or is not appropriate to their profession.

2. Which statement most effectively paraphrases the topic sentence of paragraph 4?

    a. Once considered an annoying distraction from the serious business of solving crimes, journalists are now held in high esteem by most members of the police force.

    b. Some journalists are more interested in playing detective than they are in pursuing the news.

    c. A growing number of journalists have contributed important information to police investigations and helped solve some serious crimes.

    d. Helping the police solve crimes is a legitimate journalistic activity.

3. Which statement most effectively paraphrases the topic sentence of paragraph 5?

    a. By focusing on crime stories, news organizations encourage the public to think of themselves as potential crime victims.

    b. For some reason, television viewers are fascinated by crime stories, and crime is a ratings magnet.

    c. With their extreme emphasis on crime stories, news organizations only serve to encourage our country's love affair with lawsuits.

4. The topic sentence of paragraph 5 suggests which pattern of organization?

    a. classification

    b. cause and effect

    c. comparison and contrast

    d. definition

5. In paragraph 7, the author describes two disappearance cases. The purpose of these details is to

   a. illustrate the frequency of child abduction cases.

   b. show the compassionate nature of the TV stations that helped retrieve the missing children.

   c. illustrate the competition that drives most TV stations to cover sensational news stories.

   d. show how television journalists can become involved in the stories they report.

6. In his discussion of Chuck D's career in journalism (paragraphs 10–12), the author strongly implies that

   a. everyone in the news has a personal agenda, with Chuck D being the rule rather than the exception.

   b. no self-respecting journalist should have a personal agenda when it comes to reporting the news.

   c. Chuck D's entertainment background will serve him well as a journalist.

   d. its a mistake to assume that being a journalist requires no special training.

7. Throughout the reading, the author encourages readers to associate the postmodern era with

   a. repeated attempts to redefine journalistic ethics.

   b. the complete absence of any journalistic ethics or standards.

   c. the longing to return to a more clearly defined set of journalistic ethics.

   d. the use of new technology to gather the news.

8. What issue does the author want to illustrate in case study 1?

   a. The author wants readers to ask whether or not it is appropriate for reporters to pay so much attention to the doings of athletes.

   b. The author wants readers to question if it is acceptable for members of the media to accept gifts from owners of professional sports teams.

    c. The author wants readers to ask if it's right for members of the media to openly take sides on local issues when they are supposed to be objective about covering the news.

    d. The author wants to criticize the Tampa Bay Buccaneers.

9. Case study 2 illustrates what issue about television journalism?

    a. Live broadcasts of sensational events have become common on televised news.

    b. Intent on getting a sensational event live, television crews often make no attempt to help people with serious psychological problems because to do so would interfere with their scoop.

    c. Live broadcasts of sensational events encourage people to be violent toward themselves or others as a way of getting attention.

    d. The public fully supports sensational news programming that focuses on violent events.

10. In case study 5, Madonna is used to illustrate what point?

    a. Celebrities are often suspicious of interviews because they are so often misquoted.

    b. Celebrity interviews are a popular staple of television and newspapers.

    c. Celebrities are demanding and getting control over how they are presented in print.

DEEPENING YOUR UNDERSTANDING

Directions: Answer the following questions by circling the letter of the correct response and filling in the blanks where required.

1. What would you say is the author's purpose?

    a. to describe for readers the various ethical questions facing media journalists in the postmodern era

    b. to persuade readers that media journalism in the postmodern era has lost sight of the ethical standards once supposed to guide journalistic behavior

2. How would you describe the author's tone?

   a. relaxed

   b. objective

   c. concerned

   d. friendly

3. Would you say that the author's tone is similar to or different from

the tone of the previous readings? _____

Please describe the similarities or differences you noticed.

_____

_____

4. The author uses allusions to Ed Murrow to make what point?

_____

5. Which of the following is a rhetorical question*?

   a. "Has the greedful will overtaken American news organizations in postmodern America?" (12)

   b. "What responsibilities do newspapers and magazines have in checking the factual accuracy of stories they print?" (32)

   c. "How can young journalists be encouraged to act ethically in the performance of their duties?" (32)

6. In paragraph 5, the author says, "Mass communication researchers have studied the degree to which television 'cultivates' a particular view of crime in viewers." After reading that statement, what kind of questions should you ask about the author's evidence?

_____

_____

* Refer to glossary (pp. 13–15) if you need to refresh your understanding of rhetorical questions.

7. In paragraph 8, the author says, "These incidents—and they are only two among many—clearly demonstrate the willingness of news organizations to participate in a story." Would you label that statement as

a. fact?

b. opinion?

c. a blend of both?

Please explain your answer.

_____

_____

8. In paragraphs 33–38, the author describes actions taken by David Brinkley. Would you say

a. the author is openly biased in favor of Brinkley's behavior?

b. the author is openly biased against Brinkley's behavior?

c. the author does not express his personal feelings?

9. Overall, how would you describe the author's attitude toward journalism in the postmodern era?

_____

10. Many top journalists get large fees for speaking engagements, but most don't like to talk about it. How do you think the author would respond if he heard, say, that Dan Rather spoke at a meeting of the American Medical Association? What would be

his response to this strictly fictional event? _____
Please explain your answer.

_____

_____

AIRING YOUR OPINIONS

1. In discussion or on paper, explain why you think it is or is not acceptable for journalists to accept money for speaking to corporate lobbyists, as the author claims they do in paragraph 37.

2. Explain how the author's description of local news programs fits or does not fit the local programs you yourself watch.

_____

_____

Reading 3   # Creating a Culture of Fear

GETTING FOCUSED

Like the author of the previous reading, the author of the following reading agrees that crime gets too much attention from journalists. But he focuses less on the journalists obsessed by crime stories and more on the consequences of their obsession.

Textbook Features and Readers' Strategies

Feature:	_This author uses a long opening anecdote to start the reading._
Strategy:	An opening anecdote this long isn't there just to stir up reader interest. It has to be important. Thus, you need to understand more than the chain of events. When you finish, ask yourself: "What point does the author want to make by telling me this story?"
Feature:	_The reading contains general headings that divide it into sections._
Strategy:	Like the title, the headings are very general: "Oops, Wrong Story;" "Oops, Wrong Crisis." It's your job to make them more specific each time you finish a reading. For example, if the heading were to read, "Oops, Wrong Man," you might make a marginal note at the end of the section that reads something like this: "For a number of different reasons, eyewitnesses to crimes have often identified the wrong person as the perpetrator of the crime."
Feature:	_The author devotes a good deal of attention to discrediting common beliefs about the dangers afoot in the world._
Strategy:	Look hard at the evidence the author uses to contradict some traditional ideas about the problems afflicting our society. Make sure you understand how well the evidence does or does not discredit the existing notions about the dangers we face.

Textbook Features and Readers' Strategies (continued)

Feature: *The author relies heavily on the reader's ability to draw inferences.*

Strategy 1:   Pre-read the opening anecdote and the first paragraph following each heading. Predict the point of the entire section.

Strategy 2:   Although the book from which this reading was taken is used as a text-book, it was originally written for the general public. Thus, the author does not rely as heavily on topic sentences as most textbook authors do. If you are reading a paragraph or section, and none of the sentences seem to sum up the author's point, you need to infer one.

Evaluating Your Background Knowledge

The author of this reading is relying on your knowledge of these words and terms. Look over this list carefully to make sure you know everything on it. *Note:* The number in parentheses indicates the paragraph where the word can be found while an asterisk accompanies the word's first appearance in the reading.

Gulf War (3):   In 1990, Saddam Hussein invaded the country of Kuwait. The United States and its allies waged a victorious war that drove the Iraqis out.

Pentagon (13):   the United States military establishment

grunts (13):   ordinary foot soldiers

pass muster (20):   be considered acceptable

pandemic (21):   widespread

surreptitiously (32): on the sly; undercover

innocuous (33):   harmless

unequivocal (34):   clear-cut; easy to grasp

advocacy (42):   favoring, supporting

1   The mystery about baseless scares is how they are sold to a public that has real dangers to worry about. . . . We *ought* to have concerns about crime, drug addiction, child abuse, and other afflictions to be discussed. The question is, how have we gotten so mixed up about the true nature and extent of these problems?

2   In no small measure the answer lies in stories like one that broke on March 19, 1991. If you read a newspaper or turned on a TV or radio newscast that day or the several days thereafter you were told that the streets of America were more dangerous than a war zone.

3   The press had been provoked to make this extreme assertion not by a rise in violent crime but by a dramatic event. The Gulf War* had just ended, and a soldier who returned home to Detroit had been shot dead outside his apartment building.

4   The front-page story in the *Washington Post* portrayed the situation this way:

> Conley Street, on this city's northeast side, is a pleasant-looking row of brick and wood homes with small, neat lawns, a street that for years was the realization of the American dream for middle-income families. But in the past few years, Conley has become a street of crack, crime and occasional bursts of gunfire. And at 2:15 A.M. Monday, the bullets killed Army Spec. Anthony Riggs, something that all of Iraq's Scud missiles could not do during his seven months with a Patriot missile battery in Saudi Arabia.

> Described by his mother as a man who deeply loved his family and his country, Riggs had written home from Saudi Arabia, "There's no way I'm going to die in this rotten country. With the Lord's grace and his guidance, I'll walk American soil once again." But before that letter even arrived, while Riggs was moving his wife and three-year-old daughter to a new apartment, five shots rang out and witnesses heard the sound of screeching tires. Some faceless thug had killed him just to get his car. "His wife, Toni, found him dying in a gutter," the *Post* reported.

5   TV newscasts showed Mrs. Riggs sobbing. She had warned her husband that there had been a shooting on the street earlier in the day, but he wouldn't listen. "He said he'd just got back from having missiles flying over his head, and a few shots weren't going to bother him," according to Toni's aunt, quoted in the *Los Angeles Times*. That of course was the larger point, or as the *Post* put it, "Riggs's death was a tragic reminder of President Bush's words recently when he announced a new crime bill: 'Our veterans deserve to come home to an America where it is safe to walk the streets.'"

Oops, Wrong Story

6   From the point of view of journalists and editors an ideal crime story—that is, the sort that deserves major play and is sure to hold readers' and viewers' attention—has several elements that distinguish it from other acts of violence. The victims are innocent, likable people; the perpetrator is an uncaring brute. Details of the crime, while shocking, are easy to relay. And the events have social significance, bespeaking an underlying societal crisis.

7   The murder of Anthony Riggs seemed to have it all. The only problem was, very little of this perfect crime story was true. Reporters named the right victim but the wrong perpetrator, motive, and moral.

8   It was the massive media attention, ironically, that resulted in the real story coming out. Confronted with demands from politicians and citizen groups to catch Riggs's killer, the Detroit police launched an all-out investigation. While digging through garbage cans around the Conley Street neighborhood, an officer came upon a handgun that turned out to belong to Michael Cato, the brother of Riggs's wife, Toni. Nineteen years old at the time and currently serving a life sentence for murder, Michael said in a confession that his sister had promised him a share of $175,000 in life insurance benefits.

9   Reporters cannot be blamed for failing to possess this information prior to its discovery by the police, but had they been a little skeptical or made a few phone calls they almost certainly would have stumbled on at least some aspects of the truth. They might have learned, for example, that Toni had been making noises about dumping Anthony for some time, or that it was she who arranged a hefty life insurance policy for her husband before he went off to war. Reporters might also have checked into Mrs. Riggs's past and discovered previous irregularities, such as the fact that she had not yet divorced her previous husband when she married Anthony.

10   Journalists also might have discovered the existence of a letter Riggs wrote to his mother from Saudi Arabia. "Toni has wrecked my car. She is now bouncing checks. . . . She is never home: 2:30 A.M., 4 A.M. . . . I would put my head through the neck of a hot sauce bottle to please her, but now I need happiness in return," *People* magazine, the only major publication that subsequently ran a full-fledged account of the true story, quoted him penning.

11   Had news writers checked with knowledgeable criminologists or homicide detectives they might have been impressed as well by the improbability of a car thief murdering someone execution-style when

a simple shot or two would have done the job. Carjacking victims seldom get shot at all, particularly if they do not resist.

12   Journalists generally pride themselves on being suspicious about information they are given. Your average journalist "wears his skepticism like a medieval knight wore his armor," Shelby Coffey, head of ABC News and former editor of the *Los Angeles Times,* has said. Yet when it comes to a great crime story, a journalist will behave like the high school nerd who has been approached by the most popular girl in school for help with her science project. Grateful for the opportunity, he doesn't bother to ask a lot of questions.

13   There are discernible differences, though, between reporters for electronic versus print media. Unlike their colleagues at local television stations, who will go for any story that includes a police chase or a humiliated celebrity, journalists at newspapers and magazines have a particular fondness for crime stories that help them make sense of some other phenomenon they are having trouble covering in its own right. In the Riggs murder the phenomenon in question was the Gulf War. The news media had difficulty reporting accurately on the war because the Pentagon* kept the press away from the action and used tightly scripted briefings to spoonfeed only what the generals and the president wanted known. As part of that spin Generals Colin Powell and Norman Schwarzkopf were defined as the war's heroes. Grunts* on the battlefield and in the air seemed almost irrelevant to a war fought with smart bombs. Their homecoming consequently had little intrinsic meaning or news value. So when the Riggs murder came along, reporters eagerly used it to mark the end of the war on Iraq and the start of the next phase in the ongoing domestic war on crime.

Oops, Wrong Crisis

14   If the news media merely got the facts wrong about an occasional homicide, that would be no big deal. But the significance they attach to many of the homicides and other violent crimes they choose to spotlight is another matter. The streets of America are not more dangerous than a war zone, and the media should not convey that they are.

15   Some places journalists have declared crime ridden are actually quite safe. Consider an article *Time* magazine ran in April 1994 headlined across the top of two pages: "Not a month goes by without an outburst of violence in the workplace—now even in flower nurseries, pizza parlors and law offices." One of literally thousands of stories

published and broadcast on what was dubbed "the epidemic of workplace violence," *Time*'s article presented a smorgasbord of grisly photographs and vignettes of unsuspecting workers and managers brutally attacked by their coworkers or employees. "Even Americans who see a potential for violence almost everywhere like to suppose there are a few sanctuaries left. One is a desk, or a spot behind the counter, or a place on the assembly line," the writer sighed.

16   More than five hundred stories about workplace violence appeared in newspapers alone just during 1994 and 1995, and many included some seriously scary statistics: 2.2 million people attacked on the job each year, murder the leading cause of work-related death for women, the number-three cause for men. "How can you be sure," asked a reporter for the *St. Petersburg Times,* "the person sitting next to you at work won't go over the edge and bring an Uzi to the office tomorrow?" Her answer was, "You can't."

17   At least one journalist, however, grew leery of his colleagues' fear mongering. Erik Larson, a staff reporter for the *Wall Street Journal* having come upon the same numbers quoted time and again, decided to take a closer look. The result was an exposé in the *Journal* titled "A False Crisis," in which Larson revealed how the news media had created an epidemic where none existed. Of about 121 million working people, about 1,000 are murdered on the job each year, a rate of just 1 in 114,000. Police, security guards, taxi drivers, and other particularly vulnerable workers account for a large portion of these deaths. Cab drivers, for instance, suffer an occupational homicide rate twenty-one times the national average. On the flip side of that coin, people in certain other occupations face conspicuously low levels of risk. The murder rate for doctors, engineers, and other professionals is about 1 in 457,000, Larson determined.

18   Another vocational group with relatively low rates, it turns out, is postal workers. The expression "going postal" became part of the American vernacular after some particularly bloody assaults by U.S. Postal Service employees against their supervisors. Yet postal employees are actually about two and a half times *less* likely than the average worker to be killed on the job.

19   All in all fewer than one in twenty homicides occurs at a workplace. And while most of the media hoopla has been about disgruntled workers killing one another or their bosses—the Uzi-toting fellow at the next desk—few workplace murders are actually carried out by coworkers or ex-workers. About 90 percent of murders at workplaces are committed by outsiders who come to rob. The odds of being

killed by someone you work with or employ are less than 1 in 2 million; you are several times more likely to be hit by lightning.

20   Larson deconstructed as well the survey that produced the relentlessly reproduced statistic of 2.2 million people assaulted at work each year. Most of the reported attacks were fairly minor and did not involve weapons, and once again, the great majority were committed by outsiders, not by coworkers, ex-employees, or bosses. What is more, the survey from which the number comes would not pass muster* among social scientists, Larson points out. The response rate is too low. Fewer than half of the people contacted responded to the survey, making it likely that those who participated were not typical of employed Americans as a whole.

21   Given that workplace violence is far from pandemic,* why were journalists so inclined to write about it? Perhaps because workplace violence is a way of talking about the precariousness of employment without directly confronting what primarily put workers at risk—the endless waves of corporate layoffs that began in the early 1980s. Stories about workplace violence routinely made mention of corporate downsizing as one potential cause, but they did not treat mass corporate firing as a social ill in its own right. To have done so would have proven difficult for many journalists. For one thing, whom would they have cast as the villain of the piece? Is the CEO who receives a multimillion dollar raise for firing tens of thousands of employees truly evil? Or is he merely making his company more competitive in the global economy? And how would a journalist's boss—or boss's boss at the media conglomerate that owns the newspaper or network—feel about publishing implicit criticism of something they themselves have done? Pink slips arrived with regularity in newsrooms like everywhere else in corporate America in recent years, and they didn't exactly inspire reporters to do investigative pieces about downsizing.

22   To its great credit, the *New York Times* did eventually run an excellent series of articles on downsizing in 1996. In one of the articles the authors noted off-handedly and without pursuing the point that about 50 percent more people are laid off each year than are victims of crime. It is an important comparison. From 1980 through 1995 more than 42 million jobs were eliminated in the United States. The number of jobs lost per year more than doubled over that time, from about 1.5 million in 1980 to 3.25 million in 1995. By comparison, during that same period most crime rates—including those for violent crimes—declined. A working person was roughly four to five times

more likely to be the victim of a layoff in any given year than to be the victim of a violent crime committed by a stranger.

23   For many, job loss is every bit as disabling and demoralizing as being the victim of a crime. You can lose your home, your health insurance, your self-esteem, your sense of security, and your willingness to report harassment or hazardous working conditions at your next place of employment. During the economic boom of the late 1990s layoffs occurred at an even higher rate than in the 1980s. In what former Secretary of Labor Robert Reich dubbed "down-waging" and "down-benefiting," highly profitable companies replaced full-time workers with part-timers, temps, and lower-paid full-timers, and they subcontracted work to firms that paid lower wages and provided poorer benefits. Yet throughout the past two decades the news media printed and broadcast exponentially more stories about crime. In the early and mid-1990s 20 to 30 percent of news items in city newspapers concerned crime, and close to half of the news coverage on local television newscasts was about crime.

Unhappy Halloween

24   Workplace violence was not the first false crime crisis used by journalists as a roundabout way to talk about other matters they found difficult to address directly. Even the *New York Times* has been known to engage in the practice.

25   "Those Halloween goodies that children collect this weekend on their rounds of 'trick or treating' may bring them more horror than happiness," began a story in the *Times* in October 1970 that launched a long-running crime panic. "Take, for example," the reporter continued, "that plump red apple that Junior gets from a kindly old woman down the block. It may have a razor blade hidden inside. The chocolate 'candy' bar may be a laxative, the bubble gum may be sprinkled with lye, the popcorn balls may be coated with camphor, the candy may turn out to be packets containing sleeping pills."

26   Similar articles followed in the nation's news media every autumn for years to come. In 1975 *Newsweek* reported in its edition that hit newsstands at the end of October, "If this year's Halloween follows form, a few children will return home with something more than an upset tummy: in recent years, several children have died and hundreds have narrowly escaped injury from razor blades, sewing needles and shards of glass purposefully put into their goodies by adults."

27   In her columns of the mid- and late 1980s even "Dear Abby" was reminding parents around trick-or-treat time that "somebody's child will become violently ill or die after eating poisoned candy or an apple containing a razor blade." An ABC News/*Washington Post* poll in 1985 showed that 60 percent of parents feared their kids could become victims.

28   This time no journalist stepped forward to correct the media's and public's collective fantasy, even though, as Jan Harold Brunvand, the folklorist and author observed, "it's hard to imagine how someone could shove a blade into a fruit without injuring himself. And wouldn't the damage done to the apple by such a process make it obvious that something was wrong with it?"

29   The myth of Halloween bogeymen and bogeywomen might never have been exposed had not a sociologist named Joel Best become sufficiently leery that he undertook an examination of every reported incident since 1958. Best, currently a professor at the University of Southern Illinois, established in a scholarly article in 1985 that there has not been a single death or serious injury. He uncovered a few incidents where children received minor cuts from sharp objects in their candy bags, but the vast majority of reports turned out to be old-fashioned hoaxes, sometimes enacted by young pranksters, other times by parents hoping to make money in lawsuits or insurance scams.

30   Ironically, in the only two known cases where children apparently did die from poisoned Halloween candy, the myth of the anonymous, sadistic stranger was used to cover up the real crime. In the first incident family members sprinkled heroin on a five-year-old's Halloween candy in hopes of fooling the police about the cause of the child's death. Actually, the boy had found and eaten heroin in his uncle's home. In the second incident a boy died after eating cyanide-poisoned candy on Halloween, but police determined that his father had spiked the candy to collect insurance money. Bill Ellis, a professor of English at Penn State University, has commented that both of these incidents, reported in the press at first as stranger murders, "reinforced the moral of having parents examine treats—ironically, because in both cases family members were responsible for the children's deaths!"

31   Yet if anonymous Halloween sadists were fictitious creatures, they were useful diversions from some truly frightening realities, such as the fact that far more children are seriously injured and killed by family members than by strangers. Halloween sadists also served in news

stories as evidence that particular social trends were having ill effects on the populace. A psychiatrist quoted in the *New York Times* article held that Halloween sadism was a by-product of "the permissiveness in today's society." The candy poisoner him- or herself was not directly to blame, the doctor suggested. The real villains were elsewhere. "The people who give harmful treats to children see criminals and students in campus riots getting away with things," the *Times* quoted him, "so they think they can get away with it, too."

32   In many of these articles the choice of hero also suggests that other social issues are surreptitiously* being discussed. At a time when divorce rates were high and rising, and women were leaving home in great numbers to take jobs, news stories heralded women who represented the antithesis of those trends—full-time housewives and employed moms who returned early from work to throw safe trick-or-treat parties for their children and their children's friends in their homes or churches, or simply to escort their kids on their rounds and inspect the treats.

Kiddie Porn and Cyberpredators

33   The Halloween tales were forerunners of what grew into a media staple of the last quarter of the twentieth century: crime stories in which innocent children fall victim to seemingly innocuous* adults who are really perverts. The villains take several familiar forms, two of the more common being the child pornographer and his or her pedophile customers.

34   A report on NBC News in 1977 let it be known that "as many as two million American youngsters are involved in the fast-growing, multimillion dollar child-pornography business"—a statement that subsequent research by criminologists and law enforcement authorities determined to be wrong on every count. Kiddie porn probably grossed less than $1 million a year (in contrast to the multibillion dollar adult industry), and hundreds, not millions, of American children were involved. Once again, facts were beside the point. The child pornographer represented, as columnist Ellen Goodman observed at the time, an "unequivocal* villain" whom reporters and readers found "refreshingly uncomplicated." Unlike other pornographers, whose exploits raise tricky First Amendment issues, child pornographers made for good, simple, attention-grabbing copy.

35   A conspicuous subtext in coverage during the late 1970s and 1980s was adult guilt and anxiety about the increasing tendency to turn over

more of children's care to strangers. Raymond Buckey and Peggy Buckey McMartin, proprietors of the McMartin Preschool in Manhattan Beach, California, were the most famous alleged child pornographers of the era. Their prosecution in the mid-1980s attracted a level of media hoopla unsurpassed until O. J. Simpson's double-murder trial nearly a decade later, and from the start they were depicted as pedophiles and child pornographers. The local TV news reporter who first broke the McMartin story declared in his initial report that children had been "made to appear in pornographic films while in the preschool's care." The media later quoted officials from the district attorney's office, making statements about "millions of child pornography photographs and films" at the school.

36   Not a single pornographic photograph taken at the McMartin School has ever been produced, despite handsome offers of reward money and vast international police investigations. Yet thanks to the media coverage, when social scientists from Duke University conducted a survey in 1986, four out of five people said they believed that Raymond Buckey was part of a child pornography ring.

37   In more recent years child pornographers and pedophiles have come in handy for fear mongering about the latest variety of baby-sitter: the Internet. In the 1990s politicians and the news media have made much of the existence of pedophilia in cyberspace. Speaking in 1998 on behalf of legislation he drafted that makes it easier to convict "cyberpredators" and imprison them longer, Representative Bill McCollum of Florida made the customary claim: "Sex offenders who prey on children no longer need to hang out in parks or malls or school yards." Nowadays, warned McCollum, child pornographers and pedophiles are just "a mouse click away" from their young prey.

38   This time the panic did not rely so much on suspicious statistics as on peculiar logic. With few cases of youngsters having been photographed or attacked by people who located them on-line, fear mongers found it more convenient simply to presume that "as the number of children who use the Internet continues to boom . . . pornography and pedophilia grow along with it" (*New York Times*). Reporters portrayed the inhabitants of cyberspace, children and adults alike, in somewhat contradictory ways. About the kids they said, on the one hand, "Internet-savvy children can also easily access on-line pornography" (*New York Times*). On the other hand, reporters depicted computer-proficient kids as precisely the *opposite* of savvy. They described them as defenseless against pedophiles and child

pornographers in cyberspace. "Depraved people are reaching right into your home and touching your child," Hugh Downs told viewers of ABC's "20/20."

39   To judge from reports by some of the people featured in news reports, cyberspace was largely devoid of other adults who could protect children from these creeps. The Internet is "a city with no cops," the *New York Times* quoted a district attorney from Suffolk County, even though law enforcement officials actually do a great deal of lurking and entrapping. Since 1993 the FBI has conducted an operation code-named "Innocent Images" in which agents assume false identities and post seductive messages on the Internet and on-line services. In one of the more highly publicized busts that resulted from the operation, a thirty-one-year-old Washington, D.C., attorney was arrested when he showed up at a shopping mall to meet a fourteen-year-old girl whom he had propositioned on-line for sex. In reality he had been corresponding with an adult FBI agent who had assumed a provocative on-line name—"One4fun4u"—and had sent the man messages stating that she'd had experience with an older man and "it was a lot of fun." In another arrest, a fifty-eight-year-old man was snagged by agents who used the names "Horny15bi" and "Sexcollctr" and described themselves on-line as "dreaming of kinky sex." One of them gave as her motto, "vice is nice but incest is best."

40   Cyberspace has been policed by other adults as well. Reporters for newspapers and television stations, posing as young teens or preteens, have responded to solicitations for sex, only to arrive at the agreed-on meeting place with cameras and cops in tow. Groups with names like "Cyber Angels" and "Safeguarding Our Children" collect information on pedophiles via e-mail from children who say they have been approached or molested. Members of adult vigilante groups make it a practice to disrupt Internet chat rooms where child pornography is traded and pass along information to police.

41   While judicial experts continue to debate which of these intervention strategies constitute entrapment or invasion of privacy, there is an extralegal question as well. David L. Sobel, an attorney with the Electronic Privacy Information Center, framed the question succinctly. "Are we making the world a better place," he asked rhetorically, "by tempting some of these people to commit crimes they may not have otherwise committed?"

42   Subtract from the battery of accounts in news stories all instances where the "children" lured out of cyberspace were actually undercover

adults, and what remains? Several of the most widely covered incidents involving real children turn out to be considerably more ambiguous than they seem on first hearing. Take for instance the murder of eleven-year-old Eddie Werner in a suburb in New Jersey in 1997. Defined in the media as the work of a "Cyber Psycho" (*New York Post* headline) and proof that the Internet is, as an advocacy* group put it, "a playground for pedophiles," the killing actually bore only a tertiary connection to the Net. Eddie Werner had not been lured on-line. He was killed selling holiday items door to door for the local PTA. Reporters and activists made the link to the Internet by way of Werner's killer, Sam Manzie, a fifteen-year-old who had been having sex in motel rooms throughout the previous year with a middle-aged man he had met in a chat room.

43   In an essay critical of the reporting about the Werner murder *Newsweek* writer Steven Levy correctly pointed out: "Cyberspace may not be totally benign, but in some respects it has it all over the often overrated real world. After all, one could argue, if young Eddie Werner had been selling his candy and gift-wrapping paper on the Internet, and not door to door, tragedy might not have struck."

44   In that same vein, consider a suspenseful yarn that took up much of the space in a front-page piece in the *Los Angeles Times* entitled "Youngsters Falling Prey to Seducers in Computer Web Crime." It was about a fifteen-year-old whose parents found him missing. Using the boy's America Online account, they discovered that he had been sent a bus ticket to visit a man with whom he had communicated by e-mail. The parents frantically sent messages of their own to the man. "Daniel is a virgin," one of the parents' outgoing messages said. "Oh, no, he's not," came back the chilling reply. Yet when the reporter gets to the conclusion of Daniel's saga it's something of an anticlimax. The teenager returned home and informed his parents he had not been harmed by his e-mail companion, who was only a little older than Daniel himself. Nonetheless, the moral of Daniel's story was, according to the *Los Angeles Times* reporter: "Such are the frightening new frontiers of cyberspace, a place where the child thought safely tucked away in his or her own room may be in greater danger than anyone could imagine."

45   Now *there's* a misleading message. For those children most at risk of sexual abuse, to be left alone in their rooms with a computer would be a godsend. It is poor children—few of whom have America Online connections—who are disproportionately abused, and it is in the children's own homes and those of close relatives that sexual abuse

commonly occurs. In focusing on creeps in cyberspace, reporters neatly skirt these vital facts and the discomforting issues they raise.

Barry Glassner, *The Culture of Fear*, pp. 24–35.

CHECKING YOUR COMPREHENSION

Directions: Circle the letter of the correct answer.

1. Which of the following statements best paraphrases the overall main idea of the entire reading?

   a. In their pursuit of crime stories that divide the world into innocent victims or cruel villains, journalists have left the public in the dark when it comes to serious social issues and problems.

   b. By concentrating on stories about violence in the workplace, journalists have ignored more crucial stories about unemployment, which is a far greater danger to most ordinary Americans because long-term unemployment can be devastating.

   c. If it weren't for investigative reporters like Joel Best and Erik Larson, Americans would be completely uninformed about the social problems that really can have an impact on their lives.

   d. Too many journalists have focused on child pornography on the Internet and have ignored important but less sensational issues like white collar crime.

2. According to the author, the ideal crime story for journalists has these elements:

   a. The victims are poor and the villains are wealthy; the story evokes tears and is, therefore, likely to pull in readers and viewers.

   b. The victims are completely innocent and the villains are vile; the story is simple to describe yet supposedly has profound implications.

   c. The victims are poor; they gain great wealth and lose everything because of criminal behavior.

3. The author mentions Erik Larson (paragraph 17) in order to make what point?

   a. A reporter willing to check the facts could easily undermine the myth of violence in the workplace.

   b. Larson is a fine reporter who always thoroughly checks his facts.

   c. Taxi drivers and security guards are at the greatest risk when it comes to workplace violence.

   d. Doctors and engineers are unlikely to be the victims of workplace violence.

4. The author mentions Joel Best (paragraph 29) in order to make what point?

   a. Children are in more danger from abusive relatives than they are from poisoned Halloween candy.

   b. Stories about strangers trying to hurt or kill children by giving them poisoned candy have been underreported.

   c. There's almost no evidence suggesting that children are in serious danger from strangers likely to give out Halloween candy with razor blades or poison inside.

   d. Sociologists make good journalists.

5. Which statement best paraphrases the topic sentence of paragraph 13?

   a. In contrast to newspaper and magazine journalists, local TV journalists like their crime stories to illustrate larger social issues.

   b. Journalists on local television stations resemble print journalists in their desire to make one person's story illustrate a larger social issue.

   c. In contrast to journalists on local television stations, print journalists favor crime stories that can help make sense of more complex social problems.

   d. Television and print journalists are alike in their unending pursuit of crime stories that they believe will win ratings or readers.

6. Based on the opening sentence, you would expect that paragraph 13 relies on which pattern of organization?

    a. classification

    b. comparison and contrast

    c. definition

    d. cause and effect

7. Which statement best paraphrases the topic sentence of paragraph 23?

    a. Victims of crimes usually do a lot better psychologically than do those who suffer the effects of long-term unemployment.

    b. Being the victim of a crime is not as bad as being unemployed.

    c. For some people, losing their job can be as bad as being the victim of a crime.

    d. People who have been unemployed for a long time are likely to turn to crime.

8. What's the implied main idea of paragraph 31?

    a. Stories about Halloween monsters may not have been real, but they did serve two purposes.

    b. Journalists peddled stories about Halloween sadists because the public was riveted by such tales.

    c. People who handed out candy with poison or razor blades in them were a reflection of the breakdown in society's moral code.

9. In paragraph 34, the author implies that facts are "beside the point" where stories about child pornography are concerned because

    a. child pornography is a hot-button issue, and readers don't really want to know the facts.

    b. child pornography makes headlines.

    c. child pornography involves a clear-cut villain who is easy to write about and who will grab readers' attention.

    d. journalists don't care about hard evidence anymore.

10. Which statement more accurately sums up the author's conclusion in paragraphs 42–45?

    a. By focusing on the dangers of Internet pedophiles, journalists are trying to do society a service and keep children safe; however, they are far from achieving their goal because they do not have the appropriate facts at their disposal.

    b. By focusing on the dangers posed by Internet pedophiles, journalists have managed to ignore the fact that poor children are the most likely victims of sexual abuse; furthermore, the threat comes from relatives, not the Internet.

    c. If they were dedicated to improving the lives of children, journalists would be more inclined to explore and describe how poverty and homelessness stunt the lives of the young.

DEEPENING YOUR UNDERSTANDING

Directions: Answer the following questions by circling the letter of the correct response or filling in the blanks where necessary.

    1. How would you describe the author's tone?

        a. skeptical

        b. objective

        c. irate

        d. friendly

    2. What would you say is the author's purpose?

        a. to inform readers about a possible problem with the way journalists report news

        b. to persuade readers that there is a serious problem with the way journalists report the news

    3. With which of the following statements do you agree?

        a. The author believes that most journalists are doing their best to keep the public informed and deserve more appreciation.

b. The author believes that most journalists are not working to the best of their ability and are therefore not keeping the public informed.

c. The author doesn't express any personal bias.

Please explain your answer.

_____

_____

4. The author says in paragraph 12 that journalists wear their "skepticism . . . like a medieval knight wore his armor," but when it comes to a crime story, they "behave like the high school nerd who has been approached by the most popular girl in school for help with her science project." In your own words, what point is the author trying to make with these two very different similes?

_____

_____

5. In paragraph 19, the author offers two statistics to discredit the widely held notions about the dangers lurking _in_ the workplace.

What are those statistics? _____

Do you think these statistics are relevant or irrelevant to the author's claim that the workplace is not so dangerous after all? Please explain your answer.

_____

6. In your own words, describe the flaws in the survey referred to in paragraph 20.

_____

_____

7. The columnist Ellen Goodman is quoted in paragraph 34. What conclusion about her column can you draw from the four words quoted?

_____

8. What did Joel Best do in order to discredit the belief that children were in serious danger on Halloween?

_____

How did Best's work differ from that of journalists who had reported on the same subject?

_____

9. In paragraph 38, the author quotes Hugh Downs from the ABC news program *20/20*. According to Downs, "Depraved people are reaching right into your home and touching your child." Based on what you read, do you think the author does or does not believe

Downs's claim? _____ Please explain your answer.

_____

_____

10. In paragraph 44, the author refers to a "suspenseful yarn." What does the author want to suggest with the use of the word *yarn*? *Note:* Feel free to look the word up in a desk dictionary.

_____

AIRING YOUR OPINIONS

1. Do you find the author's claim that journalists have made us anxious about the wrong issues somewhat convincing, very convincing, or not at all convincing? _____

Please explain your answer.

_____

_____

2. In discussion or in writing, explain why you think that the authors of this reading and the previous one would or would not agree about the standards of today's journalists.

Reading 4

Can the Press Keep the Government's Secrets During Wartime?

GETTING FOCUSED

In the abstract, it seems impossible to quarrel with the claim that the press must be free from censorship to report the world's events and give readers the necessary information on which to base their opinions or perhaps even take action. But as the authors of this textbook excerpt point out, wartime can alter the rules.

Textbook Features and Readers' Strategies

Feature: *The title and one of the headings include plural words (secrets and challenges).*

Strategy: Read with the intent of identifying each secret and each challenge. Take marginal notes on both, numbering each one.

Feature: *Numerous dates and events are mentioned throughout the selection.*

Strategy: Each time you finish reading about a particular date and event, mark the date in some way (for example, put a box around it). Then see if you can mentally summarize the event and identify its relationship to the overall point of the section.

Feature: *Like earlier textbook excerpts, this one frequently opens paragraphs with topic sentences.*

Strategy 1:   Pre-read the first sentence of every paragraph before you read the selection from beginning to end.

Strategy 2:   Paraphrase the topic sentences and jot the main ideas in the margins. As the list of main ideas continues to grow, keep searching for a main idea that would be general enough to cover or unite all of those individual points. You'll need a main idea for each section. You'll also need an even more general main idea that sums up the entire reading.

Evaluating Your Background Knowledge

The author of this reading is relying on your knowledge of these words and terms. Look over this list carefully to make sure you know everything on it. *Note:* The number in parentheses indicates the paragraph where the word can be found while an asterisk accompanies the word's first appearance in the reading.

Communist scares in the 1950s (1): Period when members of the American government, in the grip of anti-Communist hysteria, insisted that anything labeled Communist propaganda had to be severely censored

civil libertarians (1): People who are determined to protect individual rights such as the right to privacy and freedom of speech

Vietnam (3):   Between 1963 and 1975, the United States sided with South Vietnam in a civil war between North and South Vietnam. The bloodshed caused by the Vietnam War was heavily televised, which was one reason why the war became so unpopular with the American public.

kept at bay (3):   held back, controlled

sedition (5):   conduct or language encouraging rebellion against a law

Axis powers (6):   the nations—mainly Germany, Italy, and Japan—that opposed Britain, France, and the United States during World War II

Soviet Union (7):   Also known as the Union of Soviet Socialist Republics, a former country in eastern Europe and northern Asia. The Soviet Union fell apart in 1991 when several of the republics comprising it declared independence.

contentious (14): argumentative

1   In times of national crises, such as during wars, reporting some kinds of information can give the enemy a clear advantage. Recognizing the security risks, Americans have generally accepted some form of censorship during wars and politically sensitive periods including Communist scares in the 1950s,* the Cold War, and others. Espionage is frequently an issue whether there is a war or not. Even many fervent civil libertarians* agree that the government deserves and requires protection during wartime. But such censorship obviously contradicts the guarantee of a free press and limits the public's right to know.

2   In times of both peace and war, government secrecy has led to many controversies. For example, in October 1983, when the United States invaded the small Caribbean nation of Grenada, military commanders barred the press from the island, and thus the war zone. Journalists and broadcasters vigorously protested the government policy as unprecedented and unwarranted censorship; the White House replied that it was trying to protect the lives of the media people. After Grenada, a commission involving military officers, government officials, and representatives of the press was set up. It recommended guidelines for the coverage of military actions and suggested the formation of a press-broadcast pool for future operations.

3   In the next decade, when Iraq invaded Kuwait, causing the United States to send troops to Saudi Arabia, press access again became an issue in various foreign capitals and on the front lines with the troops. The 1991 Persian Gulf War against Iraq revisited the conflict between press and government. From the beginning of what was a very popular conflict, in contrast to Vietnam*—which was not only unpopular, but also the subject of massive demonstrations and other protest activity—the press complained that the rules of access to information from the front were too restrictive and prevented effective coverage. A pool system representing the entire press corps was in effect, and military "handlers" who followed reporters to their interviews were heavily used. The Pentagon argued that it was simply trying to prevent the release of information that would undermine military operations or endanger the lives of troops. The result was tightly controlled information, released at formal press briefings, and little opportunity for reporters to pursue stories independently, especially if they required access to the battlefield area. At the war's end, there was an almost universal agreement that the media had been kept at bay,* and, in effect, the media lost the information war. So strong was media dissatisfaction with the restrictions that, after the war, a unified committee representative of U.S. print and broadcast media petitioned the Pentagon and the White House to consider a set of rules and procedures for future wars.

Direct Censorship in Wartime

4   In past wars, the government has been able to use various indirect methods to protect its secrets. One of the earliest indirect ways used to control information was to deny access to telegraph, cable, and

similar facilities. Reporters then either had to let military censors screen their copy or try to transmit it in some other way. For example, when the battleship *Maine* blew up in the harbor of Havana, Cuba, in 1898, the U.S. government immediately closed the Havana cable to reporters. Similarly, at the outbreak of World War I, the British immediately severed the cables between Germany and the United States. American reporters had to use the English-controlled cables between Europe and the United States and submit their copy to rigid British censorship.

5   The government also has imposed censorship through codes, regulations, and guidelines. During World War I, the Espionage Act of 1917 stipulated fines and prison terms for anyone interfering with the war effort in any way. For example, criticism of arms manufacturers was said to be unpatriotic. This enraged newspaper publishers, and legal battles over the issue went all the way to the Supreme Court. Such censorship was later declared unconstitutional, but Congress passed new, even stricter laws to control information. The Sedition* Act of 1918 made it a crime to publish anything that abused, scorned, or showed contempt for the government of the United States, its flag, or even the uniforms of its armed forces. As a way to enforce the law, such publications could be banned from the mails.

6   On December 19, 1941, only a few days after Japanese forces attacked Pearl Harbor, President Roosevelt created the U.S. Office of Censorship and charged it with reviewing all communications entering or leaving the United States for the duration of the war. At the peak of its activity, the office employed more than ten thousand people. Its main objective was to review all mail, cables, and radiograms. A Code of Wartime Practices for the American Press was also issued to newspapers requesting voluntary cooperation from the nation's editors and publishers. Its purpose was to deny the Axis powers* any information concerning military matters, production, supplies, armaments, weather, and so on. For the most part, those responsible for the content of the print media cooperated very well, and often exceeded the guidelines set by government. A related code was issued for broadcasters, and their cooperation was also excellent. The system of codes, regulations, and guidelines in practice during World War II worked because the media cooperated voluntarily. The United States attempted to find a way to deny vital information to the enemy without using official censors, and by and large it succeeded.

7 Even during peacetime, the press has often censored itself to protect the national interest. In 1960, for example, the Soviet Union* shot down an American U2 spy plane. The incident temporarily ended attempts to improve Soviet-American relations. For a year before the plane was shot down, however, James Reston of the *New York Times* had known that American spy planes were flying over the Soviet Union, but "The *New York Times* did not publish this fact until one of the planes was shot down in 1960." Later, as a favor to President John F. Kennedy, Reston withheld information about the planned U.S. invasion of Cuba at the Bay of Pigs.

Challenges to Government Secrecy

8 Although the press often engages in voluntary censorship, there are many examples when the media and the government have been locked in conflict, disputing the government's right to censor the news. Because our shared belief in the need for freedom of the press became such a tradition very early in the life of the nation, any effort by the government to limit that freedom has always met with hostility.

9 During the Civil War, for example, the fifty-seventh Article of War stipulated a court-martial and possible death sentence for anyone, civilian and military alike, who gave military information to the enemy. However, newspapers were an indirect source of military information, and Confederate leaders went to great lengths to obtain copies of major Northern papers because they often revealed the whereabouts of military units and naval vessels. As a result, the U.S. War Department tried to prevent newspapers from publishing any stories that described the movements of troops or ships. Editors generally ignored these orders. Even after the war, General William Sherman refused to shake hands with Horace Greeley, publisher of the *New York Tribune,* maintaining that Greeley's paper had caused a heavy loss of life by revealing troop movements to the enemy.

10 Thus, even in wartime, Americans have questioned censorship, asking what kind of controls should be imposed and by whom. Clearly, the government has the need to protect itself and a duty to protect the nation. But the press claims a right to inform the public of what the government is doing, and the news media maintain that the public has the *right to know.* Therefore, an inherent conflict exists between the right to a free press and the need to control information that would be damaging to the government.

11   During the Johnson administration, the Defense Department put together a forty-seven-volume history of American involvement in Vietnam from 1945 to 1967, including secret cables, memos, and other documents. The history, which came to be known as the Pentagon Papers, was classified as *top secret*. In 1971, Daniel Ellsberg, who had worked on the papers, but later opposed the war, leaked them to the *New York Times,* hoping that their release would turn public opinion against the war and help bring about its end. Although the papers were both stolen and classified, the *Times* began publishing a series of articles summarizing the contents and some of the documents themselves.

12   The Nixon administration went to court to stop the *Times* (and later other newspapers) from printing additional articles on the papers, arguing that their publication would endanger national security. In response, the courts issued a temporary restraining order, stopping the *Times* from continuing its planned series on the papers. In effect, the courts imposed prior restraint.

13   Eventually, the case went to the Supreme Court, which ruled against the government. The government had failed to convince the Court that publication of the Pentagon Papers constituted a danger severe enough to warrant suspending freedom of the press. Relieved and triumphant, the newspapers resumed their articles. (Ellsberg was later tried for stealing the documents.) Yet the Supreme Court's decision in the Pentagon Papers case is still regarded as controversial and it resolved little of the debate between government and the press. Conflict continues over the press's right to publish, the public's right to know, and the government's need to protect the secrecy of some activities.

14   During the 1980s, the Reagan administration engaged in a contentious* tug of war with the press over access to government information. President Ronald Reagan proposed sweeping changes in the Freedom of Information Act, which provides access to the various departments and agencies of government, and issued executive orders making access to information about agencies like the FBI and CIA more difficult. Professional groups such as the Society of Professional Journalists and the American Society of Newspaper Editors campaigned vigorously against these restrictions. In this instance, there was profound disagreement between the government, which claimed that it acted in the best interest of the people by limiting access, and the press, which said that the public was better served by the free flow of information.

Melvin L. DeFleur and Everett E. Dennis, *Understanding Mass Communication*, pp. 406–409.

CHECKING YOUR COMPREHENSION

Directions: Circle the letter of the correct answer.

1. Which statement best paraphrases the overall main idea of the reading?

   a. Censorship is absolutely necessary during wartime because the press cannot be allowed to betray government secrets, as it has done in the past.

   b. Although some censorship during wartime is necessary, a balance needs to be struck between the government's need for secrecy and the public's right to know.

   c. Devised during the Persian Gulf War, the pool system successfully helped control the flow of information between the government and the press.

   d. When in pursuit of a story, members of the press seldom take the government's need for secrecy into account.

2. According to the author, it was generally agreed that the "pool system" described in paragraph 3 had what effect?

   a. The military and the press were able to find a balance between the need for military secrecy and freedom of the press.

   b. The press lost the right to any independent coverage of the war.

   c. Only a very few reporters were able to independently pursue stories about the war.

3. Which statement best paraphrases the overall main idea of the section titled "Direct Censorship in Wartime" (paragraphs 4–7)?

   a. Government censorship was at its peak during World War II, when President Roosevelt created the U.S. Office of Censorship.

   b. The press has generally not been irresponsible when it comes to protecting the government's secrets; on the contrary, as the example of James Reston shows, the press has engaged in a good deal of self-censorship.

   c. During wartime, the government has used several different methods in order to censor the press.

   d. In terms of controlling the press, indirect censorship is much more effective than direct censorship.

4. The reference to the Espionage Act of 1917 (paragraph 5) is a supporting detail used to develop which main idea?

   a. During wartime, the government could easily deny access to information without the possibility of protest.

   b. During wartime, it became a crime to publish anything that showed contempt for the government.

   c. The government has several methods of imposing censorship.

   d. Rules, codes, and laws are another means of imposing censorship during wartime.

5. The reference to the American U2 spy plane (paragraph 7) is a supporting detail used to develop which main idea?

   a. There are some members of the press who refuse to accept censorship even during wartime.

   b. Although the Soviet Union and the United States tried to improve their relationship, there was always a new spy incident to disrupt it.

   c. There have been times when members of the press willingly censored themselves.

   d. The press willingly censored itself when it came to the U.S. invasion of Cuba at the Bay of Pigs.

6. Which statement best paraphrases the overall main idea of the section titled "Challenges to Government Secrecy" (paragraphs 8–14)?

   a. The government's attempts to censor the press during wartime has often caused a great deal of controversy.

   b. When it came to censoring the press, President Richard M. Nixon was determined to keep a tight rein on the press's right to publish, and he ignored the public's right to know.

   c. The Pentagon Papers were classified as top secret, but that didn't stop their being published during wartime, which shows how little regard the press has for the government's right to secrecy.

   d. War or not, Americans are determined to uphold freedom of the press.

7. What pattern of organization is at work in paragraph 9?

    a. comparison and contrast

    b. classification

    c. cause and effect

    d. definition

8. Which statement best paraphrases the topic sentence of paragraph 10?

    a. Despite the government's demand for secrecy, the press needs to keep the public informed.

    b. The need for government security will always take precedence over the press's need to inform the public.

    c. There will always be a struggle between the right to a free press and the government's need to maintain national security.

    d. During wartime the American public tends to support the government's demand for secrecy rather than the rights of a free press.

9. The authors use Daniel Ellsberg and the Pentagon Papers (paragraphs 11–13) to illustrate

    a. the irresponsibility of the press during wartime.

    b. the government's need for secrecy during wartime.

    c. the conflict between freedom of the press and the government's desire for secrecy.

    d. the tendency of the courts to side with the public's right to a free press.

10. Which statement best paraphrases the topic sentence of paragraph 14?

    a. President Reagan did not realize that he was interfering with the free flow of information.

    b. The Society of Professional Journalists is always quick to defend the free flow of information.

    c. President Reagan's administration fought hard to limit the freedom of the press.

    d. The Freedom of Information Act was never as important to the press as some made it out to be.

DEEPENING YOUR UNDERSTANDING

Directions: Answer the following questions by circling the letter of the correct response or filling in the blanks where required.

1. What would you say is the authors' purpose?

   a. to inform readers about the inherent conflict between freedom of the press and national security

   b. to persuade readers that the press should always defer to the government's need for secrecy

   c. to persuade readers that the government is sometimes overly secretive

   Please explain your answer.

   _____

   _____

2. How would you describe the authors' tone?

   a. skeptical

   b. objective

   c. worried

   d. angry

3. The tone of this reading is similar to or different from the tone of

   the previous reading (pp. 181–192). _____ Please describe the similarities or differences you noted.

   _____

   _____

4. With which of the following statements do you agree?

   a. The authors are more sympathetic to the government's position than they are to that of the press.

   b. The authors are more sympathetic to the press's position than they are to that of the government.

   c. The authors do not take any side.

Please explain your answer.

_____

_____

5. Would you call the following statement (paragraph 3) a fact or an opinion*?

"At the [Gulf] war's end, there was an almost universal agreement that the media had been kept at bay, and, in effect, the media lost

the information war." _____ Please explain your answer.

_____

_____

6. Would you call the following statement (paragraph 8) a fact or an opinion?

"Because our shared belief in the need for freedom of the press became such a tradition very early in life of the nation, any effort by the government to limit that freedom has always met with

hostility."_____ Please explain your answer.

_____

_____

7. Would you call the following statement (paragraph 4) a fact or an opinion?

"when the battleship _Maine_ blew up in the harbor of Havana, Cuba, in 1898, the U.S. government immediately closed the

Havana cable to reporters."_____ Please explain your answer.

_____

_____

*If you need to, you can review the difference between fact and opinion on pages 14–15.

8. Identify the relationship between these two sentences in paragraph 7: "Even during peacetime, the press has often censored itself to protect the national interest."; "For a year before the plane was shot down, however, James Reston of the *New York Times* had known that American spy planes were flying over the Soviet Union, but 'The *New York Times* did not publish this fact until one of the planes was shot down in 1960.'"

   a. The first sentence is a fact, the second an opinion.

   b. Both sentences are opinions.

   c. The first sentence is an opinion followed by a supporting fact.

9. Reread paragraph 8. Would you say this passage suggests

   a. a subtle bias in favor of freedom for the press?

   b. a subtle bias in favor of government censorship?

   c. no bias toward either side?

   Please explain your answer.

   _____

10. Review paragraphs 11–13, in which the authors outline a chain of events. Those factual events are used to illustrate what opinion?

   _____

   _____

AIRING YOUR OPINIONS

1. In discussion or on paper, describe how you think the press should behave toward the government during wartime. Just remember that whatever position you take, it's an opinion so use information from the readings in this unit to support your point of view.

2. In 2003, during the war with Iraq, journalist Peter Arnett gave an interview that was aired on Iraqi television. In the interview, he said that the U.S. military had been surprised by the extent of Iraqi opposition. After the interview, Arnett was fired by his sponsor,

NBC. Should he have been fired or not?_____ **Please** explain your answer.

_____

_____

Reading 5

The Media, the Military, and Striking the Right Balance

GETTING FOCUSED

Stuart Taylor, the author of this textbook reading, like the previous authors, suggests that wartime makes it harder to balance the need for national security with the rights of a free press. As you read what he has to say, keep comparing and contrasting his position with that of the previous authors. Do they share his mind-set, or are there some differences?

Textbook Features and Readers' Strategies

Feature:	*Because this reading initially appeared in a journal, it does not have the typical textbook format. There are no headings, and the main ideas are as likely to be implied as stated.*
Strategy:	Pre-read the first sentence and last sentence of every paragraph, trying to get a sense of where the writer's thought is going. Mark any paragraph (perhaps with a check) to indicate any changes or shifts in the writer's train of thought.
Feature:	*The author uses the pronoun* we.
Strategy:	It's common practice for writers to use the pronoun *we* in order to suggest that they speak for the general population rather than just themselves. Yet most of the time, *we* really means *I*, so look closely at any *we* statements to determine the author's point of view. Then decide if you, in fact, do share the writer's point of view.
Feature:	*The author refers to numerous specific people and events.*
Strategy:	Each time you see a new name or event, ask yourself how that person or situation relates to the author's point of view. Is the reference being used to support his position, or is it being used to define the opposition?

Evaluating Your Background Knowledge

The author of this reading is relying on your knowledge of these words and terms. Look over this list carefully to make sure you know everything on it. *Note:* The number in parentheses indicates the paragraph where the word can be found while an asterisk accompanies the word's first appearance in the reading.

chafing (1):   irritating

aberrants (8):   abnormal beings

op-ed (9):   opinion piece on the editorial page of a newspaper

glib (9):   superficial, without serious content

transcendent (11): supreme

media cheerleading of the World War II era (14): Newspapers were generally proud supporters of the war effort during World War II.

corrosive (14):   burning

nihilism (14):   the rejection of all belief in morals or social values

tenable (14):   acceptable, understandable

1   This war [on terrorism] will severely test the inherently uneasy relationship between the government—especially the military—and the media. The chafing* has already begun. While the Bush Administration so far seems largely to have avoided the outright deceptions practiced by its predecessors, it has exhibited an unhealthy impulse to control the news by leaning on the media not to publish enemy "propaganda." And while much of the news coverage has been superb, some journalists have exhibited a reckless indifference to endangering military operations and the lives of our soldiers, and a reflexive hostility toward the military. The military and the Administration have ample reason to distrust some reporters and editors.

2   If we are going to get this right, the government must not resort unnecessarily to secrecy or to lightly tarring independent journalists as disloyal. The media should not frivolously cry "censorship." And each should work harder to understand the views and accommodate the needs of the other.

3   The delicacy of the task is exemplified by the Administration's requests that the media filter public statements by Osama bin Laden and his fellow mass murderers before airing them. National Security Adviser Condoleezza Rice took a small but worrisome step down a

slippery slope when she urged network executives not to broadcast bin Laden videos without first reviewing and editing them down to brief excerpts. Although her warning that bin Laden might be sending coded messages in Arabic to operatives planning new attacks was plausible, any such messages could almost as easily be sent through foreign networks, the Internet, or the mail. And while Rice's more emphatic concern about indiscriminate airing of enemy propaganda was understandable, some such propaganda is undeniably newsworthy. White House Press Secretary Ari Fleischer clumsily lurched farther down the same slope when he urged newspapers not to publish full transcripts of enemy rants. His suggestion that terrorists would look to printed English-language translations for coded marching orders was as farfetched as his notion that little-read transcripts could be an effective propaganda vehicle.

4   Such official efforts to influence editorial discretion are fraught with danger, likely to be futile, and sometimes self-defeating. Fraught with danger because when the government is talking, it is but a short step from making reasoned critiques to questioning the loyalty of reporters and editors. Futile because bin Laden's propaganda has little impact outside the Muslim world, where people will watch unedited bin Laden videos elsewhere if CNN does not show them. Self-defeating because the videos are the best public evidence by far of bin Laden's role in the September 11 mass murders and his moral depravity.

5   Similarly ill-advised was the State Department's pressure on the government-funded Voice of America radio to shelve an interview with Taliban leader Mullah Mohammed Omar. The VOA's hard-won reputation for balanced and independent news coverage accounts for its remarkable following in Afghanistan, where surveys show that 67 percent of all men tune in daily. If it becomes a one-sided official mouthpiece, skeptical listeners will switch to the BBC or the virulently anti-American tirades that pervade most other broadcasts in the Middle East.

6   History provides ample reason for *Washington Post* columnist E. J. Dionne's view that "the coming struggles between the government and the media over the public's right to know will have less to do with protecting individuals and operations than officials may argue. All governments have an interest in shielding themselves from reports of failure. The easiest alibi for cover-ups is to claim that the truth is dangerous." But the military and the Administration also have ample reasons to distrust some reporters and editors.

7   Dionne confidently claims that "no reporter I know" wants to be responsible for "blowing the cover of individuals or military operations." Perhaps he does not know Loren Jenkins, senior foreign editor of National Public Radio, who explained his ethical principles to

The Chicago Tribune: "Asked whether his team [of reporters] would report the presence of an American commando unit found in, say, a northern Pakistan village, [Jenkins] doesn't exhibit any of the hesitation of some of his news-business colleagues, who stress that they try to factor security issues into their coverage decisions. 'You report it,' Jenkins says. 'I don't represent the government. I represent history, information, what happened.'"

8   Of course, "what happens" might well be influenced—and American operations and lives endangered—by the kind of reporting that Jenkins vows to do. Are he and NPR aberrants*? Well, consider a televised 1987 roundtable discussion among some military men and two famous journalists. The hypothetical question for the journalists was what they would do if, after accepting (as both said they would) an invitation to travel behind enemy lines, they found themselves with an enemy unit preparing to ambush unsuspecting American and allied soldiers. Peter Jennings said with evident ambivalence that he would do his best to warn the Americans. But then, Mike Wallace asserted without hesitation that good reporters (clearly including him) "would regard it simply as another story they were there to cover." He berated Jennings and rejected the moderator's suggestion that he might have some higher duty than filming the slaughter of his countrymen: "No. You don't have a higher duty. No. No. You're a reporter!" Whereupon Jennings, embarrassed by his lapse into human decency, reversed himself and agreed with Wallace.

9   The military men were horrified. "What's it worth?" a former general (Brent Scowcroft) bitterly demanded of Wallace. "It's worth 30 seconds on the evening news, as opposed to saving a platoon." Marine Colonel George M. Connell spat out a more concise reaction: "I . . . feel . . . utter . . . contempt." Amen. All this gives a hollow ring to former television correspondent Marvin Kalb's assertion, in an op-ed* in *The New York Times*, that the Administration "must recognize that in this fight the press . . . is a valuable and necessary ally, if treated with . . . trust." This is the same Kalb who had previously mused in another op-ed, in *The Washington Post:* "Certain operations are to be super secret. If a reporter learns about one, should he report it? . . . And if he doesn't report it and the operation turns out to be badly conceived and costly in casualties, does his reticence serve his profession or his country? To these questions, there are no easy answers, no glib* guidelines."

10   Here's an easy guideline: No decent journalist, no decent American, would ever risk endangering the lives of American soldiers or—in this of all wars—the secrecy of military operations for something as petty

and self-serving as a lousy little scoop. Or, for that matter, a great big scoop. Kalb's implication that reporters with access to fragmentary leaks are better qualified than military commanders to judge whether secret operations are "badly conceived" is breathtaking in its arrogance. (Full disclosure: Kalb has been critical of my own work.)

11   Jenkins, Wallace, Jennings, and Kalb exemplify a mind-set that holds that beating the competition even to stories that would soon become public anyway or that smack more of sensationalism than of educating the public is so transcendent* a value as to justify virtual indifference to any harm that journalists might cause (or fail to prevent). If you were a military commander, would you want to help people like these get close to ground operations in Afghanistan, secret or otherwise? Would Jenkins's assertion (to *The Tribune*) that military officials "never tell you the truth" instill confidence in his own trustworthiness and fairness?

12   This is not to suggest that the Administration and the military should slam the doors in the face of all reporters. Most, or at least many, can be trusted. And keeping the media at a greater distance from combat operations than security requires would contribute to a bitterly adversarial military-media relationship. This, in turn, would likely hurt the war effort in the long run by inviting relentlessly negative coverage and fanning public distrust. Nor is this to deny that the media's most vital mission—keeping the government honest—requires both healthy skepticism and the fortitude to dig out and publish bad news, even in the face of official and public wrath.

13   Sometimes, as in the 1971 Pentagon Papers case, good journalism also calls for publishing important news in the face of transparently unwarranted stamps of official secrecy and attempted official censorship.

14   But in assessing alleged security risks, the media should give due weight to the fact that the officials often have more complete information and far, far more grave responsibilities. We cannot and should not recreate the uncritical media cheerleading of the World War II* era. But we must avoid the corrosive* military-media hostility that started in Vietnam and has since been fed both by official deceptions and by the mindless anti-military bias inculcated in many of us by our college professors. This war—unlike Vietnam—really does pit good against evil, civilization against barbarism, life and liberty against nihilism.* Journalistic neutrality is not a tenable* stance.

CHECKING YOUR COMPREHENSION

Directions: Circle the letter of the correct answer.

1. Which statement best paraphrases the main idea of the entire reading?

   a. A balance between freedom of the press and government security must be found if the United States is to effectively wage a war on terror.

   b. To reach a balance between the press's right to know and the government's right to secrecy, the press must acknowledge that during wartime, freedom of the press is not as important as military security.

   c. If they want the cooperation of the press, military leaders must give up their goal of complete secrecy during wartime; to some degree, they have to cooperate with the press.

   d. The hostility generated by the Vietnam War may have forever poisoned relations between the press and the military.

2. Which statement most effectively paraphrases the main idea of paragraph 2?

   a. The war on terrorism is going to destroy the already hard-to-maintain balance between the media and the government.

   b. If there is to be a balance between the media's need to inform the public and the nation's need for security, then the government will have to be less secretive.

   c. If the government and the press are to maintain a working relationship, then each side must make more of an effort to understand the other.

3. The author's reference to National Security Advisor Condoleezza Rice (paragraph 3) is a supporting detail used to make what point?

   a. Terrorists can use the press to send coded messages to other conspirators.

   b. During the war on terror, the press will have to be strictly censored.

   c. The threat of terrorism has sometimes encouraged government officials to err on the side of excessive censorship.

4. The name of Loren Jenkins (paragraph 7) is used in order to make what point?

   a. Journalists should not knowingly interfere with military operations.

b. Journalists must consider the need for military security in their decision to publish any story associated with the war.

c. Some journalists think it is acceptable to jeopardize military security in pursuit of news.

5. Why was the State Department's pressure on the Voice of America ill advised (paragraph 5)?

a. The publicity that resulted put the government in a bad light.

b. It could have discouraged listeners in Afghanistan from viewing VOA as an independent news source.

c. It encouraged the notion that the government insists on censorship when there is no real need for secrecy.

6. What inference does the author expect readers to draw from paragraph 6?

a. Although E. J. Dionne may have a point about the government's inclination toward cover-ups, there are good reasons for the government and the military to distrust journalists.

b. E. J. Dionne couldn't be more wrong-headed in his assumption that the government is less interested in protecting military security and more interested in hiding reports of mistakes.

c. E. J. Dionne is correct when he insists that the government is usually more interested in hiding its mistakes than it is in protecting operations.

7. What implied answer does the author give to the question he poses in paragraph 8: "Are Jenkins and NPR aberrants?"

a. Most self-respecting journalists would not jeopardize military security in pursuit of news.

b. When journalists become famous, they tend to forget about the ethics of their profession.

c. It's not at all unusual for journalists to disregard national security when they are in pursuit of news.

8. In paragraph 9, the author says the "military men were horrified." However, he does not explicitly say what horrified them. However, you can infer that they were horrified by the

a. accusation that they would engage in a cover-up.

    b. suggestion that some military operations are badly conceived and costly in unnecessary casualties.

    c. idea that a journalist would report a story even if it endangered the lives of soldiers.

9. In paragraph 10, the author offers a guideline for

    a. maintaining good relations with members of the press.

    b. judging the government's claims that an issue must be kept top secret.

    c. deciding when a story should or should not be covered.

10. What do the rhetorical questions at the end of paragraph 11 imply?

    a. There is no reason why the military should place any faith in the ethics of journalists like those referred to in the paragraph.

    b. Journalists like Kalb, Wallace, Jenkins, and Jennings are bound to get in the way of military operations.

    c. Journalists are right to believe that military officials are not likely to tell them the truth.

    d. There is no place for freedom of the press during wartime.

DEEPENING YOUR UNDERSTANDING

Directions: Answer the following questions by circling the letter of the correct response or filling in the blanks where required.

1. How would you describe the author's tone at the beginning of the reading? _____

What about at the end? _____

2. What would you say is the author's purpose?

    a. to inform readers about the difficulties involved in striking the right balance between freedom of the press and national security during wartime

    b. to persuade readers that during wartime, the press's commitment must be to national security and safety rather than to the gathering and reporting of information

3. Which statement do you believe is true?

> **a.** The author is inclined to give more weight to the government's need for secrecy.
>
> **b.** The author is inclined to give more weight to the media's need to report the news.
>
> **c.** The author gives no indication of his personal feelings.
>
> Please explain your answer.
>
> _____
>
> _____

4. In paragraph 10, the author says, "Kalb's implication that reporters with access to fragmentary leaks are better qualified than military commanders to judge whether the secret operations are 'badly conceived' is breathtaking in its arrogance." If you reread what Kalb is quoted as saying (paragraph 9), does he imply that a journalist reporting on a poorly planned operation

   would be relying on "fragmentary leaks"?_____

   Please explain your answer.

   _____

   _____

5. What is the author implying in paragraph 10, which ends with the statement: "(Full disclosure: Kalb has been critical of my own work.)"

   _____

6. Reread the quotations from Kalb (paragraph 9) one last time. He implies that a journalist who did not report on a poorly planned action might be faced with what consequences?

   _____

7. In paragraph 10, the author says that "no decent American, would ever risk endangering the lives of American soldiers . . . for something as petty and self-serving as a lousy little scoop." The author assumes that journalists report the news solely for which purpose?

      a. to beat the competition and make big headlines

      b. to inform the public about the government's activities

      c. to live up to the journalists' code of ethics

8. The author seems to think that journalists were right to report on and publish the Pentagon Papers (also mentioned in the previous reading). Based on what he says in this reading and what you already know about the Pentagon Papers, do you think he would have supported their publication at the time? _____

Please explain your answer.

_____

_____

9. In paragraph 14, the author says "Journalistic neutrality is not a tenable stance." Describe the reasoning used to support that claim.

_____

_____

10. Based on your reading, do you think the authors of the previous reading and the author of this one share a similar point of view? _____

Please describe the similarities or differences you noted.

_____

_____

AIRING YOUR OPINIONS

In discussion or on paper, describe what you think is the appropriate response in the following situation: A journalist has just discovered that a commander overseeing a military operation has badly underestimated the number of enemy troops his company will be facing. The journalist has learned this from the second-in-command, who also fears that the operation will turn out badly but is afraid of risking a court-martial by challenging his superior officer. What should the journalist do, and why?

Unit III   Terrorism Invades America

Before September 11, 2001, Americans did not think all that much about the threat of terrorism. Yet at least two of the readings in this unit suggest that the threat has been with us for close to a decade but wasn't taken as seriously as it should have been. Still, no matter what his or her perspective on terrorism, the authors included here all agree on one haunting point: The threat of a terrorist attack isn't going to disappear anytime soon.

Reading 1   # Warning About Terrorism

GETTING FOCUSED

This reading, which comes from a textbook written before the 9/11 tragedy, may give you an eerie feeling. The author, Professor Frank Schmalleger, comes close to predicting the events that were to occur only a few months later.

Textbook Features and Readers' Strategies

Feature: *The headings introduce the topic of each section.*

Strategy: Read to answer the question, "What does the author want to say about the topic?" referred to in the heading.

Feature: *The paragraphs are long and detailed.*

Strategy: Pre-read the first and last sentences of every paragraph to get an overview of the material. Make some predictions about what the author will say. Then, read to confirm those predictions.

Feature: *Marginal annotations define key terms.*

Strategy: Skim the annotations before reading the text. Letting your mind double-process the definitions will help you remember them.

Feature: *Transitions frequently open paragraphs.*

Strategy: As you read, pay close attention to what the transitions signal about the author's train of thought. They will tell you whether he is continuing, contradicting, or revising what came before.

Feature: *Two lists are present in the reading.*

Strategy: Lists are always important in a textbook, so look over each one before you start reading the entire excerpt. When you encounter a list for the second time, stop and see how many items on it you can remember without looking at the text.

Evaluating Your Background Knowledge

The author of this reading is relying on your knowledge of these words and terms. Look over this list carefully to make sure you know everything on it. *Note:* The number in parentheses indicates the paragraph where the word can be found while an asterisk accompanies the word's first appearance in the reading.

buffeted (1):   struck, moved around

radical (1):   profound, significant

domestic terrorism (1): the activity of groups that originated on American soil with the intention of making social change through violent acts

fundamentalists (3): people who refuse all changes to religious tradition or teachings

David Koresh's Branch Davidian followers (6): originally part of the Seventh Day Adventists, the Davidians split from the Adventists in 1942. Koresh, formerly known as Vernon Howell, took control of the group in 1987 and began emphasizing the coming battle between good and evil.

Aryan (9):   non-Jewish, white person

Rand Corporation (15): a nonprofit institution that uses research and analysis to make suggestions about social and governmental policy. The Rand Corporation might issue books or papers on anything from improving the math performance of high school students to responding to a nuclear threat.

totalitarian (17):   under the control of those who allow no dissent

provision (19):   a clause in a document that addresses a particular concern or modification

mandating (19):   making into a rule or law

paramilitary (20): following military patterns of organization

Terrorism

1   The American criminal justice system of the twenty-first century will continue to be buffeted* by the expanding power of politically oriented . . . groups with radical* agendas. Throughout the 1960s

terrorism A violent act or an act dangerous to human life in violation of the criminal laws of the United States or of any state to intimidate or coerce a government, the civilian population, or any segment thereof, in furtherance of political or social objectives. While we usually think of terrorism as involving bombings, kidnappings, and hijackings, other forms of terrorism include attacks on the information systems of financial institutions and threats to reveal trade or industry secrets.

and 1970s, domestic **terrorism*** in the United States required the expenditure of considerable criminal justice resources. . . . Bombings, kidnappings, and shoot-outs peppered the national scene. As overt acts of domestic terrorism declined in frequency in the 1980s, international terrorism took their place. The war in Lebanon; terrorism in Israel; bombings in France, Italy, and Germany; and the many violent offshoots of the Iran-Iraq and Gulf wars occupied the attention of the media and of much of the rest of the world. Vigilance by the FBI, the CIA, and other agencies largely prevented the spread of terrorism to the United States.

2   After incidents such as the terrorist attacks on Rome's Leonardo da Vinci Airport in 1987 and the 1988 bombing of Pan American's London–New York flight, however, Americans began to realize that international terrorism was knocking on the domestic door. Pan American flight 103 was destroyed over Scotland by a powerful two-stage bomb as it reached its cruising altitude of 30,000 feet, killing all of the 259 passengers and crew aboard. Another 11 people on the ground were killed, and many others injured as flaming debris from the airplane crashed down on the Scottish town of Lockerbie. Any doubts that Americans [were] being targeted by terrorists were dispelled by the June 25, 1996, truck bomb attack on U.S. military barracks in Dhahran, Saudi Arabia. Nineteen U.S. Air Force personnel were killed and more than 250 others injured in the blast that destroyed the Khobar Towers housing complex. A 40-person Pentagon task force headed by retired U.S. Army General Wayne Downing later concluded that the Pentagon had failed to take threats seriously.

3   The 1993 bombing of the World Trade Center in New York City and the 1995 conviction of Sheik Oma Abdel-Rahman and eight other Muslim fundamentalists* on charges of plotting to start a holy war and conspiring to commit assassinations and bomb the United Nations indicates that the threat of international terrorism has become a part of daily life in America. According to some terrorism experts, the bombing of the World Trade Center, which left four dead and a 100-foot hole through four subfloors of concrete, ushered in an era of serious domestic terrorism. In late 1999, the Second U.S. Circuit Court of Appeals upheld the convictions of the sheik and his co-conspirators.

4   Robert Kupperman of the Center for Strategic and International Studies believes . . . terrorism is just beginning. Kupperman says, "We're in for very deep trouble. The terrorism infrastructure operating in the United States is altogether deeper than what we've thought

so far." Many now suspect that sleeper agents, planted by nations as diverse as Libya, Syria, North Korea, Cuba, Iran, and Iraq, have taken up residence throughout the United States and are awaiting the appropriate signal to attack. Siddig Ibrahim Siddig Ali, one of the eight terrorists convicted in the Trade Center bombing, seemed to confirm such suspicions when he told reporters following his arrest, "We can get you anytime." The United States has lax security, according to Philip Jenkins, a counterterrorism expert. "In Europe," says Jenkins, "if you leave a bag at a railroad station, it will be blown up when you come back 30 minutes later. Here, it will be taken to lost and found."

5   The technological sophistication of state-sponsored terrorist organizations is rapidly increasing. Handguns and even larger weapons are now being manufactured out of plastic polymers and ceramics. Capable of firing Teflon-coated armor-piercing bullets, such weapons are extremely powerful and impossible to uncover with metal detectors. Evidence points to the black market availability of other sinister devices, including liquid metal embrittlement (LME). LME is a chemical which slowly weakens any metal it contacts. It could be applied easily with a felt-tipped pen to fuselage components in domestic aircraft, causing delayed structural failure. Backpack-type electromagnetic pulse generators may soon be available to terrorists. Such devices could be carried into major cities, set up next to important computer installations, and activated to wipe out billions of items of financial, military, or other information now stored on magnetic media. International terrorists, along with the general public, have easy access to maps and other information which could be used to cripple the nation. The approximately 500 extremely high-voltage (EHV) transformers on which the nation's electronic grid depends, for example, are entirely undefended but specified with extreme accuracy on easily available power network maps.

6   Equally worrisome are domestic underground survivalist and separatist groups and potentially violent special-interest groups, each with its own vision of a future America. In 1993, for example, a confrontation between David Koresh's Branch Davidian followers* and federal agents left 72 Davidians (including Koresh) and four federal agents dead in Waco, Texas.

7   Exactly two years to the day after the Davidian standoff ended in a horrific fire that destroyed the compound, a powerful terrorist truck bomb devastated the Alfred P. Murrah Federal Building in downtown Oklahoma City, Oklahoma. One hundred sixty-eight people died, and

hundreds more were wounded. The targeted nine-story building had housed offices of the Social Security Administration, the Drug Enforcement Administration, the Secret Service, the Bureau of Alcohol, Tobacco, and Firearms, and a day-care center called America's Kids. The fertilizer-and-diesel-fuel device used in the attack was estimated to have weighed about 1,200 pounds and had been left in a rental truck on the Fifth Street side of the building. The blast, which left a crater 30 feet wide and 8 feet deep and spread debris over a ten-block area, demonstrated just how vulnerable the United States is to terrorist attack.

8   In 1997, a federal jury found 29-year-old Timothy McVeigh guilty of 11 counts, ranging from conspiracy to first-degree murder, in the Oklahoma City bombing. Jurors concluded that McVeigh had conspired with Terry Nichols, a friend he had met while both were in the Army, and with unknown others to destroy the Murrah Building. Prosecutors made clear their belief that the attack was intended to revenge the 1993 assault on the Branch Davidian compound. Following the guilty verdicts, McVeigh was sentenced to death. . . . Terry Nichols was later convicted of conspiracy in the bombing and eight counts of involuntary manslaughter.

9   Some experts believe that the Oklahoma City attack was modeled after a similar bombing described in the *Turner Diaries,* a novel used by extremist groups to map their rise to power. Just as Hitler's [auto]biography *Mein Kampf* served as a call to arms for Nazis in Europe during the 1930s, the *Turner Diaries* describes an Aryan* revolution which occurs in the United States during the 1990s in which Jews, blacks, and other minorities are removed from positions of influence in government and society. Unsolved as of this writing is the 1996 Olympic Centennial Park bombing in which one person died and 111 were injured—an attack which many antiterrorism experts believe was the work of a separatist organization.

10   Active fringe groups include those espousing a nationwide "common law movement," under which the legitimacy of elected government officials is not recognized. An example is the Republic of Texas separatists who took neighbors hostage near Fort Davis, Texas, in 1997 to draw attention to their claims that Texas was illegally annexed by the United States in 1845. While not necessarily bent on terrorism, such special-interest groups may turn to violence if thwarted in attempts to reach their goals.

11   Sometimes individuals can be as dangerous as organized groups. In 1996, for example, 52-year-old Theodore Kaczynski, a Lincoln, Montana, recluse, was arrested and charged in the Unabomber case.

The Unabomber (so called because the bomber's original targets were universities and airlines) had led police and FBI agents on a 17-year-long manhunt through a series of incidents which involved as many as 16 bombings, resulting in three deaths and 23 injuries. Kaczynski pleaded guilty to federal charges in 1998 and was sentenced to life in prison without possibility of parole.

12   Also in 1998, radical Muslim leader Osama bin Laden showed the world how easy it can be to strike at American interests abroad. Attacks on American embassies in Nairobi, Kenya, and Dar es Salaam, Tanzania, were apparently both planned by bin Laden and carried out by his henchmen. The attacks killed 257 people, including 12 Americans. Although American military forces responded by attacking some of bin Laden's reputed strongholds in Afghanistan, the terrorist leader remains at large as of this writing.

13   The current situation leads many observers to conclude that the American justice system of today is ill prepared to deal with the threat represented by domestic and international terrorism. Intelligence-gathering efforts focused on such groups have largely failed. Military-style organization and training are characteristic of the groups that are known, making them difficult to penetrate. The armaments at their disposal include weapons of mass destruction, which the firepower and tactical mobility of law enforcement agencies cannot hope to match.

14   Even more frightening is the prospect of nuclear terrorism. The collapse of the Soviet Union at the close of the 1980s led to very loose internal control over nuclear weapons and weapons-grade fissionable materials held in the former Soviet republics. Evidence of such lack of control continues to surface. A few years ago, for example, German police were surprised to find that a gritty substance confiscated from the garage of an accused counterfeiter in the small town of Tengen-Weichs in southwestern Germany was superpure plutonium 239—a key ingredient needed in the manufacture of atomic bombs. Officials were able to determine through the identification of "chemical footprints" unique to the material that it had come from one of three top-secret Russian nuclear weapons laboratories—each of which had been among the most strictly guarded sites in the former Soviet Union. Experts tell us that oil-rich Middle Eastern countries, controlled by fanatical and dictatorial regimes, are willing to pay as much as $100 million for the plutonium needed to make one bomb—an amount that can be smuggled out of a supposedly secure area in a briefcase or even in the pocket of an overcoat.

cyberterrorism **15**
A form of terrorism that makes use of high technology, especially computers and the Internet, in the planning and carrying out of terrorist attacks.

Another new kind of terrorism, called **cyberterrorism,** is lurking on the horizon. Cyberterrorism is a form of terrorism that makes use of high-technology—especially computers, the Internet, and the World Wide Web—in the planning and carrying out of terrorist attacks. Cyberterrorism was first identified in a 1996 report by Rand Corporation* that warned of an emerging "new terrorism" which is being implemented by the way in which terrorist groups organize and use technology. The report warned of a coming "netwar," or "infowar," consisting of coordinated cyberattacks on our nation's economic, business, and military infrastracture.

Characteristics of Terrorism

16 According to criminologist Gwynn Nettler, any terrorism, domestic or international, has six characteristics. They are:

- *No rules.* There are no moral limitations upon the type or degree of violence which terrorists can use.

- *No innocents.* No distinctions are made between soldiers and civilians. Children can be killed as easily as adults.

- *Economy.* Kill one, frighten 10,000.

- *Publicity.* Terrorists seek publicity, and publicity encourages terrorism.

- *Meaning.* Terrorist acts give meaning and significance to the lives of terrorists.

- *No clarity.* Beyond the immediate aim of destructive acts, the long-term goals of terrorists are likely to be poorly conceived or impossible to implement.

Controlling Terrorism

17 Terrorism represents a difficult challenge to all societies. The open societies of the Western world, however, are potentially more vulnerable than are totalitarian* regimes such as dictatorships. Democratic ideals of the West restrict police surveillance of likely terrorist groups and curtail luggage, vehicle, and airport searches. Press coverage of acts of terrorism encourage copycat activities by other fringe groups or communicate information on workable techniques. Laws designed to limit terrorist access to technology, information, and physical locations are stopgap measures at best. The federal Terrorist Firearms Detection Act of 1988 is an example. Designed to prevent the development of plastic firearms by

Osama bin Laden. The exiled Saudi terrorist leader now operates out of Afghanistan. In 1998, bin Laden ordered attacks against American embassies in Kenya and Tanzania that killed 257 people, including 12 Americans.

AP/Wide World Photos

requiring handguns to contain at least 3.7 ounces of detectable metal, it applies only to weapons manufactured within U.S. borders.

18   In 1996, the Antiterrorism and Effective Death Penalty Act (AEDPA) became law. The act:

- Limits federal appeals in death penalty cases.

- Bans fund-raising and financial support within the United States for international terrorist organizations.

- Provides $1 billion for enhanced terrorism-fighting measures by federal and state authorities.

- Allows foreign terrorism suspects to be deported or to be kept out of the United States without the need to disclose classified evidence against them.

> And say, finally, whether peace is best preserved by giving energy to the government, or information to the people—this last is the most certain, and the most legitimate engine of government. Educate and inform the whole mass of the people.
> —Inscription on the atrium wall, Jefferson Hall, FBI National Academy, Quantico, Virginia

- Permits a death sentence to be imposed upon anyone committing an international terrorist attack in the United States, if a death occurs.

- Makes it a federal crime to use the United States as a base for planning terrorist attacks overseas.

- Orders identifying chemical markers known as *taggants* to be added to plastic explosives during manufacture.

- Orders a feasibility study on marking other explosives (except gunpowder).

19   Sponsors of the 1996 legislation, a direct response to the 1995 Oklahoma City bombing, had originally proposed mandating the addition of taggants to all powerful explosives during the manufacturing process, as well as to chemical compounds which could be used to make such explosives. It was also proposed to include a powerful wiretap provision* which would have made it easier for government agents to listen in on conversations of alleged terrorists. A political coalition led by the National Rifle Association and the American Civil Liberties Union, however, was successful in excluding both provisions from the final version of the legislation. Other special interests were successful in adding a separate provision to the act mandating* the creation of a five-member committee to study the activities of federal law enforcement agencies in dealing with right-wing groups.

20   There are no signs that either international or domestic terrorism will abate anytime soon. If diplomatic and other efforts fail to keep terrorism at bay, the criminal justice system may soon find itself embroiled in an undeclared war waged on American soil. The system, whose original purpose was to resolve disputes and to keep order among the citizenry, cannot be expected to adequately counter well-planned, heavily financed, covert paramilitary* operations. As long as terrorists can find safe haven among sympathizers antagonistic to the rule of law, their activities will continue. As Nettler has observed, "Terrorism that succeeds escalates."

Frank Schmalleger, *Criminal Justice Today,* pp. 675–678.

CHECKING YOUR COMPREHENSION

Directions: Circle the letter of the correct answer.

1. Which statement most effectively sums up the main idea of the entire reading?

    a. Despite the growing threat of international terrorism, America has not even begun the necessary preparations to ward off an attack.

    b. Although domestic and international terrorism are a serious threat, neither the government nor the justice system is fully prepared for the possibility of a terrorist attack.

    c. While it's true that organized terrorist groups are dangerous, it is the violence-prone individual like the Unabomber who can do the most serious damage.

    d. The radical Muslim leader Osama bin Laden is currently the most serious threat to America's security.

2. In paragraph 4, the reference to sleeper agents is used to support which main idea?

    a. Security in America is not as tight as it should be.

    b. The European security system is better than that of the United States.

    c. The threat of terrorism is going to increase.

    d. Domestic terrorists are presently being trained throughout the United States.

3. In paragraph 5, the reference to "Teflon-coated armor-piercing bullets" is there to support which main idea?

    a. Terrorism is on the rise.

    b. State-sponsored terrorism is a particularly dangerous and growing threat.

    c. State-sponsored terrorists are becoming increasingly adept at using advanced technology.

    d. Attacks by terrorists are going to become increasingly violent and vicious.

4. Paragraph 7 opens with a transition that signals

    a. the addition of similar material.

    b. the order of events in time.

    c. a contrasting point of view.

    d. the description of a cause.

5. The mention of the Oklahoma City bombing (paragraph 7) is used to support which main idea?

    a. The Davidian standoff ended in a tragic fire that killed more than seventy people.

b. In 1997, Timothy McVeigh was sentenced to death for his role in the Oklahoma City bombing.

c. The Oklahoma City attack was an act of revenge for the assault on the Davidian compound.

d. Domestic terrorists driven by their vision of what America should be are as big a danger as international ones.

6. In paragraph 11, the reference to Theodore Kaczynski illustrates which main idea?

a. The Unabomber was responsible for three deaths and twenty-three injuries.

b. The Unabomber was so called because he originally targeted universities and airlines.

c. A single person can be as much of a threat as a terrorist group.

d. Theodore Kaczynski attacked those working for universities and airlines.

7. What patterns of organization are at work in paragraph 14?

a. classification; comparison and contrast

b. comparison and contrast; definition

c. cause and effect; time order

d. time order; classification

8. In paragraph 17, the topic sentence is

a. sentence 1.

b. sentence 2.

c. sentence 3.

9. What main idea do you think is implied by paragraph 19?

a. Sponsors of the 1996 Antiterrorism and Effective Death Penalty Act put together exactly the kind of law that America needs.

b. Sponsors of the 1996 Antiterrorism and Effective Death Penalty Act put together a tough law that was then weakened by special-interest groups.

c. The 1996 Antiterrorism and Effective Death Penalty Act was bound to fail because it violated Americans' right to privacy.

10. What two patterns organize the reading?

    a. cause and effect; classification

    b. cause and effect; time order

    c. comparison and contrast; time order; classification

DEEPENING YOUR UNDERSTANDING

Directions: Answer the following questions by circling the letter of the correct response or filling in the blanks where required.

1. How would you describe the author's tone?

    a. objective

    b. worried

    c. confident

    d. disgusted

2. What would you say is the author's purpose?

    a. to inform readers about terrorist groups

    b. to persuade readers that America is facing a terrorist threat

3. Would you say that the following statement (paragraph 1) is a fact or an opinion?

"The American criminal justice system of the twenty-first century will continue to be buffeted by the expanding power of politically

oriented groups with radical agendas."_____

Please explain your answer. _____

_____

4. In paragraph 3, the author cites "terrorism experts" to support a statement. What would a thoughtful reader want to know about those experts?

_____

5. What would a thoughtful reader want to know about the word *observers* mentioned in paragraph 13?

_____

6. In paragraphs 18 and 19, the author describes the 1996 Anti-terrorism and Effective Death Penalty Act. Would you say the author

   a. approves of the changes?

   b. disapproves of the changes?

   c. gives no indication of his personal feelings?

7. Summarize the author's argument in paragraph 17. The point

   of the argument is that _____

   _____

   The following are the reasons the author gives for his claim:

   (1) _____

   (2) _____

   (3) _____

8. Do you think the author would approve or disapprove of the Patriot Act legislation passed as a result of the attack on September 11, 2001? The legislation, among other things, reduced some of the restrictions on law enforcement activity that involves terrorism. In particular the Patriot Act would make it easier for the government

   to engage in the surveillance of suspected terrorists. _____

   Please explain your answer. _____

   _____

9. According to the author, what makes the Terrorist Firearms Detection Act of 1988 ineffective in the battle against international

   terrorism? _____

10. Explain what criminologist Gwynn Nettler means when he says,

    "Terrorism that succeeds escalates." _____

    _____

AIRING YOUR OPINIONS

This reading was written shortly before 9/11. Do you think that when the author revises the textbook for its next edition he will be as pessimistic about the country's ability to deal with terrorism? Please explain your answer.

Reading 2   # Unwitting Accomplices?

GETTING FOCUSED

As you know from Unit II, journalists have been criticized for concentrating too much on stories that excite or terrify rather than inform. But according to author Robert J. Samuelson, 9/11 gave journalists a story so big, and so compelling, it erased trivial stories about celebrity love affairs or sensational ones about violent crime. Yet the author of this reading suggests that members of the media could now make another, altogether different, mistake.

Textbook Features and Readers' Strategies

Feature:	*The title poses a question.*
Strategy:	By the end of the reading, make sure you understand the author's answer to that question. If you can't, reread the article.
Feature:	*This is a newspaper article, not a textbook excerpt; many of the main ideas are implied rather than stated in topic sentences.*
Strategy:	If none of the first few sentences seem to state the main idea, start thinking about what main idea might be implied.
Feature:	*Numerous transitions mark the twists and turns in the writer's train of thought.*
Strategy:	Every time you see a transition, use it to understand how the new line of thought adds to or contrasts with the old.

Evaluating Your Background Knowledge

The author of this reading is relying on your knowledge of these words and terms. Look over this list carefully to make sure you know everything on it. *Note:* The number in parentheses indicates the paragraph where the word can be found while an asterisk accompanies the word's first appearance in the reading.

titillating (1): sensational, exciting

Gary Condit (1): A Congressman from California, Condit was forced to admit his affair with a young woman on his staff who mysteriously disappeared and whose body was not discovered until more than a year after her disappearance.

sects (2): religious groups

parochialism (4): a tendency to be narrowly limited in scope or outlook

zealousness (10): excessive enthusiasm

1   The news media rank as one of the big winners of Sept. 11: Terrorism gave us a huge story and restored our seriousness of purpose. Because this good fortune seems almost indecent, hardly anyone mentions it. But before Sept. 11, the press was caught in a prolonged process of self-trivialization. We seemed to live in an era dominated by the personal, the small and the titillating.* The summer's big stories were Gary Condit* and shark attacks. Before that, there was Monica Lewinsky. Great national issues with heavy moral, political or social significance were disappearing, consigned to back pages or ignored altogether. Among media stars, many were enthusiastically self-absorbed, gleefully shrill and blissfully uninformed on matters of substance. Attitude was king or queen.

2   Now what we do has shifted dramatically. Here is a story that truly matters. It's about good and evil, life and death, war and peace, religion, technology, the clash of cultures—our future as a society. Suddenly, we are no longer focused obsessively on the latest sex scandal. Substance counts. We need science reporters to distinguish between a microbe and a molecule, defense reporters to explain B-2s, and foreign correspondents to interpret various Islamic sects* that—until a few weeks ago—were unknown to most Americans. The story is thrilling, and people thirst for it. Great.

3   However, journalistic hazards lurk. The most obvious and, in my view, the least worrisome is the danger of becoming a propaganda

arm for the government—passive, uncritical and gullible. Of course no one should expect the news media to be neutral. Are we supposed to be indifferent to the outcome? As ordinary Americans, reporters, editors and their families are as vulnerable to terrorism as anyone else. And news organizations are special targets.

4   But just because our sympathies are clear doesn't mean we've lost our skepticism. Already, papers and TV news programs are filled with stories suggesting that the "war on terrorism" is going badly and that the Pentagon, the CIA and the FBI don't know what they're doing. For better or worse, modern journalism is reflexively skeptical of government officials (though not necessarily of government). Vietnam and Watergate have left their marks. The other safeguard against parochialism* is the war's international character. Coverage is global; foreign media—monitored by our own media—ensure different perspectives.

5   The greater danger, I suspect, is just the opposite. It is that our new obsession with terrorism will make us its unwitting accomplices. We will become (and have already partly become) merchants of fear. Case in point: the anthrax fright. Until now, anthrax has been a trivial threat to public health and safety: four people have died of the 17 known to have been infected. So far, it's the functional equivalent of a mad gunman on the loose or a biological Unabomber. By contrast, there were 42,000 deaths from car accidents and 17,000 from homicides in 1998.

6   Yet, the news media have treated anthrax as a lurking scourge that might quickly strike all. I understand the causes of this: the closeness of Sept. 11; the fact that it's in the mail system; its appearance at highly visible places (Congress, the Supreme Court, news organizations); the speed with which it kills, if inhaled; the fear of the unknown and the specter of a broader attack. Still, the coverage has so far been all out of proportion to the actual threat.

7   No self-respecting editor wants to be accused—after some future terrorist act—of not having pointed out the obvious risks beforehand. Sensationalism seems justified. The ensuing explosion of stories has highlighted our multiple vulnerabilities: to chemical, biological and nuclear devices; or at airports, reservoirs, stadiums and nuclear plants. Similarly, no public figure wants to be crucified for having concealed warnings of terrorist attacks if the attacks actually occur, because the warnings would almost certainly be revealed. On its simplest level, this is why we've had two warnings from the Bush administration against unspecified terrorist threats and one from California

Gov. Gray Davis about threats to the state's bridges. Public officials and the news media both have understandable incentives to be alarmist.

8 The perverse result is that we may become the terrorists' silent allies. Terrorism is not just about death and destruction. It's also about creating fear, sowing suspicion, undermining confidence in public leadership, provoking people—and governments—into doing things that they might not otherwise do. It is an assault as much on our psychology as on our bodies.

9 Let me admit: I have no superior insight about where and how to draw the line. Because what happened on Sept. 11 was so unimaginable, almost any threat—no matter how implausible it once seemed—now seems conceivable. But I do know that the sort of saturation coverage that we're now getting may create false fears and false expectations. It may take years to find the source of anthrax; the Unabomber was caught almost two decades after his first bomb, and not until he was turned in by his brother. Nor can we protect ourselves against every possible threat. But exaggerated fears may stimulate hoaxes or convert minor terrorist acts into large public events.

10 The fate of the war against terrorism will be determined more by the nation's ability to roll up terrorist networks and prevent the spread of weapons of mass destruction than by our ability to fortify every potential target against every potential danger. The effort to do that could prove enormously costly and disruptive of everyday life without, in the end, actually improving our security. Pursuing this important story, we media types need to recognize that our very zealousness* makes us part of the story and, possibly, not for the good.

CHECKING YOUR COMPREHENSION

Directions: Circle the letter of the correct answer.

1. What's the implied main idea of the entire reading?

   a. Given enough time, the media can make any issue seem trivial.

   b. The tragedy of 9/11 gave the media a renewed sense of purpose, and most news people are determined to recover the respect they had lost.

    c. Although the tragedy of 9/11 gave the media a renewed sense of purpose, there is still the danger that the media will not just report on terrorism but also contribute to it.

    d. The news media's skepticism of the government is only further contributing to the atmosphere of fear in the United States.

2. In paragraph 1, Gary Condit and Monica Lewinsky are mentioned to illustrate the main idea, which appears in

    a. sentence 1.

    b. sentence 2.

    c. sentence 3.

3. The transitions *But* and *Before that* in paragraph 1 signal

    a. contrast and time order.

    b. addition and consequence.

    c. time order and similarity.

    d. time order and consequence.

4. What main idea is implied in paragraph 2?

    a. Journalists must now focus on serious reports about scientific matters.

    b. Journalists now need to understand the various Islamic sects.

    c. Journalists now have to write stories that have a serious purpose.

    d. Journalists today must understand and report on complex defense matters.

5. What is the main idea of paragraph 3?

    a. Journalists cannot be completely objective.

    b. Journalists may well end up reporting pure propaganda.

    c. Journalists can now pursue stories of real importance, but even with this goal, there are dangers.

    d. Journalists can no longer afford to be objective.

6. With what type of sentence does paragraph 5 open?

    a. an introductory sentence

b. a topic sentence

c. a transitional sentence

7. Which statement best expresses the main idea of paragraph 5?

 a. The media did a superb job reporting on the anthrax scare.

 b. Anthrax can no longer be considered a trivial threat to public safety.

 c. The media may help terrorists by reporting on their activities and making the public fearful.

 d. Car accidents are a bigger threat to our lives than terrorism is.

8. Which statement best expresses the main idea of paragraph 7?

 a. Every news editor wants to be the first to point out the risks facing the American public.

 b. No one wants to be accused of having ignored the threat of a terrorist attack; thus there is a natural tendency in both the media and the government to overreact.

 c. Any public figure who ignores the threat of a terrorist attack will be the object of intense criticism should an attack really occur.

 d. Although their intentions may be good, members of the media who insist on staying in an alarmist mode are doing the public a great disservice.

9. What's the implied main idea of paragraph 8?

 a. Terrorists do not care about the amount of the death and destruction they cause.

 b. Terrorism attacks the mind more than the body.

 c. By reporting on terrorists and their actions, the media may unintentionally become their accomplices.

10. Overall, the reading is organized by which pattern?

 a. comparison and contrast

 b. time order

 c. classification

 d. cause and effect

DEEPENING YOUR UNDERSTANDING

Directions: Answer the following questions by circling the letter of the correct response or filling in the blanks where required.

1. How would you describe the author's tone?

    a. skeptical

    b. concerned

    c. objective

    d. irate

2. What would you say is the author's purpose?

    a. to describe the media's response to the 9/11 tragedy

    b. to persuade both the media and the public that alarmism is dangerous

3. Why does the author allude to Gary Condit and Monica Lewinsky in paragraph 1?

    _____

    _____

4. Would you call the following statement (paragraph 1) a fact or an opinion?

    "But before Sept. 11, the press was caught in a prolonged process of self-trivialization."

    _____

5. The author of this reading alludes to Watergate and Vietnam in paragraph 4. You have encountered these two allusions in previous readings. Why does the author use them here? What point does he want to make?

    _____

    _____

6. How does the author support his claim in paragraph 3 that the press is unlikely to become a "propaganda arm for the government"?

_____

_____

7. The author uses the phrase "merchants of fear" in paragraph 5. What figure of speech is that?

   a. simile

   b. metaphor

   The author uses this figure of speech to make what point?

   _____

8. The author compares the threat of anthrax to that of a "mad gunman on the loose or a biological Unabomber" (paragraph 5). What is the point of the comparison?

   _____

   _____

9. According to paragraph 4, the author believes that the foreign press will be a safeguard against parochialism. But he never says why parochialism is bad. Why do you think he believes we need to safeguard ourselves against parochialism?

   _____

   _____

10. Describe how the author sees the role of the foreign press in our fight against terrorism.

    _____

    _____

AIRING YOUR OPINIONS

1. Do you agree or disagree that the news media are facing the "journalistic hazards" described by the author? Please explain your answer.

2. Do you agree or disagree with the author's description of the news media prior to 9/11? Please explain your answer.

3. Do you share the author's opinion that the tragedy of 9/11 transformed the media and gave members back a seriousness of purpose? Please explain your answer.

Reading 3

Arab and Muslim America: A Snapshot

GETTING FOCUSED

In the aftermath of the terrorist attacks on 9/11, writer Shibley Telhami feels it necessary to offer readers a "snapshot" of Arab and Muslim America. He also tries to explain how terrorism on the part of Muslim fundamentalists made Muslim and Arab Americans think more deeply about where their loyalties lay.

Textbook Features and Readers'. Strategies

Feature:	*Use of the word* snapshot *in the title suggests that the author wants to give you a picture of Arab and Muslim Americans.*
Strategy:	As the author adds detail after detail, keep asking yourself: What does each piece of information add to my picture, or "snapshot," of Arab and Muslim Americans?
Feature:	*The title and the first heading suggest a comparison and contrast pattern that focuses on both similarities and differences.*
Strategy:	Read to get a clear sense of the similarities and differences between Arab and Muslim Americans. Ask yourself what each difference or similarity contributes to the author's "snapshot."

Textbook Features and Readers' Strategies (continued)

Feature: *The main ideas are not always stated in topic sentences; the author often relies on readers to draw the appropriate inferences.*

Strategy: When there's no topic sentence, make sure you infer a main idea that can sum up the statements the author actually makes.

Feature: *Some of the paragraphs are quite long.*

Strategy: The longer the paragraph, the more likely it is that the main idea will emerge later in the paragraph.

Feature: *The word* identity *appears repeatedly in the reading.*

Strategy: Each time you see the word, pay special attention to how it's being used.

Evaluating Your Background Knowledge

The author of this reading is relying on your knowledge of these words and terms. Look over this list carefully to make sure you know everything on it. *Note:* The number in parentheses indicates the paragraph where the word can be found while an asterisk accompanies the word's first appearance in the reading.

Mohamed Atta (1): the man considered to be the leader of the terrorists who crashed planes into the World Trade Center and the Pentagon

Sikhs (6):   followers of a religion that combines elements of Hinduism and Islam

resonated (7): had a profound, or deep, response

Palestinian-Israeli conflict (10): The dispute between Israelis and Arabs over ownership of what was historically called Palestine, or "the Holy Land" (because of its importance to Judaism, Christianity, and Islam). Despite progress toward peace, the conflict continues to this day. From the perspective of many Arabs, the United States has been more supportive of the Israeli than of the Arab cause.

profiling (11): a procedure whereby law enforcement officials focus on a particular group on the assumption that members are more likely to commit crimes

1 In a *New York Times* article appearing a week after the horror that befell America on September 11, a Muslim woman described her dilemma this way: "I am so used to thinking about myself as a New Yorker that it took me a few days to begin to see myself as a stranger might: a Muslim woman, an outsider, perhaps an enemy of the city. Before last week, I had thought of myself as a lawyer, a feminist, a wife, a sister, a friend, a woman on the street. Now I begin to see myself as a brown woman who bears a vague resemblance to the images of terrorists we see on television and in the newspapers. I can only imagine how much more difficult it is for men who look like Mohamed Atta* or Osama bin Laden."

2 Excruciating moments like those the nation experienced last September test the identity of all Americans, but especially those whose identity may be caught in the middle. Many Arab and Muslim Americans lost loved ones and friends in the attacks in New York and Washington, and others had loved ones dispatched to Afghanistan as American soldiers to punish those who perpetrated the horror (Muslims are the largest minority religion in the U.S. armed forces). But many also had double fears for their own children. On the one hand, they shared the fears of all Americans about the new risks of terror; on the other, they were gripped by the haunting fear of their children being humiliated in school for who they are.

Two Partially Overlapping Communities

3 There is much that's misunderstood about Arabs and Muslims in America. Although the two communities share a great deal, they differ significantly in their make-up. Most Arabs in America are not Muslim, and most Muslims are not Arabs. Most Arab Americans came from Lebanon and Syria, in several waves of immigration beginning at the outset of the 20th century. Most Muslim Americans are African American or from South Asia. Many of the early Arab immigrants assimilated well in American society. Arab-American organizations are fond of highlighting prominent Americans of at least partial Arab descent: Ralph Nader, George Mitchell, John Sununu, Donna Shalala, Spencer Abraham, Bobby Rahal, Doug Flutie, Jacques Nasser, Paul Anka, Frank Zappa, Paula Abdul, among many others. Like other ethnic groups in America, Arabs and Muslims have produced many successful Americans whose ethnic background is merely an afterthought.

4 Arab Americans now number more than 3 million, Muslims roughly 6 million (though estimates range from 3 million to 10 million). The

income of Arab Americans is among the highest of any American ethnic group—second only to that of Jewish Americans. Arab Americans have become increasingly politicized over the years. According to a recent survey, proportionately more Arab Americans contribute to presidential candidates than any other ethnic group—and the groups surveyed included Asian Americans, Italian Americans, African Americans, Hispanic Americans, and Jewish Americans. Over the past decade especially, Arab-American political clout has increased. Although Arab Americans were long shunned by political candidates, President Clinton became the first sitting president to speak at conferences of Arab-American organizations, and both President Clinton and President Bush have normalized ongoing consultations with Arab- and Muslim-American leaders. In the fall 2000 election, presidential candidates sought the support of Arab Americans, not only for campaign contributions, but also as swing voters in key states, especially Michigan. The September 11 tragedy, coming just as Arab-American political clout was ascendant, has provided a real test for the community's role in American society and politics.

Impact of September 11

5   For Arab and Muslim leaders, the terrorist crisis has been like no other. It has forced them to contemplate profoundly their identity. Are they Arabs and Muslims living in America, or are they Americans with Arab and Muslim background? The answer came within hours after the terrorist attacks. Major Arab and Muslim organizations issued statements strongly condemning the attacks, refusing to allow their typical frustrations with issues of American policy in the Middle East to become linked to their rejection of the terror. Rarely have Arab and Muslim organizations in the United States been so assertive.

6   The enormity of the horror, the Middle Eastern background of the terrorists, and the terrorists' attempt to use religion to justify their acts have inevitably led to episodes of discrimination against Arabs and Muslims, as well as against those, such as Sikhs,* who resemble them. But the support that both Arabs and Muslims received from thousands of people and organizations far outweighed the negative reaction. Arab and Muslim organizations were flooded with letters and calls of empathy from leaders and ordinary Americans, including many Jewish Americans, for most understood that at stake were the civil liberties of all Americans.

7   In large part, the public reaction was a product of quick decisions and statements by President Bush and members of his cabinet, members of

Congress from both parties, and local political leaders. The president in particular acted quickly to make two central points that seem to have resonated* with most of the public. The first was that the terrorists did not represent Islam and that Osama bin Laden must not be allowed to turn his terror into a conflict between Islam and the West. The second was that Muslim and Arab Americans are loyal Americans whose rights must be respected. Bush's early appearance at a Washington, D.C., mosque with Muslim-American leaders underlined the message.

8   The message seems to have gotten through. Despite the fears that many Americans now associate with people of Middle-Eastern background, a survey conducted in late October by Zogby International found that most Americans view the Muslim religion positively and that the vast majority of Arabs and Muslims approve the president's handling of the crisis. (Among Arab Americans, 83 percent give President Bush a positive performance rating.) Moreover, 69 percent of Arab Americans support "an all-out war against countries which harbor or aid terrorists."

9   Certainly, the events of September 11 will intensify the debate within the Arab and Muslim communities in America about who they are and what their priorities should be. One thing is already clear. Although both communities have asserted their American identity as never before and although 65 percent of Arab Americans feel embarrassed because the attacks were apparently committed by people from Arab countries, their pride in their heritage has not diminished. The October survey found that 88 percent of Arab Americans are extremely proud of their heritage. So far, however, the terrorist attacks have not affected the priorities of the Arab public in America as might be expected, given Arab Americans' deep fear of discrimination.

10   Typically, Arab-American organizations highlight such domestic issues as secret evidence and racial profiling and such foreign policy issues as Jerusalem, Iraq, and the Palestinian-Israeli conflict.* While Arab Americans, like other minorities, are involved in all American issues and are divided as Democrats and Republicans, as groups they inevitably focus on issues about which they tend to agree. The situation is no different from that of American Jews, who are also diverse, but whose organizations largely focus on issues of common interest.

11   Given the fear of profiling* that Arab Americans had even before September, one would expect this issue to have become central for most of them since September 11. And for many it certainly has.

Arab-American organizations, especially, have focused on it. But the findings of the Zogby poll among Arab Americans in October were surprising. Although 32 percent of Arab Americans reported having personally experienced discrimination in the past because of their ethnicity, and although 37 percent said they or their family members had experienced discrimination since September 11, 36 percent nevertheless supported profiling of Arab Americans, while 58 percent did not. Surprisingly, 54 percent of Arab Americans believed that law enforcement officials are justified in engaging in extra questioning and inspections of people with Middle Eastern accents or features.

12   Though their views on profiling have been mixed since September 11, Arab Americans have been considerably more unanimous on one subject—the need to resolve the Palestinian-Israeli dispute. Seventy-eight percent of those surveyed agreed that "a U.S. commitment to settle the Israeli-Palestinian dispute would help the president's efforts in the war against terrorism." Although most Arab Americans are Christian and mostly from Lebanon and Syria—and only a minority are Palestinians—their collective consciousness has been affected by the Palestinian issue in the same way that Arab consciousness in the Middle East has been affected. In a survey I commissioned in five Arab states (Lebanon, Syria, United Arab Emirates, Saudi Arabia, and Egypt) last spring, majorities in each country consistently ranked the Palestinian issue as "the single most important issue to them personally." The role of this issue in the collective consciousness of many Arabs and Muslims worldwide is akin to the role that Israel has come to play in contemporary Jewish identity.

13   Like all Americans since September 11, Arab and Muslim Americans are searching for solutions to terrorism. Like all Americans, they are also finding new meaning in aspects of their identity to which they might have given little thought a few short months ago.

CHECKING YOUR COMPREHENSION

Directions: Circle the letter of the correct answer.

1. Which of the following statements best paraphrases the main idea of the entire reading?

   a. Following the 9/11 terrorist attacks, Arab and Muslim Americans no longer feel at home in the United States.

b. Like the rest of the country, Muslim and Arab Americans were appalled by the terrorists' use of religion as a justification for their attacks.

c. The 9/11 terrorist attacks have forced Muslim and Arab Americans to think more about how their religious or ethnic identity affects their identity as U.S. citizens.

d. Thanks to the efforts of President Bush, and their own decency and common sense, most U.S. citizens refused to accept that the beliefs of the 9/11 terrorists were shared by all members of the Arab and Muslim communities.

2. What inference should readers draw from the last sentence in paragraph 1?

    a. The woman believes she has become the object of prejudice because of her ethnic identity.

    b. The woman believes that Muslim or Arab men will be the special object of threats and prejudices because they will remind people of the terrorists involved in the 9/11 attacks.

    c. The woman believes that Arabs and Muslims have always been the object of prejudice, but that after 9/11, it is easier to express that prejudice out in the open.

3. The topic sentence of paragraph 3 suggests which pattern of organization?

    a. definition

    b. cause and effect

    c. comparison and contrast

    d. time order

4. In paragraph 5, the author asks: "Are they Arabs and Muslims living in America, or are they Americans with Arab and Muslim background?" What answer can you infer from the details given?

    a. They are Americans with Arab and Muslim backgrounds.

    b. They are Arabs and Muslims living in America.

    c. They no longer know how to identify themselves.

    d. They are afraid to say that they are Arabs and Muslims living in America.

5. Which statement best paraphrases the main idea of paragraph 6?

   a. Because of the terrorist attacks, discrimination against Arab Americans has increased, and many fear that the situation will worsen with time.

   b. Although the events of 9/11 led to some discrimination against Arabs and Muslims, the discrimination was offset by the outpouring of public support.

   c. Jewish Americans were quick to show their support for Arab and Muslim Americans.

   d. Because members of the Sikh community are often perceived to be Arabs or Muslims, they too were the victims of discriminatory acts.

6. Which pattern of organization dominates paragraphs 5–7?

   a. comparison and contrast

   b. cause and effect

   c. definition

   d. time order

7. What's the implied main idea of paragraph 11?

   a. Many Arab Americans have been the object of discrimination in the past and are therefore strongly opposed to the use of profiling in the fight against terrorism.

   b. Even before 9/11, the issue of profiling was of great concern to Arab Americans.

   c. Profiling has long been an issue of concern to Arab Americans, and it has become even more so since the events of 9/11.

   d. Profiling is not a concern for Arab Americans.

8. In paragraph 12, the survey cited supports which main idea?

   a. Most Arab Americans are Christians rather than Muslims.

   b. Arab Americans are unanimously against the use of profiling in the war against terror.

   c. The majority of Arab Americans are deeply concerned about the Palestinian-Israeli dispute.

   d. Most Muslim Americans believe that the U.S. government has not given enough attention to the Palestinian-Israeli conflict.

9. In paragraph 8, the survey by Zogby International is used to support which main idea?

    a. President Bush reacted quickly to protect the rights of Arabs and Muslims after the 9/11 tragedy.

    b. The message that the terrorists did not represent all Muslims, most of whom are loyal Americans, seems to have gotten through to the American public.

    c. Unfortunately, in the aftermath of 9/11, many Americans became mistrustful of anyone who came from the Middle East.

    d. The majority of Arab Americans fully support the idea of an all-out war with any country harboring terrorists.

10. In paragraph 9, the second sentence is a

    a. topic sentence.

    b. transitional sentence.

    c. supporting detail.

DEEPENING YOUR UNDERSTANDING

Directions: Answer the following questions by circling the letter of the correct answer or filling in the blanks where required.

1. How would you describe the author's tone?

    a. concerned

    b. neutral

    c. skeptical

    d. outraged

2. What would you say is the author's purpose?

    a. to explain the differences between Arab and Muslim Americans

    b. to persuade readers that 9/11 has left Arab and Muslim Americans with a sense of split identity

3. In paragraph 1, the author quotes from an article in the *New York Times*. What does the quotation illustrate about the effect of 9/11 on the lives of Arab and Muslim Americans?

_____

_____

4. Why do you think the author thought it important to mention in paragraph 2 that "Muslims are the largest minority religion in the U.S. armed forces"?

_____

_____

5. What purpose do the allusions to people such as consumer activist Ralph Nader, former senator George Mitchell, and football player Doug Flutie (paragraph 3) serve?

_____

_____

6. In paragraph 5, the author poses a question about the identity of Arabs and Muslims living in the United States. He says the response to that question came within hours after the terrorist attacks but doesn't tell us what the answer was. Rather, he relates what Arab and Muslim organizations did. What answer is implied by those actions?

_____

_____

7. How would you label the following statement: "Surprisingly, 54 percent of Arab Americans believed that law enforcement officials are justified in engaging in extra questioning and inspections of people with Middle Eastern accents or features" (paragraph 11).

a. fact

b. opinion

c. a blend of both

Please explain your answer. _____

_____

8. Is the word *snapshot* in the title a metaphor or a simile?

_____

9. Look up the words *snapshot* and *photograph* in a desk dictionary to answer the following question: The words *snapshot* and *photograph* can, in some cases, be used synonymously. Is this reading's title—"Arab and Muslim America: A Snapshot"—one of those instances

where the word *photograph* would have done just as well?_____

Please explain your answer.

_____

_____

10. The author ends the reading with the repetition of the phrase, "Like all Americans. . . ." When writers consciously repeat a phrase, they do it for emphasis. What does the author want to emphasize in this instance?

_____

AIRING YOUR OPINIONS

Imagine that you are standing in line at the bus station when two men who appear to be of Arab descent are pulled from the line and questioned before they are allowed to get on the bus. They are also asked to show identification before they can board. The bus company is clearly engaged in profiling. What's your response to this situation? Do you approve or disapprove of the bus company's behavior? Please explain your answer.

Reading 4   # Airline Insecurity

GETTING FOCUSED

In this reading, journalists Barry Yeoman and Bill Hogan outline the changes in airline security that were a result of the 9/11 tragedy. They also offer a disturbing explanation of why those changes didn't happen sooner.

Textbook Features and Readers' Strategies

Feature: *The title takes a stand announcing that the airlines are or were lacking in security.*

Strategy: From the very first sentence, keep asking yourself why the authors believe that the airlines were or are insecure.

Feature: *Using a pro and con pattern of development, the authors repeatedly cite a person who disagrees with their point of view; then they respond to that person's claim.*

Strategy: Underline the point made by the opposition. Then, mentally or in the margins, sum up the authors' response.

Feature: *The reading does not use headings to indicate a change in the authors' thinking.*

Strategy: Pre-read the first and last sentence of every paragraph. Put checks next to those paragraphs where you think the authors shift direction. As you read, keep asking yourself if the current passage is picking up on, modifying, or contradicting the ideas already introduced.

Feature: *The reading returns again and again to two topics: the Federal Aviation Administration (FAA) and airline-industry lobbyists.*

Strategy: Every time you see references to these subjects, give those passages extra attention.

Feature: *The reading makes numerous references to specific people.*

Strategy: Pay closest attention to those names that appear more than once. Note what they stand for or represent. In the margins, write the name of the person along with a brief comment about the position expressed.

Evaluating Your Background Knowledge

The author of this reading is relying on your knowledge of these words and terms. Look over this list carefully to make sure you know everything on it. *Note:* The number in parentheses indicates the paragraph where the word can be found while an asterisk accompanies the word's first appearance in the reading.

"Mother Jones" (5): a magazine with a strong liberal bias

scuttled (5):   abandoned, eliminated

formidable (7):   impressive, strong

Evaluating Your Background Knowledge (continued)

breach (8):   invade, break

mandatory (10):   forced

kissing the ring (13): an allusion to the way nobles would kiss the pope's ring to show their respect

resonance (15):   echo, similarity

rubber-stamp (16): approve without question

myriad (26):   many

bureaucratic process (31): a system that requires numerous and complex procedures that hinder action

1   Federal regulators have known for years that the nation's system of airport security was "seriously flawed." But the FAA repeatedly placed politics and profits above the public's safety.

2   The buzzer sounded at an awkward moment for Rep. Don Young. The Alaska Republican was halfway through a press conference on October 17, explaining why he was trying to derail efforts to turn over the screening of airline passengers to federal law enforcement officers. Six days earlier, the Senate had unanimously passed a bill that would overhaul the way airports staff their metal detectors and X-ray checkpoints. Rather than relying on private security companies, whose minimum-wage workers routinely fail to detect guns and bombs, the bill called for hiring 28,000 better-paid and better-trained government agents. But Young considered this a "knee-jerk" reaction to the September 11 terrorist attacks. "My wife Lu flies quite a lot, as do my two daughters," he told reporters. "I want my family and all Americans to have the best air security possible." Still, he added, he did not want "to tie the president's hands and force him to hire only federal employees."

3   As Young started to field questions, a mechanical screech alerted House members that they were needed across the street at the Capitol for a vote. The congressman huddled with his fellow Republicans behind the podium. "We'll be back," he said—and with that, he handed over the microphone to a man named Kenneth Quinn, who wasted no time blasting the Senate bill. "A nationalized approach to

security is a step backward in the war against terrorism," Quinn declared. Rather than relying on "civil servants," he said, the government should "inspire the private sector's competitive juices."

4   Quinn was no congressional aide filling in for absent lawmakers. He works for the Aviation Security Association, a lobbying group for private screening companies. His clients, who are paid $700 million by the airlines each year to screen passengers and baggage, have been cited repeatedly for sloppy performance. Many pay their employees so little—wages are sometimes $11,000 a year, with few benefits—that workers must hold down two jobs to make ends meet. Almost all wind up quitting: On average, airports are forced to replace their entire screening workforces every year. In October 2000, a federal judge ordered the largest company, Argenbright Security, to pay a fine of $1 million for hiring violent felons, falsifying their background checks, and "training" the new hires with 45-minute videos. As reporters took notes at the press conference, however, Quinn declared that taking business away from companies like Argenbright would be "a huge mistake."

5   A month later, Congress voted to replace private screeners with federal employees. But Young's decision to leave a corporate lobbyist running the show underscores why airports have remained unsafe for so long. A review by *Mother Jones** of court documents, lobbying disclosure forms, campaign finance records, government audits, and the docket of the Federal Aviation Administration—as well as interviews with numerous experts—shows that when it comes to airline security, the aviation industry has remained firmly in control. With the cooperation of the FAA, industry leaders have scuttled* or watered down just about every significant reform that has been proposed over the past dozen years, including the recommendations of two high-profile presidential commissions.

6   They've accomplished this, in part, through generous campaign contributions: The airlines gave almost $4.2 million to both political parties during the 2000 elections. They've also deployed a squadron of lobbyists that includes the best—and best-connected—talent that money can buy. More than half of the airline industry's 200 lobbyists used to work on Capitol Hill or in the executive branch, including 10 former members of Congress, 2 former transportation secretaries, 3 former high-ranking FAA officials, and 15 former White House aides. Quinn was the FAA's top lawyer under the elder President Bush. Linda Hall Daschle, the wife of Senate Majority Leader Tom Daschle, worked for the Air Transport Association, a lobbying group

composed of the major airlines, before serving as the FAA's acting administrator under President Clinton; she now lobbies for American and Northwest airlines. All told, the top nine U.S. airlines and their lobbying group typically spend more than $15 million a year lobbying Congress, the Department of Transportation, the FAA, the National Transportation Safety Board, and the White House.

7   "Clearly, from my experience, the airline industry has one of the most formidable* and most aggressive groups of lobbyists representing any industry," says Senator Peter Fitzgerald, a Republican from Illinois. "In the three years that I've been in Washington, I don't think I've seen anything the airlines favor die, or anything they oppose pass."

8   Since September 11, Americans have become all too familiar with the flaws in the nation's aviation security. Throughout the 1990s, government inspections designed to intentionally breach* airport security met with extraordinary success. Federal inspectors found they could smuggle firearms, hand grenades, and bomb components past screening checkpoints at every airport they visited. They could walk onto planes and place objects in the cabins. They could get into cargo holds. In one probe conducted in 1999, they successfully boarded 117 airplanes—some filled with passengers—and were asked to show identification only one-fourth of the time. Mary Schiavo, the inspector general for the Department of Transportation from 1990 to 1996, says her office repeatedly recommended security improvements, including a system to match checked bags with onboard passengers. "The FAA simply didn't want to hear about it," she says. "They said since we had never had a major domestic terrorist incident against aviation, the risk was low."

9   Ever since 1988, when a bomb in a suitcase destroyed Pan Am Flight 103 over Lockerbie, Scotland, experts have sounded increasingly forceful alarms. "The U.S. civil aviation security system is seriously flawed and has failed to provide the proper level of protection for the traveling public," concluded a 1990 report by the President's Commission on Aviation Security and Terrorism, appointed by then-President Bush. "This system needs major reform."

10   The Bush commission's report recommended dozens of new measures. It called for more rigorous training of the workers who screen passengers entering airport terminals. It proposed a system to ensure that a would-be bomber doesn't check a suitcase full of explosives onto a plane and then fail to board himself. And, upon learning that some of the baggage clerks working for Flight 103 had criminal records, the

commission recommended the FBI run background checks on everyone working at airports. "The case for mandatory* criminal-record checks for airport employees is at least as compelling as for employees in industries such as securities and banking," the panel concluded.

11   But the airline industry used its clout to block implementation of the new criminal-check rule. The Air Transport Association argued the measure would cost the airlines more than $1 billion, with limited effectiveness. To press its case, it hired a man who could normally be expected to advocate background checks: William Webster, the former director of the FBI and CIA. Webster argued the reform "would subject the industry to a very heavy diversion of resources" without catching would-be bombers. The lobbying worked: It took the FAA five years to adopt a rule to weed out criminals—and in the end, it required the industry to conduct background checks only on employees with access to secure areas who had long gaps in their employment histories.

12   Few regulatory agencies give industry lobbyists as warm a welcome as the FAA. For its first 38 years, the close relationship was codified into the law: The agency's twofold mission was to safeguard the traveling public and to promote the aviation industry. Although Congress eliminated the FAA's promotional role in 1996, airline executives and lobbyists continue to enjoy "direct and frequent access to the administration," says Gerald Dillingham, director of civil aviation issues for the General Accounting Office, the investigative arm of Congress. "Not only do they lobby the administration, but oftentimes they serve on advisory panels the agency puts together." The agency frequently holds "industry days," in which airline executives are briefed on hot issues and given an opportunity to make recommendations behind closed doors. The calendars of FAA officials are filled with appointments with lobbyists, and many of the agency's senior employees wind up leaving to work for the private sector. Besides Quinn and Linda Daschle, former FAA Chief Counsel E. Tazwell Ellet now lobbies for the Air Transport Association, and former Assistant Chief Counsel Albert Randall works for American and Northwest.

13   As a result, many officials acknowledge, the agency has come to perceive issues the same way industry does. The process begins as soon as FAA administrators are nominated. "In order to get confirmed, they have to go around kissing the ring* of the powers-that-be in the industry," says Jim Burnett, who chaired the National Transportation Safety Board under President Reagan. "It's a process

of visiting with people who have power and trying to reassure them that you will not be a threat."

14   By 1995, when the FAA finally passed its rule requiring limited background checks, a leading congressional expert on airline security was growing concerned about how little progress had been made since the Lockerbie crash. That May, Rep. Jim Oberstar, a Minnesota Democrat, wrote to President Clinton, urging him to convene a blue-ribbon panel to review the system from top to bottom. For a year, nothing happened. It took another air disaster to trigger the next flurry of high-level discussions.

15   Just before the 1996 Olympics, TWA Flight 800 went down off the coast of Long Island in what was initially believed to be a bombing or missile attack. The explosion had eerie resonance* for Victoria Cummock, who had lost her husband over Lockerbie. The Miami widow, who had become an advocate for air crash victims, flew to New York to meet the families of TWA passengers. In a hangar at Kennedy Airport, she met with President Clinton, who invited her to serve on the brand-new White House Commission on Aviation Safety and Security. The commission would be chaired by Vice President Al Gore, lending it considerable credibility and power. It would include scientists, military experts, and high-ranking government officials. "My heart sang," Cummock says, recalling her conversation with the president. "I thought, 'Oh my God, thank God.'"

16   Her enthusiasm was short-lived. The Gore commission, as it was known, became one of the clearest examples of how politics and profit have eclipsed public safety. At their very first meeting, the commissioners were surprised to receive a pre-written set of recommendations prepared by staff members. "We were just going to rubber-stamp* them," Cummock recalls. "With each recommendation, I remember saying, 'With all due respect, Mr. Vice President, do you realize that . . . ?' People were horrified that I was interrupting the flow. They kept telling me, 'Ms. Cummock, the vice president has a press conference, then he needs to get on to other meetings.'"

17   Cummock didn't know it at the time, but the commission's initial report was a done deal before she ever saw it. A CIA memo written the day before the meeting indicates that the agency was working with the staff behind the scenes to ensure that the panel offered no dissent to the preapproved proposals. "The government members of the commission are lined up to support the recommendations," Richard Haver, a CIA official assigned to assist the committee, reported to his agency's director. Cummock, though, was a different

matter. "She is a very intelligent, intense, and attractive individual," he wrote, noting that he had tried "schmoozing" her several weeks earlier. "My estimate is that she can be kept in line if she believes progress is going to result from the effort. If she believes the effort is headed in the direction of appeasing the airlines, whom she distrusts, then she could become a major problem."

18   Immediately after the first meeting, Gore and his aides held press conferences to highlight the panel's "common-sense solutions." One of the proposals, which Cummock endorsed, was called "full bag match." Every piece of luggage loaded onto an airplane would have to be matched to a passenger on board. Any unmatched suitcase, like the one containing the bomb that killed Cummock's husband, would have to be removed before takeoff. The airlines claimed that matching bags would be time-consuming and expensive, but a study by the University of California, partly funded by the FAA, found that full bag match would take barely one minute per flight. "You probably won't even notice it," said Elaine Kamarck, one of Gore's top political advisers, at a press briefing held on September 11, 1996.

19   The airlines noticed. "We were vigorously opposed to it," says Dick Doubrava, managing director of security for the Air Transport Association. Insisting that the delays from bag matching would "impact the whole integrity of the system," the association and its member airlines launched a full-bore lobbying campaign. They met with the commission staff. They made the rounds on Capitol Hill. They leaned on members of Congress, who in turn pressured the commission to back off. And although Kamarck insists that "the vice president never met with the industry," officials at the Air Transport Association recall otherwise, noting that their president, Carol Hallett, had plenty of access to the White House. "She would routinely see Gore all the time," Doubrava says.

20   Eight days after Kamarck's press briefing, Gore sent a letter to Hallett backing off on his call for an immediate move toward full bag match. "I want to make it very clear that it is not the intent of this administration or of the commission to create a hardship for the air transportation industry or to cause inconvenience to the traveling public," he wrote. Instead of sticking with the original plan to match all bags to passengers, Gore began calling for an industry-backed alternative, in which a computerized profiling system would monitor suspicious travelers and remove their bags if they failed to board planes. The new plan was blasted by security experts, who concluded it would be simple for terrorists to evade the profiling system.

21   The nation's airlines wasted no time in expressing their thanks. The day after Gore's letter, TWA sent $40,000 to the Democratic National Committee, which was headed into the final weeks of the 1996 campaign. A month later, American Airlines came through with three contributions of $83,333 made over five days—a $250,000 burst of beneficence that it has never again matched. In the last days of the push to re-elect Clinton and Gore, Democratic Party committees also raked in $83,000 from Northwest Airlines, $117,465 from United Airlines, and $15,000 from US Airways. In all, the major airlines poured more than $500,000 into various Democratic soft-money accounts in the weeks following Gore's letter—two and a half times what they gave Republicans during the same period.

22   Michael Wascom, vice president of the Air Transport Association, calls the contributions "strictly coincidental." Kamarck, the Gore political adviser, says the prospect of campaign donations had no influence on Gore's decision to write the letter. "It didn't make a f— difference," she says. "It was October of an election year. We were 15 points ahead of Bob Dole. Everyone was giving money." In fact, the commission's staff seemed as intent on raising money as it was on improving airline safety. According to documents obtained by *Mother Jones*, campaign aides on the staff used the commission's offices, fax machine, and letterhead to draft a speech for the Democratic National Convention and to assist Maria Hsia, the party operative later convicted in the Buddhist temple fundraising scandal. When industry executives were asked to assist the commission, the requests often came from staffers who were assisting the campaign.

23   As the commission kept meeting in preparation for the release of its final report, the industry continued to lean on commissioners. A few months after the election, Billie Vincent, former director of civilian aviation security for the FAA, spoke with commission member Brian Jenkins, an antiterrorism consultant whose clients included the airlines. "He was distraught," recalls Vincent. "He related to me that somebody from the airline industry—he wouldn't say who—had contacted him and told him they were angry with his positions. They told him he should remember how much business the airlines were giving him."

24   In public hearings, commissioners sat quietly through testimony by various experts, rarely asking tough questions. In the final months, they grew even less interested in security issues after the crash of TWA Flight 800 was traced to faulty wiring rather than an act of terrorism. The FBI and CIA continued to warn the commission that serious

holes remained in the security system, and Cummock urged her colleagues not to back off. When she pressed for more meaningful give-and-take on security issues, a commission staff member pulled her aside and told her that the Christmas decorations had been put up at the White House. "If you'd like," she recalls the aide telling her, "we could arrange a VIP tour."

25   When the Gore commission issued its final report in February 1997, the industry was pleased. The commission called for a slow approach to bag match, calling it a "contentious and difficult area." It suggested private security companies be certified by the government, but made no mention of improving wages or benefits. And it gave the FAA two more years to implement FBI fingerprint checks on airport workers. The Air Transport Association praised the document as a "good compendium of the issues that the industry and the FAA and the government at large have been looking at for some time."

26   Armed with the report, the FAA vowed to develop rules to accomplish the broad mandates outlined by the commission. Over the next four years, however, the airlines mounted an all-out campaign to forestall or weaken the already-diluted security proposals. The industry filed myriad* objections to the rules, asking for delays and calling for public hearings. "The rule-making process is very easily manipulated by someone with a lot of money and expertise, and the airlines have that in spades," says Rep. Peter DeFazio, an Oregon Democrat. "Anything that would cost them money they could fight, and delay rule making for years and years." According to Elaine Kamarck, federal regulators didn't bother to fight back. "The FAA decided to pick its battles with the airlines," she says. "You had a sluggish bureaucracy under pressure from the corporate world. They paid lip service, but let the rules drag on."

27   Paul Takemoto, a spokesman for the FAA, insists the agency took the rules seriously but needed input from the airlines. "We move as fast as we can, with the understanding that we need to make sure that we're doing it right," he says. But according to a study by the General Accounting Office, it sometimes takes the agency 5 years or more to begin the rule-making process—and up to 15 years to complete it. All that while, says DeFazio, "the Air Transport Association, with its huge staff and budget, is working day in and day out to prevent things from happening."

28   The FAA did suggest criminal-background checks on more airport employees with gaps in their employment records, including workers who screen passengers, baggage, and cargo. But the airlines claimed

that vetting their current workers would be an administrative headache. "They have been good employees and do not pose a threat to aviation," TWA argued in a letter to the FAA in May 1997. "This proposed requirement would not do anything to increase aviation security. It would only add unnecessary costs and paperwork to the industry." The same day, a lobbying group for airport-service companies called the National Air Transportation Association weighed in, protesting that it would be difficult to run checks on baggage and cargo screeners, fuel truck operators, and other workers whose previous employers often kept few records.

29   In the end, the FAA narrowed its rule even further. It exempted baggage and cargo screeners from background checks, and called for checks only on new applicants for passenger-screening jobs with long employment gaps—less than 1 percent of all airport workers hired. Federal agents are now investigating the possibility that the September 11 hijackers were aided by renegade airport employees.

30   While the FAA did issue a modest rule on criminal checks, it issued no rule at all on another key recommendation of the Gore plan. The commission had recommended that before an airline hires a private security firm to screen passengers and baggage, the federal government must certify that the company provides minimal training for workers and periodically tests their performance. Congress ordered the FAA to create a certification rule by May 2001.

31   The Air Transport Association insists it has always supported screening-company certification. "There was no resistance," says Doubrava, the group's security chief. But a review of government dockets shows that the airlines themselves were quietly working to delay and weaken the regulation that the FAA eventually came up with. "The proposed rule will have a major economic impact on Alaska Airlines' long-term conducting of business," a company executive wrote to the FAA in April 2000. The letter enumerated three pages of specific objections, arguing that it would "not be costeffective" to recertify companies every five years and adding that the airline didn't want to be held responsible if one of its screening companies violated the law. The next day, Midway Airlines chimed in, calling it an "unnecessary burden" to require that employees have a week of full-time experience before training newcomers. And United Express said it supported screener certification—as long as the FAA exempted all existing security firms from the "rigorous application process." In the end, the FAA missed its congressional deadline, and the rule plodded its way through the bureaucratic process* without being approved.

32   In the first weeks after the September 11 attacks, measures that had previously been stalled were suddenly put on the fast track. FAA administrator Jane Garvey ordered criminal-history checks for all airport workers with access to secure areas. She also ordered the acceleration of a program to put in new machines to detect explosives at the nation's largest airports. "Everything has changed," says Takemoto, the FAA spokesman. "It's a completely different environment. It should make it easier to accomplish things that, sadly, we would not have been able to accomplish before September 11."

33   Those emergency measures, though, didn't solve the underlying problems. A month after the hijackings, a passenger made it through the security checkpoint in New Orleans International Airport and onto a Southwest flight carrying a loaded derringer. Two weeks later, workers employed by Argenbright Security failed to detain a man who passed through a checkpoint at Chicago's O'Hare International Airport with a stun gun, a can of pepper spray, and nine knives.

34   Nevertheless, industry officials continued to fight measures to help prevent airline terrorism, citing their concerns for the bottom line. At one recent congressional hearing, Alaska Airlines president John Kelly spoke out against a $2.50 to $3 surcharge to pay for enhanced security, suggesting the fee would scare away potential passengers. "The people do not respond to anything other than the total price," he told the House Transportation Committee. "That is strictly supply and demand." When Rep. DeFazio suggested that airline tickets could say "security surcharge" in large letters, Kelly remained unmoved. "People still make decisions on whether to fly based on how much it costs," he said.

35   Private security companies also fought efforts to place airport screening in the hands of federal law enforcement officers. "No one would think of contracting out the FBI," said Senator Fritz Hollings, a South Carolina Democrat, during a debate in October over the Senate bill to federalize the screening workforce. "No one would ever think about contracting out the security and protection of the president." But despite the unanimous vote in the Senate to eliminate private contractors, Republicans in the House sided with the security firms, passing an alternative bill on November 1 that would have kept the screening business in the hands of private companies unless the president ordered otherwise. Bush backed the measure, and the airlines bowed out of the fight, saying only that they no longer wanted responsibility for overseeing screeners.

36   On November 16, lawmakers finally agreed on a compromise to make all airport screeners federal employees. But in a nod to private screening companies, airports will be given what Rep. Don Young calls the "flexibility" to opt out of the system after three years and resume contracting with private firms.

37   Even with the increase in federal oversight, security experts note that it will take more than a single law to make air travel truly secure. Jim Burnett, the former head of the National Transportation Safety Board, says that unless federal regulators take a tougher approach—one that doesn't place the industry's profit margins above all else—security reforms will continue to drag on for years, stalled by industry lobbying and regulatory inaction. "If the FAA doesn't move away from the consensus-type regulatory behavior," he says, "we may walk away from these things with a lot of visible steps being taken, but without really having put in an effective security system."

CHECKING YOUR UNDERSTANDING

Directions: Circle the letter of the correct answer.

1. Which of the following statements best paraphrases the main idea of the entire reading?

   a. Americans have learned the hard way that airline security, even if it means higher ticket prices and longer waits in line, is worth every dollar and every inconvenience.

   b. Without the FAA, airline passengers would be in even greater danger.

   c. Up until the 9/11 tragedy, lobbyists continuously worked against increasing airline security, but they abandoned their efforts in the wake of the terrorists' attack.

   d. Because of the FAA's close ties to the airline industry, airline security has never been as tight as it should be.

2. According to the authors, Kenneth Quinn's taking over for Congressman Don Young (paragraphs 2–5) illustrates what point?

   a. Congress works too closely with lobbyists when creating legislation.

b. Lobbyists for the airlines have frequently hindered improvements in airline security.

c. Journalists should not be listening to lobbyists when covering issues related to airline security.

d. Despite appearances, Congress is not influenced by lobbyists.

3. Based on what the authors say, you can infer that

   a. only the Republicans have been influenced by airline lobbyists.

   b. only the Democrats have been influenced by airline lobbyists.

   c. airline lobbyists have heavily influenced the actions of both parties.

4. What inference do the authors want you to draw from paragraph 8?

   a. Despite inspections in the 1990s showing how easy it was to avoid airport security, the FAA failed to take appropriate actions.

   b. Because there had never been a terrorist incident involving an airline, federal inspectors were not concerned about possible security breaches.

   c. If federal inspectors had publicly complained about the possibility of security breaches, the FAA would have acted to bring about changes.

   d. Federal inspections throughout the 1990s revealed only a few minor problems with airport security.

5. In paragraph 11, William Webster's argument is a supporting detail used to show how

   a. the FBI and CIA were intent on reforming airline security.

   b. people in Washington are constantly changing sides.

   c. the airlines used political influence to defeat a needed security measure.

   d. slow the FAA is to act, no matter how great the threat to national security.

6. The fact that a former FAA chief counsel E. Tazwell Ellet (paragraph 12) now works as an airline lobbyist is used to illustrate what point?

   a. Most Washington lobbyists are homegrown.

   b. The FAA has an incredibly close relationship with airline lobbyists.

   c. Everyone who ever worked for the FAA has ended up becoming a lobbyist for the airlines.

   d. The FAA hosts industry days to make sure the airlines are fully apprised of new developments.

7. According to the authors (paragraph 16), the Gore commission illustrated how

   a. political commissions are often used to convince the public that things will change when they will actually stay the same.

   b. the airlines sabotaged public safety.

   c. public safety can be ignored in favor of money and politics.

   d. an outsider willing to challenge those in established positions of power can make a difference.

8. Which inference do the authors expect readers to draw from paragraph 27?

   a. Despite complaints, the FAA moves as quickly as possible to resolve security problems.

   b. Despite Paul Takemoto's claim that the FAA move as quickly as possible, the record shows it takes the FAA years to make changes.

   c. It's naive to assume that large-scale changes can be made in a matter of months, but the FAA is clearly doing its best to act in a timely fashion.

   d. The FAA wants to avoid making any changes in airline security.

9. What inference do the authors want readers to draw from this reading?

   a. Improvements in airline security have been made and there are more to come.

   b. If the FAA doesn't change its methods, we may never have an effective airline security system.

   c. The FAA will eventually be dismantled and once that happens, we will have an effective airline security system.

10. What pattern organizes this reading?

    a. cause and effect

    b. definition

    c. comparison and contrast

    d. classification

DEEPENING YOUR UNDERSTANDING

Directions: Answer the following questions by circling the letter of the correct response or filling in the blanks where required.

1. How would you describe the authors' tone?

    a. neutral

    b. sympathetic

    c. angry

    d. concerned

2. What would you say is the authors' purpose?

    a. to describe the process by which changes in airline security are made

    b. to persuade readers that the airlines fight changes in security if those changes would diminish their profits

3. Why do you think Victoria Cummock was able to speak her mind during meetings of the Gore commission while others were horrified that she was "interrupting the flow" (paragraph 16)?

_____

_____

4. Do you think the authors believe that one political party is better

than the other at avoiding lobbyists' influence?_____

Please explain your answer. _____

_____

5. Which statement best describes the authors' attitude toward the FAA?

   a. The authors are so biased against the FAA, they wouldn't be able to recognize its real efforts to make changes in airline security.

   b. The authors are highly critical of the FAA, but they do not ignore evidence that contradicts their position.

   c. The authors show no evidence of bias.

   Please explain your answer. _____

   _____

6. In paragraph 31, the authors cite the Air Transport Association's security chief, who says the airlines showed no resistance to changes in security measures. How do the authors respond to this claim?

   _____

7. In paragraph 33, the authors say that new emergency measures implemented after 9/11 don't solve the "underlying problems." What evidence do they offer for that claim?

   _____

   How would you evaluate that evidence? Is it both relevant and

   adequate? Please explain your answer. _____

   _____

   _____

8. In paragraph 35, Senator Fritz Hollings is quoted as saying: "No one would ever think about contracting out the security and protection of the president." What's the point of his statement?

   _____

9. In paragraph 36, the authors describe how airports will be given the "flexibility" to opt out of using federal employees as screeners, calling that option "a nod to private screening companies." What does the use of the word *nod* imply?

   _____

10. Would you say that the reading ends on an optimistic or a pessimistic note?_____

Please explain your answer. _____

AIRING YOUR OPINIONS

1. Imagine you have to fly somewhere in the next six months. Did this reading make you feel more or less secure about flying? Please explain your answer.

2. The authors do not hold the FAA in high esteem. Do you think that they offer a convincing argument as to why readers should share their point of view? Please explain your answer.

It's Not About the Money

GETTING FOCUSED

Shortly after the tragedy of 9/11, Congress passed legislation that guaranteed compensation for the victims of the terrorists' attacks. At the time, a few lone voices warned that the compensation, although well intentioned, was a bad idea. Now, as writer Lisa Belkin points out, those voices have swelled to a chorus.

Textbook Features and Readers' Strategies	
Feature:	*This is a long article with no headings to signal shifts in the writer's train of thought.*
Strategy:	Before reading in earnest, pre-read the first and last sentence of every paragraph. Anytime a paragraph seems to veer away from the point of the previous one, put a check next to the paragraph to signal a change in direction. When you read the article from beginning to end, slow down your reading rate for the paragraphs that are checked. Make sure you understand how the author's train of thought has changed.
Feature:	*The author usually introduces a main idea and then follows with three or four paragraphs that explain it.*
Strategy:	Every time you find a new idea developed over several paragraphs, jot that idea in the margins and use arrows or double lines to identify the paragraphs that develop that one point.

Textbook Features and Readers' Strategies (continued)

Feature: *There are repeated references to the Victim Compensation Fund set up for the relatives of 9/11 victims.*

Strategy: As you read, see if you can summarize the fund's goals and recount the way in which it came about.

Feature: *This reading comes from the* New York Times Magazine. *Like most articles from that source, this one will develop a specific position about the Victim Compensation Fund.*

Strategy: From the moment you start reading, your focus should be on determining the author's point of view by answering the question: What is the author's opinion of the Victim Compensation Fund?

Feature: *Early on in the reading, the author uses a series of questions to suggest her point of view.*

Strategy: Imagine how you might answer those questions to figure out what the author's questions imply.

Feature: *The author doesn't include a thesis statement but instead develops her position over the course of the reading.*

Strategy: As you read, keep asking yourself what each paragraph adds to your understanding of the author's point of view.

Feature: *The author has included a number of personal stories.*

Strategy: Make sure you can identify what point each story is meant to illustrate.

Evaluating Your Background Knowledge

The author of this reading is relying on your knowledge of these words and terms. Look over this list carefully to make sure you know everything on it. *Note:* The number in parentheses indicates the paragraph where the word can be found while an asterisk accompanies the word's first appearance in the reading.

tangible (3):   touchable

tony (4):   fancy, rich

arbiter (4):   person who makes a final decision about how a problem should be resolved

emissary (5):   messenger

Evaluating Your Background Knowledge (continued)

slippery slope (7): The slippery slope method of thinking assumes that one set of actions is going to have a snowball effect and cause an additional and even worse chain of events. Although often identified as an error in logic, the phrase can be used to accurately identify a chain of increasingly negative effects.

contingent (12):   dependent

tort (12):   an act which results in an injury and entitles the victim of that injury to compensation

precedent (14):   previous case or instance that acts as a model for others

Agent Orange (15): a chemical used during the Vietnam War that many believe left soldiers who served in that war with a host of serious ailments

erroneously (15):   mistakenly; out of error

culpable (22):   blameworthy

red herring (29):   something that diverts people from thinking about what's really happening

disconcerting (32): disturbing

discretion (33):   ability or power to decide responsibly

intractable (33):   stubborn or difficult

DES (33):   diethylstilbestrol, a drug that caused women to bear children who were statistically more likely to get cancer

crucible (51):   a container in which substances are heated to high temperatures; a severe test

surrogate (51):   substitute

intifada (52):   Palestinian uprising

1   In the early days there were the leaflets, thousands of frantically scribbled posters, created of the need to do something. Then there were the funerals, many without bodies to bury, cobbled from a need for structure and ceremony. Now there are the meetings—with lawyers, with investment counselors and, whenever possible, with Kenneth Feinberg, the special master of the Victim Compensation Fund. Feinberg, the man granted full power by Congress to repay the families of 9/11

victims, came into their lives one year ago, a result of legislation created in the same lurching haze as the leaflets and the funerals, legislation born of the reflex to act. "I cannot make you happy," Feinberg says to a woman at one such meeting—a mother protesting that her firefighter son's memory is being cheapened by the government's offer of $500,000, far less than a bond broker's family will get. "I cannot bring people back," he says, his elongated vowels betraying his Massachusetts roots. "I can't." "It's not about the money," she answers in her sharper New York tones. "This is not ever about the money."

2   But of course it is.

3   Tragedy, particularly American tragedy, is always and inevitably about the money. As much as we rail against this and insist that it is not true, as much as we would prefer to talk about love and honor and legacy, in the end we find our talk turning to dollars. We do this in part because we need to eat, and to pay the rent, and to continue on with our lives in the face of death. We also do this because cash is the only tangible* way to measure infinite loss.

4   And so, one by one the families take the microphone in meeting after meeting to talk about cash. Feinberg has traveled to tony* towns in New Jersey to meet the families of bond traders, to the Bronx to meet the families of laborers, to Staten Island, where the victims were largely police officers and firefighters. The families speak the language of their new universe, this complex world sprung fully formed from one hasty congressional act. They use phrases they had probably never heard a year ago, terms like "collateral offset" (money from other sources, like life insurance) and "presumptive amount" (what their loved one's projected lifetime income looks like on a government chart). Presumptive amount minus collateral offset equals the payment they will get unless they choose to challenge the number; if they appeal, Feinberg is the final arbiter* there too. "One of my husband's benefits was supposed to be a line-of-duty mayoral payout equivalent to one year's salary," says the wife of a Port Authority security officer when it is her turn at the mike. "I've been told that amount will be deducted as an offset, but I never got it. They never paid it." "My mother-in-law was murdered 60 days before her 60th birthday," another says. "She was helping to support us. She was healthy. She was vibrant. But your projections assume that she would have stopped at 62 or 65." "I'm the first wife," another explains. "My ex-husband's will left everything, including his $1 million life insurance policy, to the new wife, and once that is offset, then the children are left with less than $200,000 each for their father's death."

5   Question after question. But the most important questions are left unasked. How did the government get into the business of saying that one victim's life is worth three times as much as another's? Or that the grief of these families is worth millions while the grief of other crime victims, or accident victims, or even other terror victims, is not? Should an emissary* with unlimited power be granting children money when their father chose to leave them nothing? Should an emissary with unlimited taxpayer funds—current projections put the cost as high as $6 billion—have such power over people's lives at all? And what about next time? Are we going to be making these sorts of payoffs—for that is what they are—every time we are attacked?

6   These are difficult questions to ask, and even harder ones to answer. "The senator will never go on record with that," a Washington aide says after spending half an hour explaining why said senator thinks the plan should not have been passed in the first place. But around the country—where as a rule we like to shower victims with charity and then criticize them when they accept it—people are asking. "I am very bothered by what I perceive as greedy people when it comes to the distribution of funds to the victims of Sept. 11," reads a comment posted on the Victim Compensation Fund's Web site. Another reads: "What about the victims of Oklahoma City, the U.S.S. *Cole* and the embassies in Africa?"

7   "However generous the intentions, it's a slippery slope,"* says Prof. Peter H. Schuck, who teaches tort law at Yale Law School and studies compensation systems. "It's impossible to justify this money in terms of a defined system of justice. We should not be saying that a death caused by one terrorist is worth more than a death caused by another, or that a death caused by a terrorist is worth more than a death caused by a drunk driver. And isn't that what this fund is saying?"

8   On the evening of Thursday, Sept. 20, 2001, with the country still reeling and the wreckage still smoldering, President Bush addressed a joint session of Congress. A group of congressional aides barely heard the speech. Instead, they sat huddled over their computers, banging out the language that would become the Victim Compensation Fund. According to key participants in the process, almost no time was spent discussing the moral or the philosophical whys of the plan. There simply wasn't time. The entire $6 billion program took 72 hours, just three days, from Wednesday the 19th through Saturday the 22nd, from first glimmer to presidential signature.

9   The Victim Compensation Fund was not really created to help the 9/11 families. The bill that authorizes the fund is titled the Air Transportation Safety and System Stabilization Act, and the victims' families are not mentioned until the fourth of six sections. The first draft offered no help to the families at all. They were an afterthought to a bill designed to save the airlines.

10   It happened like this: Within days of the attacks, executives at the highest levels of the airline industry informed Congress and the White House that unless the government provided immediate and extensive help, the nation's planes would stop flying. The airlines were in shaky economic shape before 9/11; now their insurance was in danger of being revoked. United Airlines and American Airlines in particular argued that they were in need of help because the threat of lawsuits made it impossible to borrow money that would keep them operating. In response, the White House began circulating a proposed $15 billion bailout of the industry. It would provide cash and loans and, most significant, put a cap on liability from lawsuits. Victims' families could sue, but damages would be limited to the insurance carried by each plane, for a total of less than $7 billion. (Compare this with current damage estimates, which amount to $40 billion.)

11   About midday on Wednesday, Sept. 19, a week and a day after the attacks, lobbyists for the Association of Trial Lawyers of America approached Representative Richard Gephardt and Senators Patrick Leahy and Tom Daschle with a counterproposal. "You can't just take away their rights and not replace them with something else," one lobbyist recalls saying. They suggested that victims' families who waived their rights to sue be entitled to a payment from the government equal to the monetary damages that would result from such a suit. This plan was adopted by the Democrats, who proposed to fold it into the Air Transportation Safety Act.

12   The Republicans resisted, but the Democrats made their vote for the bailout contingent* on inclusion of victim compensation. Because the plan was a replacement for the tort* system, they said, it should operate like the tort system, taking projected lifetime earnings into account. When talk briefly turned to the high price tag that would result, Daschle reportedly ended the discussion by asking: "Do you want to put a value on human life right now? I don't."

13   When the president finished speaking that evening, the congressional leadership and their aides gathered in Speaker of the House J. Dennis Hastert's office to work out the details long into the night.

The Democrats wanted the fund to be overseen by a senior judge subject to Senate confirmation. The Republicans instead wanted a special master appointed by the attorney general—a special master with sweeping powers, whose decisions could not be appealed—and that's what they got.

14   What they presented to the public and the rest of Congress the following morning was a plan with no precedent.* Nothing in the history of the country is comparable to the system of compensation set in place during those three hectic days. Never before had the government made such payments to victims of an attack—not after Pearl Harbor or Oklahoma City, not after the attack on the Marine barracks in Lebanon or even after the first World Trade Center bombing.

15   Nor has the country ever paid money in this way to victims of natural disasters or epidemics. There have been occasional compensation programs—for uranium miners exposed to radiation, for instance, or for soldiers exposed to Agent Orange*—but not with payments anywhere as large as these. American survivors of the Holocaust were compensated, but by the country that wronged them, not by the United States. And our government, in turn, has paid foreigners it has wronged—like the families of those who died in the Chinese Embassy in Serbia when it was erroneously* targeted by American bombs. But nothing like this had ever been done before.

16   On the evening of Sept. 21, 2001, hours after it was finalized in Hastert's office, the Air Transportation Safety Act passed the House by a vote of 356 to 54 and the Senate by 96 to 1.

17   The message, as it stood that day, was therefore this: If your death involves an industry that the government feels compelled to protect, you're in luck. But if it's an industry that the government would let go under, you are on your own.

18   On the day the compensation plan became law, Kathleen Treanor was traveling back and forth across the Hudson River, escorting grieving families who were viewing ground zero for the first time. Every trip to the site, every hug for a new widow, brought back searing memories of her own loss. Her 4-year-old daughter, Ashley, had been with her in-laws, Luther and LaRue, who were running an errand in the Alfred P. Murrah Federal Building in Oklahoma City on April 19, 1995; they were among the 168 who died in what had been, until Sept. 11, the worst terrorist attack on American soil.

19   Treanor spent Sept. 11 in front of her television "weeping for the people who were dying and the people who loved them. I knew what they were going through now. I knew what they were going to

go through for years and years." She thought of P. J. Allen, 18 months old at the time of the Oklahoma blast, who survived with blackened lungs; he still can't go to school for fear of infection, and he and his grandmother live on Social Security and financial aid from the Red Cross. She thought of Brandon Denny, 3 at the time; Brandon was left with severe brain damage. She thought of Tim Hearn, who gave up a scholarship to come back home and raise his orphaned siblings; he was working three jobs at one point and, until the Red Cross stepped in to help recently, was on the verge of losing his home. And now, she thought, there were going to be thousands more Dennys and Allens and Hearns. Rallying, Treanor contacted the Red Cross (she had come to know many of the volunteers well) and said: "You have to get me to New York. These people need me." It was from one of the families, while standing on a boat in New York Harbor, that she first heard about the planned 9/11 compensation fund.

20   Until that moment, she says, "I didn't really buy into this whole victim-compensation idea." Her own family lost her father-in-law's farm after he died, and they were still paying off his debts. She had had to ask a charity worker for money for schoolbooks for her remaining children. Still, she said, she had always thought that "it wasn't the government's responsibility to make everything right."

21   But at that moment in New York, she changed her mind. Equal treatment for Oklahoma City families became her single-minded cause. "How come you didn't stand up for us?" she asked in repeated phone calls to the Oklahoma congressional delegation. "Why is it right for a New York stockbroker's widow to be given millions of dollars and not a poor farmer's family in Oklahoma? It's been nearly eight years since the Oklahoma City bombing. It took them days to pass this legislation. Why is my daughter worth less than these people?"

22   Treanor founded a group called Fairness for OKC and has gone from House to Senate and back with the attorney and lobbyists she hired. "All we heard was no, no, no," she says of the Republicans. "They all said they were afraid of opening the barn door and letting everybody in." The Democrats were more sympathetic, but she still got nowhere. So she fought harder. Noting that the World Trade Center families were being paid to prevent lawsuits against the airlines, she drafted a lawsuit of her own—against the United States government. "Timothy McVeigh perpetrated his crime as a sole result of the bungling by the government in Waco and Ruby Ridge," she says. "So was the government culpable* in what happened here in Okla-

homa? They've admitted they'd done some things very wrong. You could make the argument that they were somewhat guilty."

23   Her lawsuit also questions the legitimacy of protection for a single set of terror victims. "The 14th Amendment guarantees equal protection under the law," she says. "This is not equal. They told me that my daughter was not worth as much as a New York victim, and that's an ugly, ugly thing to say."

24   Treanor's voice was soon joined by others. "I don't begrudge those people getting a nickel," says Howard Kavaler, a retired foreign service officer, whose wife, Prabhi, was among the 12 killed and two dozen injured in the bombing of the American Embassy in Nairobi on Aug. 7, 1998, when their children were 5 an 10. "But what do I tell my daughters? Your mother didn't count?"

25   For four years, Kavaler and the other embassy families have been petitioning the State Department for $1.5 million in compensation for each victim (which is the same amount the United States government paid to those killed in the Chinese Embassy in Serbia). They claim that Secretary of State Madeleine Albright failed to act on warnings that the Nairobi embassy and the embassy in Tanzania, which was attacked the same day, were "sitting ducks," as Kavaler puts it. He and the other embassy families say they will sign away their right to sue on those grounds in return for being grandfathered into the 9/11 fund.

26   Families of sailors on the U.S.S. *Cole* have also asked to be included, as have relatives of the six people who died in the 1993 World Trade Center bombing. There has been some talk of including the victims of the anthrax letters as well. "It's begun to look like a Christmas tree," says one Senate aide of the fund. "Everyone wants to hang something on it."

27   Each of these groups has an argument for why they are deserving. As is the way of these things, the arguments that serve to include them simultaneously serve to exclude someone else. "Just like the trade center, ours was an attack on American soil," Treanor says, implying that this gives the Oklahoma City families a claim the others do not have. "And like the trade center, most of the victims were civilians," she continues, leaving unstated the comparison with embassy and military victims.

28   "We were the first victims of Al Qaeda," responds Kavaler, who is more direct. "Oklahoma City is completely different. McVeigh and Nichols were just homegrown malcontents. They were criminals. Where do you draw the line?" As for those on the U.S.S. *Cole*, he says, "They had weapons; my wife didn't."

29   In May, by an overwhelming 391 to 18, the House voted to include the embassy bombing victims into the Sept. 11 fund. The vote was seen as the first step to including other groups, but neither that bill nor any other has as yet been passed by the Senate. Technically, the legislation is being held up over the question of lawyers' fees. The 9/11 fund included no caps on fees, but members of the Judiciary Committee say they are troubled that some lawyers are charging . . . fees for an application process that shouldn't even require a lawyer. The Association of Trial Lawyers of America—which is providing free legal help to many of the victims—says that this is a red herring* and that the real reason is that Congress is loath to expand the fund and therefore the precedent.

30   In one of the many interesting wrinkles and reversals by politicians on this subject, the sponsor of the embassy bill in the House was Representative Roy Blunt. Months earlier, however, when asked why those same victims were not included in the 9/11 fund, he replied: "Well, a lot of things in life are not fair, and this may turn out to be one of them. Some unlucky victims are more unlucky than others."

31   In the world according to Kenneth Feinberg, the Victim Compensation Fund raises two fundamental questions. The first is asked by people who are not included under the law. "Dear Mr. Feinberg," he says, reciting examples of comments he has heard, "My husband died in the World Trade Center in '93. Why aren't I eligible?" "Dear Mr. Feinberg, Last year my husband saved three little girls from drowning in the Mississippi River, and then he went under and died, a hero— why aren't I eligible?" "Dear Mr. Feinberg, Last year I got rear-ended by a hit-and-run driver and got laid up for six months. Where's my $1.8 million?" His answer to this sweeping philosophical question— why is one group of victims more deserving than others—is simple. "Congress decided," he says. And he is but the executor of that decision.

32   The second question is asked by the families who are eligible. Why, they wonder, are some among them worth more in death than others? At first blush, Feinberg's answer to this question is the same: Congress decided. The act could have given the same "award" (a disconcerting* term in this context, making it seem as if the survivors had won a prize) to every family. Instead, the rules specify that the special master is to repay each family for its "economic losses," defined as "the loss of earnings or other benefits related to employment, medical expense loss, replacement-services loss, loss due to death, burial costs and loss of business or employment opportuni-

ties." In other words, he is bound by statute to treat every victim differently. Then, the statute continues, he must subtract from that number the offsets agreed to in the late-night negotiation—specifically "life insurance, death benefits and pension funds."

33   But despite his insistence that he is just the messenger, Feinberg is permitted a remarkable degree of discretion* within those limits. His decisions include setting the exact formulas of the payouts and adjusting each award as circumstances warrant. When he was first appointed last year, the feeling in Washington was that he was perfectly suited to wield such power. A former chief of staff for Senator Edward Kennedy ("The last thing you want is a buddy of the president's in that job," says Senator Chuck Hagel, a Republican from Nebraska, who recommended Feinberg to Attorney General John Ashcroft in the first place), he negotiated a settlement in the seemingly intractable* Agent Orange case, served as special master in the DES* case and negotiated for Dow Corning when it was sued by 450,000 women over breast implants.

34   In some respects, this is the simplest case he has wrestled with. "Qualitatively, these are all traumatic deaths and injuries," he says. "This isn't a question of 'Did the chemical cause the cancer or did the medical device cause the injury?' The causation here is pretty much a given." But there are two central differences between huge tort cases and these cases. The first, Feinberg says, clipped and brusque as always, is "the raw emotion": "There's never been a mass case like this, where the compensation scheme is created so soon after the triggering event, where the emotion is so new. Most of these cases take years to percolate up the ladder. By the time I got to Agent Orange, it was eight years in litigation."

35   The second difference is that in previous cases the goal of the court was to create a pot and then divide it among the plaintiffs. But this legislation does not put a cap on spending. This pot is unlimited, its size dependent only on the special master's decisions, and the division of it is, by definition, unequal. In the year since he was appointed, Feinberg has used his discretion to make some choices that may or may not have been what Congress intended. At least one person present at the birth of the fund, for instance, says that Congress intended charity received by the families to be offset. And at first that's what Feinberg thought he would do. But the charitable organizations, he says, made it very clear that if he did subtract charity, they would "hold up distributing the charitable money until I cut each family's check," he says, "so they wouldn't be subsidizing the taxpayer." He

chuckles. "I blinked. I'm not going to hold up $2.5 billion worth of charity. So they won that round on a technical knockout. I gave in on that one, as wisely I should."

36   He also "blinked," if you will, on some of his numbers. In a preliminary set of regulations he released in January, he allowed $50,000 to a surviving spouse and each surviving child over and above the amount paid for projected lifetime earnings. In the final regulations, released in April after months of heated comments from families and their representatives, he raised that amount to $100,000. Similarly, he decided to use national averages for calculating the costs to be subtracted from those earnings projections—the amounts that would have been spent by the victims on housing, transportation and food had they survived to earn that projected salary—rather than average costs from the New York area, which would have been higher.

37   In other areas, however, he refused to blink, most notably on the decision to work from presumptive income tables. (Enter victim's age, salary, number of dependents, get a ballpark figure.) He also would not vary the amount added to each award for pain and suffering. Except in very rare cases (involving, for example, a second death in the family), it is $250,000 per victim, regardless of the specific and horrific details of each death. "I refuse to make distinctions," he says. "I refuse to go down the road of 'He was on the 103rd floor and died a slow death; she was on the 84th floor and was killed instantly.' I'm not getting into that."

38   He seems far less certain of how he will act on the final remaining question: What to do about the highest earners—those whose salaries were more than $231,000 a year. It is unclear exactly how many there were, but data supplied by the investment firm Cantor Fitzgerald, which lost 658 people in the tragedy, suggest that in that company alone about a quarter of the employees fell into this group in 2001. The charts posted on the compensation fund's Web site, however, do not include these victims. Feinberg has so far released no estimates of what they will receive, because, he says, he cannot decide. Neither the limiting details of the law nor the expansive powers it provides give him the answer he needs.

39   "It's a problem," he says. "It's a philosophic problem, and it's a financial problem. What to do with some of these people—the Cantor Fitzgerald people or the Sandler O'Neill people—with incomes of a million or two million. Are there no limitations? If somebody is earning $1 million a year, and you run the model, and they could, after offsets, get $10 million—should the taxpayer and this program subsi-

dize a $10 million lifestyle and a $10 million tax-free award? Should 15 percent of the people get 85 percent of the money? That isn't what Congress intended. If Congress had thought this through for more than a few hours, I don't believe that's what they would have said."

40   It is this last question, he says, that makes him wonder about the wisdom of the entire fund. Not that he disagrees with paying the victims' families, he says, but he does struggle with paying them in this way. Should it be the goal of the government to give families everything they might have had if their loved one had not died, he asks, or should it instead be the goal to try to help, to provide enough money to get them on their feet again? "If I were writing the program today—and I don't fault Congress; they were acting under the gun—I would have clarified the public-policy foundation," he says. "Is it tort or is it social welfare? And I'd think long and hard about this: Is a flat sum better than variations? I think perhaps it might be." . . .

41   He also knows well that public support for the plan fades as the arguments center more and more on money. He is not shy about pointing that out to those who seek the largest amounts. "I saw a lawyer the other day, and he said, 'My client wants $12 million,'" he says. "I said, 'That client's not getting $12 million.' He said, 'Well, then, he'll litigate.' I said: 'Go ahead. Go litigate. And do me a favor, hold a press conference, O.K.? And tell everyone how that $4 million I was willing to give you was too low, and say you wanted 12. Go on national TV and all the networks and let people know how unfair Feinberg's been in not giving you $12 million.'"

42   Twelve days after the collapse of two of the tallest buildings in the world, there was an explosion at the deepest mine shafts in the country. The twin towers went straight up, 110 stories each; the Blue Creek No. 5 mine went straight down, roughly 210 stories underground. The calamity that unfolded in Brookwood, Ala., on Sept. 23, 2001, took place in two parts: first, a falling rock apparently struck a battery charger and ignited a pocket of methane gas, damaging the ventilation system. Next, some 45 minutes later, a much larger explosion was apparently caused by methane mixing with fresh air as a result of the damaged ventilation shafts. Thirteen miners were killed, and 12 of them died when they raced into the burning tunnel after the first explosion to help a miner who was trapped. The underground fire smoldered for weeks.

43   Aside from the eerie parallels to the World Trade Center, the story of Blue Creek No. 5 is striking because the country barely noticed.

This was the largest mining accident in the United States in nearly 20 years, but the nation's gaze was fixed on another drama, and the nation's psyche was too saturated for any more tears. What happened in Brookwood, Ala., therefore, is what usually happens in America when disaster strikes—a smaller audience bears witness and then moves on. The miners' widows say their hearts went out to the families of 9/11 on the day the towers fell. "He wrote 'airplane' with a black marker on the calendar on Sept. 11," says Wanda Blevins, of her husband, David, who was a miner for 34 years. And since their own fiery tragedy, the widows say that they feel for the earlier victims even more.

44   Important people stopped into town to eulogize the dead miners using metaphors from the trade center. "Just yesterday," said Elaine Chao, the secretary of labor, when she spoke at a Brookwood memorial service, "I was in New York, standing at the spot that the entire world now knows as ground zero. And this afternoon, I visited another ground zero not very far from here. In both places we have seen images of destruction that have forever seared our memory. And in the deepest darkness of these tragedies, we have also seen the best that America has to offer."

45   After the speeches were over, however, it was the widows of Brookwood who lived the similarities of Sept. 11. They came to understand what it meant to wait for a body to be brought up from underground and what it's like to retrieve only part of one. "Joe was down there for 46 days before his body was retrieved," says Betty Riggs, who is haunted by the image of her husband's decomposed remains. "When I buried him, he weighed 100 pounds. Before he died, he was 180 pounds. I got my husband's autopsy. I've wished a million times I had not read it." "You get out of bed in the morning and you just pray for the night to come so you can go back to bed," says Blevins, who has still not returned to her job as a nurse in a dermatology office. "You live on pills." Like many in New York, Washington and Pennsylvania, the Brookwood families are financially vulnerable. "The house needs a new roof," says Linda Mobley, who was married to Dennis for almost 40 years. "The flooring needs to be replaced. He isn't here to handle that."

46   In contrast to the tragedy of Sept. 11, there is no federal program, however confusing and controversial, to help. There is a fund—the No. 5 Mine Memorial Trust Fund—which was created with the donations received right after the explosion, mostly from around Alabama. Jim Walter Resources, which owns the mine, said it would accept and

then match all contributions, for a total of $1.28 million. That should divide out to a bit less than $100,000 per family, but the widows say they have seen nothing close to that. "They made us a smaller disbursement a year ago Thanksgiving," Mobley says—a disbursement the company says was about $19,000. "And there were other, smaller disbursements for people who made specific requests. But to get that money, it was on an as-needed basis, and we had to fill out a form: Do you have drinking water? Do you have a car to drive? Do you have indoor plumbing? Our neighbors, friends, strangers donated to this fund. It's none of Jim Walter's business if I have indoor plumbing. The money is for us, but aren't you greedy for asking for it."

47   Kyle Parks, a spokesman for the company, says that I.R.S. requirements mean that some of the money must be set aside for victims of future mining accidents, which is why the entire amount has not been disbursed. He adds, writing in an e-mail message, that "J.W.R. covered the funeral costs for the 13 families" and "provided the following benefits: lifelong health insurance unless a widow remarries or earns more than $2,000 a month, $110,000 in life insurance and two months' pay. (The first two benefits are as called for in the union contract; two months' pay is not included in the contract.)" In addition, the widows of the miners are receiving $549 a week in workers' compensation for their husbands, and some, whose husbands were near retirement age, are entitled to a partial pension.

48   Talk of the World Trade Center and the Pentagon roils already raw emotions in Brookwood. "That 9/11 thing overshadowed everything," Mobley says. "I can sympathize and understand what a disaster that was. But we were terribly overlooked. My husband was a hero, too. I don't want him to be forgotten like he was never here."

49   A few months ago the company offered each family $29,000 more. In exchange, the families were asked to sign an agreement not to sue the company over how the money was disbursed. Only two of the families have accepted. Altogether, 10 families have filed 11 wrongful-death lawsuits against the company, alleging a pattern of safety violations at the mine (a pattern the company denies). "It's not about the money," says Mobley, who is among those who have filed suit. "I don't want this to happen to anyone else's husband. I want the company to make things safer. But money is the only thing you are allowed to sue for."

50   It is an uncomfortable truth to admit, but it is about the money.

51   In America, at this moment, money has come to stand not only for what it can buy—security, revenge—but also for what cannot be bought. Living through the crucible* of tragedy is something only

those who have done it can understand. This must be true, because time and time again we see victims act in ways that seem obsessive and masochistic to those on the outside looking in. It's not about the money, they say, while pursuing money with a single-mindedness that is puzzling to everyone else. "We have made money a surrogate* for tragedy," says Philip K. Howard, a lawyer, who does not represent any 9/11 victims and is the author of *The Collapse of the Common Good: How America's Lawsuit Culture Undermines Our Freedom*. "But we learn and relearn that it is not a very good surrogate." "Victims fight for the money, but even as they do it, they feel their suffering isn't adequately recognized," Peter Schuck of Yale says. "It's human nature. Suffering is such a totalizing experience. You can't allow yourself to suggest the wrong has ever been repaid."

52   This is not the pattern everywhere in the world. In Israel, for example, more than 500 people have died in terrorist attacks since Sept. 11 [2001]. That country has a population of six million, making it roughly one-fiftieth the size of the United States. Proportionately, then, these deaths would be like 25,000 people dying in the United States—the equivalent of one Sept. 11 every month or two. And this does not include the almost 5,000 people injured since the intifada* began.

53   And yet there are no lawsuits—not the type that Congress feared would be brought against the airlines. There have not been waves of lawsuits against the companies that owned the buses on which some victims were killed or the pizza parlors and catering halls where others died. There have been lawsuits of another kind—brought against Yasir Arafat and the Palestinian Authority, charging that they provided the funds to launch these attacks. But the first of these was not filed until a little less than three years ago. "People don't sue the bus companies, although they are very angry at them," says Nitsana Darshan-Leitner, the lawyer who brought those first suits (and is now handling more than 100 more). "In a time of war, you have to go after your real enemies. The bus companies did not intend to kill any Israelis."

54   Those 500 Israeli families were not left with nothing, however. The survivors of every "hostile action" against Israel are well cared for by the government and receive the same compensation as the families of soldiers killed in battle: a monthly payment equivalent to the average national monthly salary (more if they have more than two children), education for their children and a lifetime of psychological care. "Unfortunately, we have a lot of experience doing this," says Aviva Abrahami, who was an administrator in Israel's equivalent of Social Security for 32 years and now lives in New York. "Our experience is something the Americans can learn from."

55   And it seems that we have a lot to learn. At the very least, we have gone into this backward. When asked, "Why are we paying the Sept. 11 families?" Congress answered, "To save the airlines." And when asked, "Why aren't we paying the victims of other attacks?" Congress is saying: "Because lawyers would take too large a share. Because it would cost too much. Because it would never end."

56   No doubt all of this is true, but these are not reasons, Abrahami and others warn, that will satisfy history. Or the 9/11 families. As of the last week in November [2002], only 820 applications for compensation had been received by Feinberg's office, about 25 percent of the total number eligible to apply.

57   Among those who have not yet applied is Jacqui Eaton, whose 37-year-old husband, Robert, worked for eSpeed. She is waiting to see what Feinberg decides about the earners at the top of his charts. "We're made to feel bad for wanting everything that was promised by Congress," says Eaton, who explains that her husband misread his company insurance policy and left her only $100,000. "When we were paying 50 percent of our money to the government in taxes, did anyone have a problem with that?" Ellen Mariani, whose husband, Neil, 58, died aboard United Airlines Flight 175, has also not applied. Instead, she has filed the very type of lawsuit the fund was created to prevent. More than 150 such suits have been filed so far, against the airlines, the Port Authority and the security companies at the airports. "It's not money I'm after, or I would take their package," says Mariani, whose husband left no life insurance and little savings. "I want answers. I want justice. I want it investigated so it doesn't happen that way again." Lynn McGuinn is also waiting, holding out the possibility of suing the special master himself, on the grounds that he has misapplied the law. She was left with three children and no life insurance (the unsigned policy, for $1 million, was on her insurance broker's desk on 9/11) after the death of her husband, Frank, 48, who worked at Cantor. "Congress put all this power in the hands of one man," she says. "They say his word is final." Because the process requires families to sign away their rights to sue before Feinberg calculates their final compensation package, "it's like playing 'Let's Make a Deal,'" she says. "We don't get to know what's behind door No. 3."

58   And so the question remains: How did we get here? How did we get to this deeply flawed policy, creating so much frustration for families struggling in the present and with no plan for the future?

59   We got here, I would argue, because we never paused for a key philosophical debate. It takes more than three days to face the kind of questions that arise from a different sort of war. What is our

government's responsibility for its citizens—and what are the limits of that responsibility? Is it the government's role to compensate victims in the first place? And if so, exactly how?

60   Are we a country like Israel that accepts the inevitability of such deaths and treats compensation matter-of-factly, as a way to address a surviving family's basic needs? Or is money for us a metaphor, meant to signal our regret?

61   Is our collective compassion triggered equally by all deaths, or only by those caused by forces beyond our borders? Is it numbers that make the difference? Three thousand dead requires national action? One hundred sixty-eight does not?

62   These are not easy questions and will not yield easy answers. But they must be asked—and answered—because, inevitably, we'll have to face them again.

CHECKING YOUR COMPREHENSION

Directions: Circle the letter of the correct answer.

1. What main idea or overall point does the author want to convey to readers?

   a. The tragedy of 9/11 has no precedent; therefore, the government had to find a whole new way to respond to and help the victims of those horrific events.

   b. The Victim Compensation Fund was a mistake, and the government needs to rethink how it should respond to victims of terrorism because the chances are good that it will have to do so again.

   c. After the initial outpouring of sympathy for the victims of 9/11, the American public forgot about all the suffering and needs to be reminded that for such grief, there is no quick fix.

   d. Established charities lacked adequate funds to help the 9/11 victims, so the government stepped in with a plan to compensate families based on what the victims might have earned over a lifetime; what the government did, in effect, was legislate inequality of payment.

2. Paragraphs 3 and 4 develop which main idea?

   a. The families of the 9/11 victims come from different classes and from all parts of New York.

b. The families of 9/11 victims will receive a payment equal to the income the victim would have earned minus money from sources like life insurance.

c. In the United States, we often use money as a way to measure the pain and suffering caused by tragedy.

d. We can pretend that money is compensation for tragedy, but in our hearts, we know that it is not.

3. Which paragraph shifts the writer's focus from describing problems with the Victim Compensation Fund to outlining how the fund came into being?

   a. paragraph 6

   b. paragraph 7

   c. paragraph 8

4. Which idea is developed in paragraphs 10–17?

   a. The Republicans and the Democrats had a hard time agreeing on how the victims' fund should be administered.

   b. The Victim Compensation Fund came into being because the government was intent on saving the airlines.

   c. The Air Transportation Safety Act was passed by majorities in both the House and the Senate.

   d. The Victim Compensation Fund was initially promoted mainly by lawyers.

5. Kathleen Treanor (paragraphs 18–23) and her family are mentioned in the article to illustrate what point?

   a. Treanor's compassion for the victims of 9/11 moved her to action.

   b. Treanor was one of the first to raise the issue of unequal compensation for victims of terrorism.

   c. Treanor was one of the many people who suffered a devastating loss as a result of the Oklahoma City bombing.

   d. Despite her own devastating loss, Kathleen Treanor found the strength to reach out to the families of 9/11 victims.

6. In paragraph 28, the author claims that Howard Kavaler is "more direct." However, she doesn't say specifically what he is direct about. What inference does she expect readers to draw?

a. He is willing to say how angry he is about the way the Victim Compensation Fund came into being, and he is not afraid to voice his complaints.

b. He is willing to directly challenge the decisions of Kenneth Feinberg.

c. He openly says that he and his family have a greater claim to compensation than do other victims of tragedies.

7. What does the story of the Blue Creek No. 5 mine (paragraphs 42–49) illustrate in the reading?

a. It shows how tragedies that happened in the wake of 9/11 got little or no national attention despite the loss of life involved.

b. It illustrates the sad fate of the miners' wives.

c. It proves what a mistake it is for the government to respond to tragedy with financial compensation.

d. It highlights just how dangerous it is to be a miner.

8. Paragraphs 52–54 develop what point?

a. In Israel, the survivors of terrorist attacks are well cared for by the government.

b. The Israelis treat all victims of tragedy the same, and the American government might consider following their example.

c. The Israelis illustrate how impossible it is to compensate families for the loss of their loved ones.

d. The Israelis know who their real enemies are, and they sue the terrorists, not the people or institutions that provide the background or context for terrorism.

9. What's the implied main idea of paragraphs 56–57?

a. Some families of victims are filing the very lawsuits the Victim Compensation Fund was meant to avoid.

b. Some relatives of 9/11 victims have been made to feel guilty for wanting the money promised to them by Congress.

c. In time, many of the victims' families will end up suing Kenneth Feinberg.

10. In paragraph 58, the author poses two questions. Which of the following statements best paraphrases her answer?

a. We ended up with the Victim Compensation Fund because Americans are too quick to think that problems can be solved with money.

b. We ended up with the Victim Compensation Fund because we rushed into it without asking hard questions about the role that government should assume when tragedy strikes its citizens.

c. We ended up with the Victim Compensation Fund because it was an easy way for Congress to look sympathetic to the victims of 9/11 while having ordinary citizens foot the bill.

d. We ended up with the Victim Compensation Fund because the public demanded action from Congress.

DEEPENING YOUR UNDERSTANDING

Directions: Answer the following questions by circling the letter of the correct response or filling in the blanks where required.

1. How would you describe the author's tone?

   a. serious and sympathetic

   b. appalled and contemptuous

   c. cool and objective

   d. casual and friendly

2. What would you say is the author's purpose?

   a. to describe the events that led to the Victim Compensation Fund

   b. to persuade readers that the Victim Compensation Fund has caused more problems than it has solved

3. With which of the following statements do you agree?

   a. The author believes that victims of terrorism should not be compensated.

   b. The author believes that there are better ways to compensate the victims of 9/11.

   c. The author believes that there are better and fairer ways to handle the victims of terrorism.

   d. It's impossible to identify the author's personal feelings.

What statements in the text helped you choose your answer?

_____

_____

4. Can the questions posed in paragraphs 58–61 be considered

   rhetorical? Please explain why or why not. _____

   _____

5. The author opens the reading with this statement (paragraph 3):
   "Tragedy, particularly American tragedy, is always and inevitably
   about the money."

   Does this statement qualify as a fact or an opinion?_____

   Please explain your answer. _____

   _____

6. In paragraph 51, the author writes, "Living through the crucible
   of tragedy is something only those who have done it can under-

   stand." The metaphor in that statement compares _____

   to _____.

   What's the point of that metaphor? _____

   _____

7. Explain Kathleen Treanor's argument (paragraphs 18–23) by
   identifying her position and her reasons for holding it.

   Position: _____

   Reasons:

   _____

   _____

   _____

8. In paragraph 28, what does Howard Kavaler suggest about the victims of the Oklahoma City bombing as well as the victims of the attack on the U.S.S. *Cole?*

_____

9. In paragraph 51, Philip K. Howard is quoted as saying, "We have made money a surrogate for tragedy." What does Howard mean by that statement?

_____

Does Howard's statement apply to the Victim Compensation Fund?

_____

Please explain your answer. _____

_____

10. In paragraph 60, the author asks if we are a country like Israel that treats financial compensation as a way to address the basic needs of people who have suffered, or are we a country where money is meant to signal our regret? What do you think her

answer is to the question she poses? _____

Please explain your answer. _____

_____

AIRING YOUR OPINIONS

Explain why you think the victims of terrorism should or should not receive government compensation. Make sure you give reasons for your position.

Individual Rights
Unit IV versus Public Safety

The opening reading in this unit suggests that the balance between the rights of the individual and the need for public safety has undergone a change. The author of reading 1 believes that as a society, we are becoming less concerned with protecting personal rights and more focused on maintaining public safety. While the other authors in Unit IV might agree that the balance has been upset and the scales of justice weighted more heavily on the side of public safety, some are not so optimistic about the change.

Reading 1   Individual Rights and Public Order

GETTING FOCUSED

The author of the following reading traces a shift in the criminal justice system that has taken place during the last decade. Twenty years ago, the emphasis in criminal justice was on the rights of the accused. Now, however, there is much greater interest in protecting the rights of the victim.

Textbook Features and Readers' Strategies

Feature:	*The text includes a number of marginal annotations.*
Strategy:	Pre-read the annotations to see what topics the author will cover and to double-process the definitions that will be central to your understanding of the material.
Feature:	*The author uses numerous examples to make a point.*
Strategy:	Every time you read a description of a crime, ask yourself what larger point the reference is supposed to make. Jot that point in the margins.
Feature:	*Numerous paragraphs in this reading open with transitions.*
Strategy:	Whenever you see a transition, ask yourself what it signals about the author's train of thought. Is he tracking key events over a period of time, describing the consequences of an event, or telling you that the point of the previous paragraph needs to be revised?
Feature:	*Like most textbook writers, the author of this excerpt favors topic sentences at the beginning of paragraphs.*
Strategy:	Pay particularly close attention to the first three sentences in a paragraph. If one of them isn't the topic sentence, start considering what implied main idea the author might have in mind.

Evaluating Your Background Knowledge

The author of this reading is relying on your knowledge of these words and terms. Look over this list carefully to make sure you know everything on it. *Note:* The number in parentheses indicates the paragraph where the word can be found while an asterisk accompanies the word's first appearance in the reading.

Evaluating Your Background Knowledge (continued)

conservative (1): having a preference for tradition

take precedence (2): be considered more important

burgeoning (3): growing

prerogatives (3): rights

perceptions (5): views, interpretations

insidious (5): subtly dangerous

inundated (5): flooded

juggernaut (11): an overwhelming, advancing force

hamstrung (16): deadlocked, frustrated

1   For many years the dominant philosophy in American criminal justice focused on guaranteeing the rights of criminal defendants while seeking to understand the root causes of crime and violence. During the last decade, however, a growing conservative* emphasis has concerned itself with the interests of an ordered society and with the rights of crime victims. This newly popular perspective has called into question some of the fundamental premises upon which the American system of criminal justice rests. In attempting to balance both points of view, the materials presented in this text are built around the following theme:

The horrific events in Oklahoma City . . . show the high price we pay for our liberties.

—Senator Orrin Hatch, Chairman of the Senate Judiciary Committee, commenting on the 1995 bombing of the Alfred P. Murrah Federal Building

There is increasing recognition in contemporary society of the need to balance (1) the respect accorded the rights of individuals faced with criminal prosecution against (2) the valid interests of society in preventing future crimes and in reducing the harm caused by criminal activity. While the personal freedoms guaranteed to criminal suspects by the Constitution, as interpreted by the U.S. Supreme Court, must be closely guarded, so too the urgent social needs of local communities for controlling unacceptable behavior and protecting law-abiding citizens from harm must be recognized. Still to be adequately addressed are the needs and interests of victims and the fear of crime now so prevalent in the minds of many law-abiding citizens.

2   Most people today who intelligently consider the criminal justice system assume either one or the other of these two perspectives. We shall refer to those who seek to protect personal freedoms and civil rights within the criminal justice process as **individual-rights advocates.** Those who suggest that under certain circumstances involving criminal threats to public safety, the interests of society (especially crime control) should take precedence* over individual rights will be called **public-order advocates.** In this [article] we seek to look at ways that the individual-rights and the public-order perspectives can be balanced to serve both sets of needs.

individual-rights advocate One who seeks to protect personal freedoms within the process of criminal justice.

public-order advocate One who suggests that, under certain circumstances involving a criminal threat to public safety, the interests of society should take precedence over individual rights.

3   Both points of view have their roots in the values which formed our nation. However, the past 30 years have been especially important in clarifying the differences between the two points of view. The 1960s and 1970s saw a burgeoning* concern with the rights of ethnic minorities, women, the physically and mentally challenged, and many other groups. The civil rights movement of the period emphasized equality of opportunity and respect for individuals regardless of race, color, creed, or personal attributes. As new laws were passed and suits filed, court involvement in the movement grew. Soon a plethora of hard-won individual rights and prerogatives,* based upon the U.S. Constitution and the Bill of Rights, were recognized and guaranteed. By the 1980s the civil rights movement had profoundly affected all areas of social life—from education through employment to the activities of the criminal justice system.

individual rights The rights guaranteed to all members of American society by the U.S. Constitution (especially those found in the first ten amendments to the Constitution, known as the *Bill of Rights*). These rights are especially important to criminal defendants facing formal processing by the criminal justice system.

4   This emphasis on **individual rights** was accompanied by a dramatic increase in criminal activity. "Traditional" crimes, such as murder, rape, and assault, as reported by the FBI, increased astronomically during the 1970s and into the 1980s. Many theories were advanced to explain this virtual explosion of observed criminality. A few doubted the accuracy of "official" accounts, claiming that any actual rise in crime was much less than that portrayed in the reports. Some analysts of American culture, however, suggested that increased criminality was the result of newfound freedoms which combined with the long-pent-up hostilities of the socially and economically deprived to produce social disorganization.

5   By the mid-1980s, popular perceptions* identified one particularly insidious* form of criminal activity—the dramatic increase in the sale and use of illicit drugs—as a threat to the very fabric of American society. Cocaine in particular, and later laboratory-processed "crack," had spread to every corner of America. The country's borders were inundated* with smugglers intent on reaping quick fortunes. Large cities became havens for drug gangs, and many inner-city areas were

all but abandoned to highly armed and well-financed racketeers. Some famous personalities succumbed to the allure of drugs, and athletic teams and sporting events became focal points for drug busts. Like wildfire, drugs soon spread to younger users. Even small-town elementary schools found themselves facing the specter of campus drug dealing and associated violence.

6   Worse still were the seemingly ineffective governmental measures intended to stem the drug tide. Drug peddlers, because of the huge reserves of money available to them, were often able to escape prosecution or wrangle plea bargains to avoid imprisonment. Media coverage of such "miscarriages of justice" became epidemic, and public anger grew.

7   By the close of the 1980s, neighborhoods and towns felt themselves fighting for their communal lives. City businesses faced dramatic declines in property values, and residents wrestled with the eroding quality of life. Huge rents had been torn in the national social fabric. The American way of life, long taken for granted, was under the gun. Traditional values appeared in danger of going up in smoke along with the "crack" now being smoked openly in some parks and resorts. Looking for a way to stem the tide, many took up the call for "law and order." In response, then-President Ronald Reagan initiated a "war on drugs" and created a "drug czar" cabinet-level post to coordinate the war. Careful thought was given at the highest levels to using the military to patrol the sea-lanes and air corridors through which many of the illegal drugs entered the country. President George Bush, who followed President Reagan into office, quickly embraced and expanded the government's antidrug efforts.

8   The 1990s began with the arrest of serial murderer Jeffrey Dahmer (in 1991), and the shocking details of his crimes later became public. Dahmer, who killed as many as 15 young men in sexually motivated encounters, cannibalized some of his victims and kept the body parts of others in his refrigerator. . . .

9   In 1992, the videotaped beating of Rodney King, an African American motorist, at the hands of Los Angeles–area police officers, splashed across TV screens throughout the country and shifted the public's focus onto issues of police brutality and the effective management of law-enforcement personnel. As the King incident seemed to show, when financially impoverished members of "underrepresented groups" come face-to-face with agents of the American criminal justice system, something less than justice may be the result. Although initially acquitted by a California jury—which contained no

black members—two of the officers who beat King were convicted in a 1993 federal courtroom of violating his civil rights. . . .

10 The year 1993 saw an especially violent encounter in Waco, Texas, among agents of the Bureau of Alcohol, Tobacco, and Firearms (ATF), the Federal Bureau of Investigation (FBI), and members of cult leader David Koresh's Branch Davidians. The fray, which began when ATF agents assaulted Koresh's fortresslike compound, leaving four agents and six cultists dead, ended 51 days later with the fiery deaths of Koresh and 71 of his followers. Many of them were children. The assault on Koresh's compound led to a congressional investigation and charges that the ATF and FBI had been ill prepared to deal successfully with large-scale domestic resistance and had reacted more out of alarm and frustration than wisdom. Janet Reno, Attorney General under President Bill Clinton, refused to blame agents for misjudging Koresh's intentions, although 11 Davidians were later acquitted of charges that they murdered the agents.

11 By the mid-1990s, however, a strong shift away from the claimed misdeeds of the criminal justice system began, and a newfound emphasis on individual accountability began to blossom among an American public fed up with crime and fearful of their own victimization. Growing calls for enhanced responsibility began to quickly replace the previous emphasis on individual rights. As a juggernaut* of conservative opinion made itself felt on the political scene, Texas Senator Phil Gramm observed that the public wants to "grab violent criminals by the throat, put them in prison [and] stop building prisons like Holiday Inns."

12 It was probably the public's perception of growing crime rates, coupled with a belief that offenders frequently went unpunished or that many received only judicial slaps on the wrists, which led to the burgeoning emphasis on responsibility and punishment. However, a few spectacular crimes which received widespread coverage in the news media heightened the public's sense that crime in the United States was out of hand and that new measures were needed to combat it. In 1993, for example, James Jordan, father of Chicago Bulls' basketball superstar Michael Jordan, was killed in a cold-blooded robbery by two young men with long criminal records. Jordan's death, which seemed to be the result of a chance encounter, helped rivet the nation's attention on what appeared to be the increasing frequency of random and senseless violence.

13 In that same year, a powerful bomb ripped apart the basement of one of the twin World Trade Center buildings in New York City. The

It is commonly assumed that these three components— law enforcement (police, sheriffs, marshals), the judicial process (judges, prosecutors, defense lawyers), and corrections (prison officials, probation and parole officers)—add up to a "system" of criminal justice. A system implies some unity of purpose and an organized interrelationship among component parts. In the typical American city and state, and under federal jurisdiction as well, no such relationship exists. There is, instead, a reasonably well-defined criminal process, a continuum through which each accused offender may pass: from the hands of the police, to the jurisdiction of the courts, behind the walls of a prison, then back onto the street. The inefficiency, fall-out, and failure of purpose during this process is notorious.

—National Commission on the Causes and Prevention of Violence

explosion, which killed five and opened a 100-foot crater through four sublevels of concrete, displaced 50,000 workers, including employees at the commodities exchanges that handle billions of dollars worth of trade in oil, gold, coffee, and sugar. The product of terrorists with foreign links, the bombing highlighted the susceptibility of the American infrastructure to terrorist activity.

14   Similarly, in 1993 the heart-wrenching story of Polly Klaas splashed across the national media. Twelve-year-old Polly was kidnapped from a slumber party at her home while her mother and little sister slept in the next room. Two other girls were left bound and gagged after a bearded stranger broke into the Klaas home in Petaluma, California. Despite efforts by hundreds of uniformed officers and 4,000 volunteers, attempts to find the girl proved fruitless. Nine weeks later, just before Christmas, an ex-con named Richard Allen Davis was arrested and charged with Polly's murder. Investigators found that Davis's life read like a litany of criminal activity and that Polly's death was due at least partially to the failure of the criminal justice system to keep a dangerous man behind bars. Three years later, in 1996, Davis was convicted of Polly's murder and sentenced to death.

15   In 1994 the attention of the nation was riveted on proceedings in the Susan Smith case. Smith, a South Carolina mother, confessed to drowning her two young boys (ages 1 and 3 at the time) by strapping them into child-safety seats and rolling the family station wagon off a pier and into a lake. Smith, who appears to have been motivated by the demands of an extramarital love affair, had originally claimed that a black man carjacked her vehicle with the boys still inside. This was also the year in which 7-year-old Megan Kanka was brutally murdered by previously convicted sex offender Jesse K. Timmendequas.

16   Senseless violence linked to racial hatred stunned the nation during the 1995 trial of Colin Ferguson. Ferguson, who was eventually convicted of killing six passengers and wounding 19 others during what prosecutors claimed was a racially motivated shooting rampage on a Long Island Rail Road commuter train in 1993, maintained his innocence throughout the trial, despite the fact that he was identified by more than a dozen eyewitnesses, including some whom he had shot. "This is a case of stereotyped victimization of a black man and subsequent conspiracy to destroy him—nothing more," Ferguson told the jury. Many were offended by the fact that Ferguson declared himself the victim when the real victims were either dead or seriously injured. Famed defense attorney William Kunstler suggested that Ferguson plead not guilty by reason of insanity, which, Kunstler argued, had

been caused by "black rage" at racial injustice in America. Instead, Ferguson claimed that he had dozed off on the train and that a white man had stolen his gun and shot the passengers. Public backlash at the increasing willingness of defense attorneys to use an "offender as victim" defense contributed to growing disgust with what many saw as a hamstrung* and ineffective criminal justice system.

17   In 1995 the double-murder trial of former football superstar and media personality O. J. Simpson received much national exposure, with daily reports on the trial appearing on television and in newspapers throughout the country. Simpson was acquitted of the brutal murders of his ex-wife Nicole and her associate Ronald Goldman, after hiring a team of lawyers whom some referred to as "the million-dollar defense"—an action which many saw as akin to buying justice. In a 1997 civil trial, however, a California jury found Simpson liable for the death of Goldman and the "battery" of his former wife, and he was ordered to pay $33.5 million in damages.

> People expect both safety and justice and do not want to sacrifice one for the other.
>
> —Christopher Stone, President and Director, the Vera Institute of Justice

18   Perhaps no one criminal incident gripped the psyche of the American people, and later galvanized the policy-making efforts of legislators, more than the 1995 bombing of the Alfred P. Murrah Federal Building in Oklahoma City by right-wing extremists. One hundred sixty-eight people died in the bombing, 19 of them children. Hundreds more were wounded, and millions of dollars worth of property damage occurred. The bombing demonstrated just how vulnerable the United States is to terrorist assault. That attack, and a bombing during the 1996 Atlanta Olympics which killed one person and injured 111, caused many Americans to realize that the very freedoms which allow the United States to serve as a model of democracy to the rest of the world make it possible for terrorist or terrorist-affiliated groups to operate within the country relatively unencumbered.

19   The strangulation murder of 6-year-old JonBenet Ramsey, the young "beauty queen" killed at Christmastime 1996 in her family's Boulder, Colorado, home added to the national sense that no one is safe. . . . In 1997, the roadside murder of 27-year-old Ennis Cosby, son of well-known entertainer Bill Cosby, heightened the public's fear of random violence. A 1997 killing spree attributed to Andrew Cunanan, which ended in his suicide (and which claimed the life of world-renowned fashion designer Gianni Versace and five other men), galvanized the nation as the public participated in a media-led hunt for the alleged killer.

20   In 1998, 21-year-old Matthew Shepard, a shy and slightly built University of Wyoming college student, was savagely beaten to death

by two men, Aaron James McKinney and Russell Arthur Henderson—both of whom were also 21. Shepard, who was gay, had been lured from a bar to a remote location outside of town. He suffered 18 blows to the head and had been pistol-whipped with a .357-caliber Magnum revolver. Shepard's body had been tied so tightly to a barbed-wire fence that sheriff's deputies had trouble cutting it free. The blood on Shepard's face had been partially washed away by tears—a sign that he had lived for some time after the beating. The killing outraged the gay community and helped focus the nation's attention on hate crimes.

21   The Columbine High School shooting and the Wedgwood Baptist Church shootings in Fort Worth, Texas, . . . provided a stunningly violent backdrop to 1999. A check of your local or national newspapers, TV news shows, or news-oriented Web sites will show that crimes, especially shocking, violent, personal, and seemingly random crimes, continue unabated.

22   Violent crimes, punctuated with seemingly random cruelty, have changed the mood of the American public or, perhaps more accurately, have accelerated what was an already changing mood. A growing national frustration with the apparent inability of our society and its justice system to prevent crimes and to consistently hold offenders who are identified and then arrested to heartfelt standards of right and wrong has led to increased conservatism in the public policy arena. That conservative tendency, which continues to thrive today, was already in place by the time of the 1994 congressional elections, where get-tough-on-crime policies won the day. Since that time, numerous other public officials have joined the get-tough bandwagon. Many have stopped asking what society can do to protect individuals accused of crimes and instead demand to know how offenders can better be held accountable for violations of the criminal law. As we enter the twenty-first century, public perspectives have largely shifted away from seeing the criminal as an unfortunate victim of poor social and personal circumstances, to seeing him as a dangerous social predator.

Frank Schmalleger, *Criminal Justice Today,* pp. 6–10.

CHECKING YOUR COMPREHENSION

Directions: Circle the letter of the correct answer.

1. Which statement best sums up the overall main idea of the reading?

    a. In the early nineties, public attitude was shifting away from protecting the rights of those accused of crimes; by the end of the decade, however, the pendulum had swung back.

    b. For several decades, the emphasis in criminal justice was on protecting the rights of the accused, but in the nineties a series of gruesome, highly publicized crimes encouraged a get-tough-on-crime approach.

    c. In the current conservative environment, our criminal justice system emphasizes the punishment of criminals rather than their reeducation.

    d. More than any other crime, the bombing of the federal building in Oklahoma City encouraged the public's desire for a get-tough-on-crime approach to criminal misbehavior.

2. Which statement best paraphrases the difference between individual-rights and public-order advocates?

    a. Individual-rights advocates seek to protect individual freedoms and are not interested in the rights of the community; public-order advocates, in contrast, focus solely on the well-being of society.

    b. Individual-rights advocates offer reasons why a crime was committed but are much less concerned with controlling criminal behavior; in contrast, public-order advocates care only about punishing crime and are relatively uninterested in its causes.

    c. Individual-rights advocates want to make sure that civil rights are not ignored by the workings of the criminal justice system; in contrast, public-order advocates believe that where crime is concerned, the good of the community is often more important than the rights of the individual.

3. Paragraphs 5, 7, and 8 all begin with transitions signaling

    a. contrast.

    b. time order.

    c. consequences.

    d. similarity.

4. In paragraph 9, the videotaped beating of Rodney King is used to illustrate which main idea?

    a. The criminal justice system is no longer functioning effectively.

    b. Two officers involved in the Rodney King beating deserved to be convicted for violating King's civil rights.

    c. When the poor are confronted by the police, they don't always receive the justice they deserve.

    d. Since the Rodney King beating, the Los Angeles police department has improved its treatment of minorities.

5. Paragraph 11 opens with which two kinds of transitions?

    a. time order; contrast

    b. addition; time order

    c. time order; similarity

    d. contrast; illustration

6. In paragraph 11, the quotation from Texas Senator Phil Gramm suggests that

    a. he does not think criminals have been pampered by the justice system.

    b. he believes that criminals have been pampered by the justice system.

    c. he hasn't made up his mind either way.

7. Paragraph 12 relies on which pattern of organization?

    a. time order

    b. comparison and contrast

    c. cause and effect

    d. classification

8. Paragraphs 12–20 are all used to illustrate which main idea?

    a. By the mid-1990s, many Americans believed that they were living through a crime wave.

    b. The public's belief that they were in the midst of a crime wave was encouraged by the media's coverage of some particularly brutal crimes.

    c. A series of particularly brutal crimes encouraged a more conservative trend in criminal justice.

d. The murder of James Jordan, father of basketball great Michael Jordan, was widely covered by the media and contributed to the public's sense of being under attack.

9. Which statement most effectively paraphrases the topic sentence of paragraph 22?

   a. Cruel and violent crimes have angered and frightened the American public.

   b. The more conservative approach to crime had already made its appearance in the 1994 congressional elections.

   c. A series of senseless and bloody crimes increased the public's more conservative attitude toward crime.

   d. Few people today are interested in what leads an individual to crime; most care only about protecting themselves and their community from criminal activity.

10. Which two patterns organize the reading?

    a. cause and effect; classification

    b. time order; cause and effect

    c. time order; classification

DEEPENING YOUR UNDERSTANDING

Directions: Answer the following questions by circling the letter of the correct answer or filling in the blanks where required.

1. How would you describe the author's tone?

   a. objective

   b. outraged

   c. concerned

   d. skeptical

2. What would you say is the author's purpose?

   a. to inform readers about a shift in the public's attitude toward crime and criminals

   b. to persuade readers that a more conservative approach toward crime is necessary

3. With which of the following statements do you agree?

   a. The author is inclined to favor a more liberal approach toward curbing crime.

   b. The author is inclined to favor a more conservative approach toward curbing crime.

   c. It's impossible to determine the author's personal sentiments.

   Please explain your answer.

   _____

   _____

4. Read the following statement: "'Traditional' crimes, such as murder, rape, and assault, as reported by the FBI, increased astronomically during the 1970s and into the 1980s" (paragraph 4). Is that statement

   a. a fact?

   b. an opinion?

   c. a blend of fact and opinion?

5. What's missing from paragraph 4's references to "theories" and "analysts"?

   _____

6. What cause-and-effect relationship do you think is implied in paragraph 4?

   _____

7. In paragraph 5, the author says that "popular perceptions identified one particularly insidious form of criminal activity. . . ." Based on what you know about the media from the reading titled "Creating a Culture of Fear" (pp. 181–192), what might be the difficulty with trusting "popular perceptions"?

   _____

8. In paragraph 21, the author says, "A check of your local or national newspapers, TV news shows, or news-oriented Web sites will

show that crimes, especially shocking, violent, personal, and seemingly random crimes, continue unabated." How would Barry Glassner, author of "Creating a Culture of Fear" (pp. 181–192), respond to the notion that one can assess crime trends by turning to "your local or national newspapers"?

_____

9. In paragraph 7, what opinion about American life in the 1980s does the author promote?

_____

What evidence does he provide? _____

_____

10. The author cites a number of particularly brutal crimes to illustrate why some people became public-order advocates. What specific illustrations does he offer in order to show why some people became individual-rights advocates?

_____

_____

Do you think both sides get equal treatment in this reading? _____

Please explain your answer. _____

_____

AIRING YOUR OPINIONS

1. Do you see yourself as an individual-rights advocate or as a public-order advocate? What led you to your point of view?

2. Do you think that a person's personal, financial, or social history should play any role in how his or her crime is judged? Please explain your answer.

Internal Security Confronts Civil Liberties

GETTING FOCUSED

The author of this reading, Richard Posner, believes that the balance between preserving individual civil liberties and protecting the general public's safety has shifted or changed in the wake of 9/11 and America's subsequent war on terrorism.

Textbook Features and Readers' Strategies

Feature:	*Unlike the author of the previous reading, who relied heavily on examples to make his point, this author varies the type of support he uses, relying on examples, reasons, and historical precedent.*
Strategy:	Start by searching out the point of the author's argument. Each time you locate a passage that offers a supporting reason, or precedent, make a note about it in the margins.
Feature:	*The writing style here is more complex than that of most of the previous readings.*
Strategy:	Pre-read the first and last sentences of every paragraph before you read the entire essay. Above all, take your time and don't rush through the paragraphs. If the meaning of a paragraph seems foggy, reread it on the spot or mark it for a second reading later.
Feature:	*The author makes heavy use of pronouns.*
Strategy:	The longer the sentences, the more likely you are to encounter pronouns. Always make sure you know exactly what a pronoun refers to; if you don't, you are liable to lose the author's train of thought.

Evaluating Your Background Knowledge

The author of this reading is relying on your knowledge of these words and terms. Look over this list carefully to make sure you know everything on it. *Note:* The number in parentheses indicates the paragraph where the word can be found while an asterisk accompanies the word's first appearance in the reading.

civil libertarians (1): people who believe that individual rights of free speech, thought, and action must be guaranteed

civil liberties (1): fundamental individual rights, such as freedom of speech and religion, along with protections against unwarranted or unnecessary government intrusions

sacrosanct (1): sacred

probable cause (2): some indication that a crime has been or is being committed

amendatory (2): corrective

judicial (3): relating to the courts

doctrinaire (4): overly rigid

diffuse (5): vague, unclear

curtailed (5): limited, restricted

secession (6): the South's decision to secede, or leave the Union, in 1861

Cuban missile crisis (6): Period in October 1962, when President John F. Kennedy publicly faced down Russian premier Khrushchev, forcing him to remove missiles from Cuba. Backstage, however, Kennedy's brother Robert brokered a deal with the Russians that traded U.S. troops in Turkey for Russian missiles in Cuba.

Tet Offensive of 1968 (6): during the Vietnam war, an attack launched by the North Vietnamese that took American forces completely by surprise

Iranian revolution of 1979 (6): The U.S. had been supporting the Shah of Iran and was surprised when the Iranians revolted and forced the Shah to leave in disgrace.

habeas corpus (7): document that forces someone to come before a judge and thereby release another person from unlawful restraint

Emancipation Proclamation (7): Lincoln's executive order that freed America's slaves

pragmatic (8): practical, realistic

Evaluating Your Background Knowledge (continued)

dogmatic (8):   rigid, inflexible

mandarin (8):   marked by refined and elaborate language

1   In the wake of the September 11 terrorist attacks have come many proposals for tightening security; some measures to that end have already been taken. Civil libertarians* are troubled. They fear that concerns about national security will lead to an erosion of civil liberties.* They offer historical examples of supposed overreactions to threats to national security. They treat our existing civil liberties—freedom of the press, protections of privacy and of the rights of criminal suspects, and the rest—as sacrosanct,* insisting that the battle against international terrorism accommodate itself to them.

2   I consider this a profoundly mistaken approach to the question of balancing liberty and security. The basic mistake is the prioritizing of liberty. It is a mistake about law and a mistake about history. Let me begin with law. What we take to be our civil liberties—for example, immunity from arrest except upon probable cause* to believe we've committed a crime, and from prosecution for violating a criminal statute enacted after we committed the act that violates it—were made legal rights by the Constitution and other enactments. The other enactments can be changed relatively easily, by amendatory* legislation. Amending the Constitution is much more difficult. In recognition of this the Framers left most of the constitutional provisions that confer rights pretty vague. The courts have made them definite.

3   Concretely, the scope of these rights has been determined, through an interaction of constitutional text and subsequent judicial* interpretation, by a weighing of competing interests. I'll call them the public-safety interest and the liberty interest. Neither, in my view, has priority. They are both important, and their relative importance changes from time to time and from situation to situation. The safer the nation feels, the more weight judges will be willing to give to the

liberty interest. The greater the threat that an activity poses to the nation's safety, the stronger will the grounds seem for seeking to repress that activity, even at some cost to liberty.

4   This fluid approach is only common sense. Supreme Court Justice Robert Jackson gave it vivid expression many years ago when he said, in dissenting from a free-speech decision he thought doctrinaire,* that the Bill of Rights should not be made into a suicide pact. It was not intended to be such, and the present contours of the rights that it confers, having been shaped far more by judicial interpretation than by the literal text (which doesn't define such critical terms as "due process of law" and "unreasonable" arrests and searches), are alterable in response to changing threats to national security.

5   If it is true, therefore, as it appears to be at this writing, that the events of September 11 have revealed the United States to be in much greater jeopardy from international terrorism than had previously been believed—have revealed it to be threatened by a diffuse,* shadowy enemy that must be fought with police measures as well as military force—it stands to reason that our civil liberties will be curtailed.* They *should* be curtailed, to the extent that the benefits in greater security outweigh the costs in reduced liberty. All that can reasonably be asked of the responsible legislative and judicial officials is that they weigh the costs as carefully as the benefits.

6   It will be argued that the lesson of history is that officials habitually exaggerate dangers to the nation's security. But the lesson of history is the opposite. It is because officials have repeatedly and disastrously underestimated these dangers that our history is as violent as it is. Consider such underestimated dangers as that of secession,* which led to the Civil War; of a Japanese attack on the United States, which led to the disaster at Pearl Harbor; of Soviet espionage in the 1940s, which accelerated the Soviet Union's acquisition of nuclear weapons and emboldened Stalin to encourage North Korea's invasion of South Korea; of the installation of Soviet missiles in Cuba, which precipitated the Cuban missile crisis;* of political assassinations and outbreaks of urban violence in the 1960s; of the Tet Offensive of 1968;* of the Iranian revolution of 1979* and the subsequent taking of American diplomats as hostages; and, for that matter, of the events of September 11.

7   It is true that when we are surprised and hurt, we tend to overreact—but only with the benefit of hindsight can a reaction be separated into its proper and excess layers. In hindsight we know that interning Japanese Americans did not shorten World War II. But was this

known at the time? If not, shouldn't the Army have erred on the side of caution, as it did? Even today we cannot say with any assurance that Abraham Lincoln was wrong to suspend habeas corpus* during the Civil War, as he did on several occasions, even though the Constitution is clear that only Congress can suspend this right. (Another of Lincoln's wartime measures, the Emancipation Proclamation,* may also have been unconstitutional.) But Lincoln would have been wrong to cancel the 1864 presidential election, as some urged: by November of 1864 the North was close to victory, and canceling the election would have created a more dangerous precedent than the wartime suspension of habeas corpus. This last example shows that civil liberties remain part of the balance even in the most dangerous of times, and even though their relative weight must then be less.

8   Lincoln's unconstitutional acts during the Civil War show that even legality must sometimes be sacrificed for other values. We are a nation under law, but first we are a nation. I want to emphasize something else, however: the malleability of law, its pragmatic* rather than dogmatic* character. The law is not absolute, and the slogan *"Fiat iustitia ruat caelum"* ("Let justice be done though the heavens fall") is dangerous nonsense. The law is a human creation rather than a divine gift, a tool of government rather than a mandarin* mystery. It is an instrument for promoting social welfare, and as the conditions essential to that welfare change, so must it change.

9   Civil libertarians today are missing something else—the opportunity to challenge other public-safety concerns that impair civil liberties. I have particularly in mind the war on drugs. The sale of illegal drugs is a "victimless" crime in the special but important sense that it is a consensual activity. Usually there is no complaining witness, so in order to bring the criminals to justice the police have to rely heavily on paid informants (often highly paid and often highly unsavory), undercover agents, wiretaps and other forms of electronic surveillance, elaborate sting operations, the infiltration of suspect organizations, random searches, the monitoring of airports and highways, the "profiling" of likely suspects on the basis of ethnic or racial identity or national origin, compulsory drug tests, and other intrusive methods that put pressure on civil liberties.

10   The war on drugs has been a big flop; moreover, in light of what September 11 has taught us about the gravity of the terrorist threat to the United States, it becomes hard to take entirely seriously the threat to the nation that drug use is said to pose. Perhaps it is time to

redirect law-enforcement resources from the investigation and apprehension of drug dealers to the investigation and apprehension of international terrorists. By doing so we may be able to minimize the net decrease in our civil liberties that the events of September 11 have made inevitable.

CHECKING YOUR COMPREHENSION

Directions: Circle the letter of the correct answer.

1. Which statement most effectively sums up the main idea of the entire reading?

   a. Law enforcement officials in America should give up the war on drugs and focus on the threat of terrorism.

   b. Civil libertarians are right to feel that our civil liberties—freedom of the press, freedom of speech, protection of privacy, and the like—must be held sacred no matter what threats the country may face.

   c. We need to accept the fact that civil liberties cannot always be preserved to the same degree as when the nation is secure; when danger threatens, individual rights may need to be curtailed.

   d. The Constitution makes no guarantee of the civil liberties some people are so anxious to preserve; thus, there is nothing wrong with abolishing them today, when the country is under siege by terrorists.

2. The pronoun *them* in the last sentence of paragraph 1 refers to

   a. civil libertarians.

   b. civil liberties.

   c. freedom of the press.

   d. terrorist acts.

3. In sentence 3 of paragraph 2, the opening *it* refers to the

   a. history of liberty.

   b. balancing of liberty and security.

    c. prioritizing of liberty.

    d. our existing civil liberties.

4. Which statement best expresses the main idea of paragraph 2?

    a. It's a mistake to assume that national security needs should always outweigh the right to civil liberties.

    b. In the balance between liberty and security, liberty always wins.

    c. In trying to find a balance between individual liberty and national security, one should not give liberty the highest priority.

    d. Amending the Constitution is an extremely difficult and lengthy procedure.

5. In paragraph 3, the pronoun *them* in the second sentence refers to

    a. constitutional provisions.

    b. the scope of these rights.

    c. competing interests.

6. In paragraph 4, the first *it* in the second sentence refers to

    a. a fluid approach.

    b. common sense.

    c. the Bill of Rights.

    d. a suicide pact.

7. Which statement best sums up the main idea of paragraph 5?

    a. The United States is in greater danger from terrorism than at any other time in its history.

    b. International terrorists are shadowy enemies, who are difficult to track, let alone capture.

    c. If the nation is under threat, civil liberties have to be restricted to some degree.

    d. The United States is still reeling from the events of September 11, 2001.

8. In paragraph 6, the topic sentence is

    a. sentence 1.

b. sentence 2.

c. sentence 3.

9. Which statement best paraphrases the main idea of paragraph 7?

   a. We now know that the interning of Japanese Americans was a tragic miscarriage of justice.

   b. It's only in retrospect that we can tell if we have overreacted to a perceived threat to national security.

   c. Abraham Lincoln was not above breaking the law in order to protect national security.

10. Which statement most effectively sums up the main idea of paragraph 9?

   a. The war on drugs has been a massive failure.

   b. Paid informants are rarely reliable, and the evidence they supply should not be used in courts of law.

   c. Those who want to protect civil liberties would do well to look at how the war on drugs has been waged.

   d. Civil libertarians always seem to miss the boat when it comes to identifying where the real threat to civil liberties lies.

DEEPENING YOUR UNDERSTANDING

Directions: Answer the following questions by circling the letter of the correct answer or filling in the blanks where required.

1. How would you describe the author's tone?

   a. timid

   b. confident

   c. sarcastic

   d. neutral

2. How would you describe the author's purpose?

   a. to describe the times in American history when civil liberties had to take a back seat to national security

   b. to persuade readers that when national security is threatened, civil liberties should be restricted

3. Which of the following statements do you consider accurate?

   a. The author is himself a civil libertarian but still believes that civil liberties must be limited in times of national security.

   b. The author is not a civil libertarian, and he has little patience with the idea that civil liberties must be preserved even during times of national security.

   c. It's impossible to tell the author's personal feelings.

   Please explain your answer. _____

   _____

4. Which statement is most similar to the position taken by Supreme Court Justice Robert Jackson in paragraph 4?

   a. The individual rights accorded by the Bill of Rights must be protected even if doing so ends up being a suicidal act.

   b. Trying to preserve all of the individual rights granted in the Bill of Rights is a grave, perhaps deadly error.

   c. We shouldn't treat the Bill of Rights as if it were a promise or a pact that should never be broken.

5. In paragraph 7, the author alludes to the internment of Japanese Americans. He says, "In hindsight we know that interning Japanese Americans did not shorten World War II. But was this known at the time?" Is that question rhetorical?_____

   Please explain your answer. _____

   _____

6. The author follows the above question from paragraph 7 with a second one: "If not, shouldn't the Army have erred on the side of caution, as it did?" What opinion about the internment of Japanese Americans is implied by those two questions?

   _____

   _____

7. Explain what the author means when he says in paragraph 8, "We are a nation under law, but first we are a nation."

_____

_____

8. In paragraph 8, the author insists that the law must be malleable. What reasons does he give in defense of that position?

_____

_____

_____

_____

9. Why does the author bring up the war on drugs in paragraph 9? What connection does he make between the war on drugs and the defense of civil liberties?

_____

_____

10. The author of the previous reading used the terms _individual-rights advocates_ and _public-order advocates_. To which group would

the author of this reading belong? _____ Given what the author says in the reading, is he likely to be a permanent

member of that group?_____

Please explain your answer.

_____

_____

AIRING YOUR OPINIONS

1. Freedom of speech has always been one of the most hotly defended civil liberties. In times of national security, do you believe that freedom of speech should or should not be preserved at all costs?

2. During the war on Iraq, the lead singer of the Dixie Chicks, Natalie Maines, harshly criticized President Bush. As a result, some disk jockeys refused to play the Dixie Chicks' songs, and some former fans made a pile of the group's recordings and set them aflame. What do you think? Is it okay to criticize the president during wartime, or should Natalie Maines have kept quiet?

Reading 3

Time to Think About Torture

GETTING FOCUSED

There was a time in the United States when using torture as a method of interrogation would never have been discussed. Yet as the authors of the first two readings pointed out, times have changed. Some Americans now argue that it is time to rethink our attitude toward the use of torture when public safety is at stake. It is this issue that Jonathan Alter addresses in the following reading.

Textbook Features and Readers' Strategies

Feature:	*As is often true in magazine articles, the title of this reading comes close to summing up the main idea of the entire reading.*
Strategy:	Read to figure out exactly *why* the author believes it's time to think about torture. Ask yourself if he places any limits on the kinds of torture he would consider acceptable.
Feature:	*The author openly takes a controversial position.*
Strategy:	When an author unabashedly takes a stance many might criticize, he or she is likely to anticipate and answer objections. Make sure you can summarize both the opposition and the author's response.
Feature:	*This author also quotes Chief Justice Robert Jackson.*
Strategy:	Try to determine if this author uses the reference to Jackson in a way that is similar to or different from the previous author.
Feature:	*The author offers examples of other countries that use torture.*
Strategy:	Make sure you can summarize some of the examples and explain what they add to the author's argument.

Evaluating Your Background Knowledge

The author of this reading is relying on your knowledge of these words and terms. Look over this list carefully to make sure you know everything on it. *Note:* The number in parentheses indicates the paragraph where the word can be found while an asterisk accompanies the word's first appearance in the reading.

ACLU (3): the American Civil Liberties Union, an organization dedicated to preserving civil liberties such as the right to privacy and freedom of speech

quibble (3): argue over small, insignificant points

tepid (3): weak, lacking in force

anachronism (4): something out of place or inappropriate to the time

patina (7): literally, the sheen or surface of an object; figuratively, a good appearance that covers flaws

1   In this autumn of anger, even a liberal can find his thoughts turning to . . . torture. OK, not cattle prods or rubber hoses, at least not here in the United States, but something to jump-start the stalled investigation of the greatest crime in American history. Right now, four key hijacking suspects aren't talking at all.

2   Couldn't we at least subject them to psychological torture, like tapes of dying rabbits or high-decibel rap? (The military has done that in Panama and elsewhere.) How about truth serum, administered with a mandatory IV? Or deportation to Saudi Arabia, land of beheadings? (As the frustrated FBI has been threatening.) Some people still argue that we needn't rethink any of our old assumptions about law enforcement, but they're hopelessly "Sept. 10"—living in a country that no longer exists.

3   One sign of how much things have changed is the reaction to the antiterrorism bill, which cleared the Senate last week [Oct. 2001] by a vote of 98–1. While the ACLU* felt obliged to quibble* with a provision or two, the opposition was tepid,* even from staunch civil libertarians. That great quote from the late Chief Justice Robert Jackson—"The Constitution is not a suicide pact"—is getting a good workout lately. "This was incomparably more sober and sensible than

what some of our revered presidents did," says Floyd Abrams, the First Amendment lawyer, referring to the severe restrictions on liberty imposed during the Civil War and World War I.

4   Fortunately, the new law stops short of threatening basic rights like free speech, which is essential in wartime to hold the government accountable. The bill makes it easier to wiretap (under the old rules, you had to get a warrant for each individual phone, an anachronism* in a cellular age), easier to detain immigrants who won't talk and easier to follow money through the international laundering process. A welcome "sunset" provision means the expansion of surveillance will expire after four years. That's an important precedent, though odds are these changes will end up being permanent. It's a new world.

5   Actually, the world hasn't changed as much as we have. The Israelis have been wrestling for years with the morality of torture. Until 1999 an interrogation technique called "shaking" was legal. It entailed holding a smelly bag over a suspect's head in a dark room, then applying scary psychological torment. (To avoid lessening the potential impact on terrorists, I won't specify exactly what kind.) Even now, Israeli law leaves a little room for "moderate physical pressure" in what are called "ticking time bomb" cases, where extracting information is essential to saving hundreds of lives. The decision of when to apply it is left in the hands of law-enforcement officials.

6   For more than 20 years Harvard Law School professor Alan Dershowitz has argued to the Israelis that this is terribly unfair to the members of the security services. In a forthcoming book, *Shouting Fire*, he makes the case for what he calls a "torture warrant," where judges would balance competing claims and make the call, as they do in issuing search warrants. Dershowitz says that as long as the fruits of such interrogation are used for investigation, not to convict the detainee (a violation of the Fifth Amendment right against self-incrimination), it could be constitutional here, too. "I'm not in favor of torture, but if you're going to have it, it should damn well have court approval," Dershowitz says.

7   Not surprisingly, judges and lawyers in both Israel and the United States don't agree. They prefer looking the other way to giving even mild torture techniques the patina* of legality. This leaves them in a strange moral position. The torture they can't see (or that occurs after deportation) is harder on the person they claim to be concerned about—the detainee—but easier on their consciences. Out of sight, out of mind.

8   Short of physical torture, there's always sodium pentothal ("truth serum"). The FBI is eager to try it, and deserves the chance. Unfor-

tunately, truth serum, first used on spies in World War II, makes suspects gabby but not necessarily truthful. The same goes for even the harshest torture. When the subject breaks, he often lies. Prisoners "have only one objective—to end the pain," says retired Col. Kenneth Allard, who was trained in interrogation. "It's a huge limitation." [Yet] some torture clearly works. Jordan broke the most notorious terrorist of the 1980s, Abu Nidal, by threatening his family. Philippine police reportedly helped crack the 1993 World Trade Center bombings (plus a plot to crash 11 U.S. airliners and kill the pope) by convincing a suspect that they were about to turn him over to the Israelis. Then there's painful Islamic justice, which has the added benefit of greater acceptance among Muslims.

9   We can't legalize physical torture; it's contrary to American values. But even as we continue to speak out against human-rights abuses around the world, we need to keep an open mind about certain measures to fight terrorism, like court-sanctioned psychological interrogation. And we'll have to think about transferring some suspects to our less squeamish allies, even if that's hypocritical. Nobody said this was going to be pretty.

CHECKING YOUR COMPREHENSION

Directions: Circle the letter of the correct answer.

1. Which statement most effectively sums up the overall main idea of the reading?

   a. In an effort to protect ourselves, we must let law-enforcement officials use any form of torture they think appropriate in order to extract information from suspects.

   b. Given the threat of terrorism that hangs over our heads, no one would question the right of law-enforcement officials to use torture when necessary.

   c. Although we shouldn't legalize all methods of torture, we need to seriously consider some forms of psychological torture in order to extract information from terrorist suspects.

   d. If we legalize torture, we become no better than the tyrants we have criticized for decades.

2. What's the implied main idea of paragraph 3?

   a. The antiterrorism bill goes overboard in its attempt to preserve freedom of speech.

   b. The current antiterrorism bill is much better than similar bills introduced during World War I.

   c. The antiterrorism bill is not excessive in its restraint of civil liberties.

   d. The ACLU generally supported the antiterrorism bill passed in the wake of 9/11.

3. Which statement accurately summarizes the author's attitude toward free speech?

   a. During times of emergency, even freedom of speech must be curtailed.

   b. Freedom of speech means that we can openly challenge the government during times of war.

   c. Even during time of war, free speech is essential to ensuring that our government remains a democracy.

4. In paragraph 5, the author uses the Israelis to illustrate what point?

   a. For years, the rest of the world has been grappling with issues we never thought we would have to address.

   b. When it comes to responding to terrorism, it would be a mistake to follow the examples of the Israelis.

   c. Like the Israelis, we too now have to consider whether torture is an acceptable method of interrogation.

   d. In a world where terrorists may strike at any moment, we cannot hold onto old ideas about right and wrong.

5. Which statement most accurately paraphrases the author's response to those who don't believe we should rethink our notions of law enforcement (paragraph 2)?

   a. People who won't reconsider traditional notions of law enforcement wrongly assume that the old ways can be adapted to the current threat.

   b. The people who won't reconsider our old notions of law enforcement just don't understand how much the world has changed.

   c. The people who are unable to admit the need for new methods of law enforcement are fearful of where those methods will lead.

6. What's the implied main idea of paragraph 6?

   a. Alan Dershowitz insists that the Israelis should leave the issue of torture in the hands of law-enforcement officials.

   b. Alan Dershowitz insists that the Fifth Amendment must not be tampered with even during a time when national security is under attack.

   c. Alan Dershowitz argues that if torture is going to be used, there needs to be something like a "torture warrant."

7. In paragraph 7, what does the author imply about judges and lawyers who don't want to legalize torture?

   a. Judges and lawyers who don't want to legalize torture are working against the good of the country.

   b. Judges and lawyers who don't want to legalize torture will eventually see the error of their ways.

   c. Judges and lawyers who don't want to legalize torture are good people who have misguided notions about justice.

   d. Judges and lawyers who won't legalize torture are hypocrites willing to let it happen as long as they don't have to approve it.

8. Why is terrorist Abu Nidal mentioned in paragraph 8?

   a. He illustrates that even the most dangerous terrorists can be captured.

   b. Nidal's capture exemplifies Jordan's success at combating terrorism.

   c. His case illustrates that torture can sometimes be effectively used in the fight against terrorism.

   d. His confession illustrates the effective use of sodium pentothal.

9. Which statement best summarizes the author's conclusion?

   a. There is no way that Americans can allow torture to become legal; to do so would undermine everything the country stands for both at home and abroad.

   b. If we are to mount an effective fight on terror, we will have to use some form of psychological torture or else allow others to torture in our name.

    c. In the fight against terrorism, we have to be ready to do whatever is necessary to ensure our safety, even if that includes torturing suspects to obtain information.

10. Overall, the reading is governed by which two patterns?

    a. time order; cause and effect

    b. cause and effect; comparison and contrast

    c. definition; time order

    d. cause and effect; definition

DEEPENING YOUR UNDERSTANDING

Directions: Answer the following questions by circling the letter of the correct answer or filling in the blanks where required.

1. How would you describe the author's tone?

    a. serious

    b. puzzled

    c. sarcastic

    d. neutral

2. How would you describe the author's purpose?

    a. to inform readers about the use of torture as a tool of interrogation

    b. to persuade readers that it's time to think about using some forms of torture as a tool of interrogation

3. Do you think the author does or does not support Alan Dershowitz's proposal for a *torture* warrant (paragraph 6)? _____

Please explain your answer. _____

_____

4. Give an example of what you think would be a "ticking time bomb case" (paragraph 5).

_____

_____

5. In paragraph 3 (second sentence), what does the author's use of the word *quibble* suggest?

   _____

6. What does the author intend to suggest with the use of the word *patina* in paragraph 7?

   _____

7. Some people have called the phrase "the morality of torture" (paragraph 5) an oxymoron. An oxymoron is an expression that links together contradictory words, for example, *jumbo shrimp, mandatory option,* and *near collision.* Explain why "the morality of torture" could be considered an oxymoron.

   _____

8. Do you think this author agrees or disagrees with Richard Posner, the author of the previous reading, when it comes to protecting

   free speech during a national emergency? _____

   Please explain your answer. _____

   _____

9. The author of the previous reading insists on the need for a "fluid" approach to civil liberties when the nation is under threat. Do you think this author is or is not in agreement with that position?

   _____ Please explain your answer. _____

   _____

10. Like the author of the previous reading, Jonathan Alter alludes to the famous quote from Chief Justice Robert Jackson. Does Alter use it in a way that is similar to or different from

    Richard Posner? _____

    Please explain your answer. _____

    _____

AIRING YOUR OPINIONS

Do you agree that it's time to think about the use of torture? Please explain.

Reading 4

No Tortured Dilemma

GETTING FOCUSED

Writer Steve Chapman believes that the issue of torture as an interrogation method needs to be openly discussed and examined. As you read what he has to say, consider how his position resembles or contradicts that of Jonathan Alter, the author of the reading on pages 317–319.

Textbook Features and Readers' Strategies

Feature:	*The word* dilemma *in the title suggests a situation with two possible solutions, neither one completely satisfying.*
Strategy:	Read to clearly understand the situation or problem. Make sure you can summarize both sides of the dilemma.
Feature:	*The writer outlines both sides of the dilemma before reaching a conclusion.*
Strategy:	Pay special attention to the final paragraphs in which the author comes to a conclusion about how best to handle the dilemma of the title.
Feature:	*The writer relies heavily on short paragraphs that either state the main idea in the first sentence or else imply it.*
Strategy:	If the main idea does not appear in the first or second sentence, start working on an inference that would summarize the implied main idea.
Feature:	*Like the author of the previous reading, this writer refers to the "ticking bomb" scenario.*
Strategy:	Ask yourself if the writers agree or disagree on their response to the "ticking bomb" scenario.
Feature:	*The author uses two literary quotations.*
Strategy:	Translate the quotations into your own words to make sure you understand what they mean, but also be certain you know how they apply to the author's argument.

Evaluating Your Background Knowledge

The author of this reading is relying on your knowledge of these words and terms. Look over this list carefully to make sure you know everything on it. *Note:* The number in parentheses indicates the paragraph where the word can be found while an asterisk accompanies the word's first appearance in the reading.

suffice (4):   to be adequate for, cover

hypothetical (5):   in theory rather than reality

holocaust (5):   great destruction causing great loss of life

coercion (6):   force

extradition (11):   forced removal to another country

1   It's the sort of question that, way back in spring semester, would have made for a good late-night bull session in a college dorm room: If an atomic bomb were about to be detonated in Manhattan, would police be justified in torturing the terrorist who planted it to learn its location and save the city? But today, the debates are starting up in the higher reaches of the federal government. And this time, the answers really matter.

2   The *Washington Post* reported great frustration in the FBI and Justice Department over the stubborn silence of four suspected terrorists arrested after September 11, including one who wanted lessons in steering a commercial aircraft but had no interest in taking off or landing. Unless they can administer truth serum or torture, law-enforcement officials fear, they may never get information about planned attacks that are still in the works. American lives could therefore be lost.

3   The question posed above is easy to answer. No one could possibly justify sacrificing millions of lives to spare a murderous psychopath a brief spell of intense pain, which he can end by his own choice. When the threat is so gigantic and the solution so simple, we are all in the camp of the Shakespeare character who said, "There is no virtue like necessity."

4   This indulgence of reality requires no great rethinking of fundamental principles. Rules that suffice* for normal circumstances often have to be suspended for emergencies. We have laws against burglary

and theft, and for good reason. Society couldn't function if homes and property had no protection. But if a starving plane-crash victim stranded in the wild broke into a locked cabin to get food, he wouldn't be sent to prison.

5   The complications of the torture issue arise once you move from the extreme hypothetical* case to the messiness and uncertainty of the real world. Almost everyone would agree it's permissible to use forcible interrogation methods to prevent nuclear holocaust.* But it's impossible to write a law that restricts the use of torture to cases where (1) a considerable number of lives are in peril, and (2) police are sure they have a guilty party who can provide the information needed to avert the catastrophe. The brutal techniques are therefore likely to spread.

6   We know that from experience. Most states that employ torture do it pretty much anytime it suits their law-enforcement purposes. And Israel, the rare government to attempt to impose clear standards and limits on the use of coercion, found that the exception threatened to swallow the rule.

7   With an eye to the "ticking bomb" scenario, Israel authorized the use of "moderate physical pressure" to persuade suspected terrorists to talk—including shaking them, covering their heads with foul-smelling hoods, putting them in cold showers, depriving them of sleep for days on end, forcing them to crouch in awkward positions, and the like. These were needed, the government said, because of the constant threat of Palestinian attacks on civilian and military targets. And, besides, they weren't really torture.

8   But this option quickly expanded beyond the cases where it might be excused. An Israeli human-rights group that successfully challenged these methods in court said that 85 percent of Arabs arrested by the General Security Service each year—including many never charged with a crime—were subjected to such abuse. That works out to thousands of victims over the years.

9   Israel found its carefully controlled approach escaping control in two ways. First, the brutal techniques were soon used in routine cases, not just extreme ones. Second, "moderate" pressure sometimes became immoderate: An estimated 10 detainees died from their mistreatment.

10   The problem is not with Israel but with human nature. To a man with a hammer, said Mark Twain, everything looks like a nail. Give police and security agents in any country a tool, and they'll want to use it, and even overuse it. If the government were to torture the

suspects arrested after September 11, it might find they don't know anything important.

11   There are, of course, other options for inducing cooperation from suspected lawbreakers, including carrots (light sentences, money, relocation with a new identity) and sticks (long sentences, extradition to countries known for harsh punishments). That strategy has worked on other terrorists, like the one caught trying to sneak explosives into the U.S. for a millennium attack.

12   So it would not be wise to formally authorize the use of torture to combat terrorism. And what if the cops someday have to try it to save New York City from a nuclear blast? I trust they'll do what they have to do, and forgiveness will follow.

CHECKING YOUR COMPREHENSION

Directions: Circle the letter of the correct answer.

1. Which statement best paraphrases the overall main idea?

   a. The "ticking bomb" scenario is no longer the lighthearted subject of late-night debate among college students; it's a real possibility that has to be addressed at the highest levels of government.

   b. Like the Israelis, we need to acknowledge the need for torture when dealing with terrorists.

   c. Israel's experience with the use of torture suggests it can effectively be controlled and therefore should be legalized.

   d. These are not ordinary times and they require extraordinary measures, even if those measures involve the legalization of torture.

2. Which statement more accurately interprets the Shakespearian quotation: "There is no virtue like necessity" (paragraph 3)?

   a. In times of emergency, vice often becomes virtue.

   b. In an emergency situation, necessity redefines what we consider virtuous behavior.

   c. Necessity often gives rise to behavior we may be ashamed of at a later date.

3. In paragraph 4, the detail about the starving plane-crash victim illustrates what point?

   a. In life or death situations, we are likely to do things we would never do under ordinary circumstances.

   b. In extreme situations, the rules governing ordinary life may need to be revised or abandoned.

   c. The threat of terrorism is not sufficient reason to abandon our entire legal system.

   d. In an emergency situation, we cannot worry about the protection of property.

4. Which statement best paraphrases the main idea of paragraph 5?

   a. The use of torture becomes much more complicated once we move from theory to practice.

   b. Even in theory, there is no way to justify making torture part of our legal system.

   c. If we make torture part of our legal system, we are no better than the people we fear.

   d. For years, the United States has harshly criticized countries that routinely used torture; we cannot now simply change our minds and claim that the new reality demands a new attitude.

5. What is the main complication the author believes will result from the legalized use of torture?

   a. The United States will lose all credibility as a representative of human rights.

   b. The laws governing torture will prohibit its effective use.

   c. If we legalize the use of torture, we won't be able to control its use.

   d. Once we legalize torture, it will be with us forever, even when terrorism is no longer a threat.

6. What is the reference to Israel used to prove (paragraphs 6–9)?

   a. Israel has given up the use of psychological torture because it doesn't work, which proves that such methods won't work here either.

   b. The use of torture in Israel grew out of control in the same way it would if we tried to use it here.

   c. Like the United States, the Israelis were forced into the legalized use of torture; it is not something they would have chosen to do without provocation.

   d. No emergency situation can justify the use of torture.

7. The reference to an "Israeli human-rights group" in paragraph 8 suggests that

   a. all Israelis are in agreement about using torture when interrogating terrorists.

   b. the Israeli population is strongly against the use of torture during interrogation.

   c. the use of torture in interrogation is also the subject of disagreement in Israel.

8. In paragraph 10, the author quotes writer Mark Twain: "To a man with a hammer, everything looks like a nail." What is Twain really saying?

   a. Under the right circumstances, men are given to destroying everything that crosses their path.

   b. Take away a man's hammer, and you take away his ability to construct a new society.

   c. If we have a certain tool at our disposal, we are inclined to use it even when it isn't necessary.

   d. Unlike women, men tend to fall in love with their tools.

9. What inference would the author like you to draw from the last paragraph?

   a. If the "ticking bomb" scenario ever does become reality, then the police will not be penalized if they do decide to use torture.

   b. The chances of the "ticking bomb" scenario ever becoming a reality are extremely slim.

   c. Eventually we will have to legalize the use of torture; it is unavoidable given the constant threat of terrorism.

10. What word in paragraph 12 implies that the author does not completely rule out the use of torture to combat terrorism?

   a. wise

   b. formally

   c. authorize

DEEPENING YOUR UNDERSTANDING

Directions: Answer the following questions by circling the letter of the correct answer or filling in the blanks where required.

1. How would you describe the author's tone?

   a. concerned

   b. angry

   c. sarcastic

   d. neutral

2. What would you say is the author's purpose?

   a. to inform readers about the dilemma surrounding the use of torture during interrogation

   b. to persuade readers that one choice is much worse than another

3. In paragraph 3, the author says, "No one could possibly justify sacrificing millions of lives to spare a murderous psychopath a brief spell of intense pain . . ." Is that statement

   a. a fact?

   b. an opinion?

   c. a blend of both?

4. The author says, "Rules that suffice for normal circumstances often have to be suspended for emergencies" (paragraph 4). With that statement, would you say the author agrees or disagrees with Richard Posner in the reading "Internal Security Confronts Civil

   Liberties" (pp. 308–311)? _____

   Please explain your answer. _____

   _____

5. In paragraphs 6–10, the author describes the problems Israel encountered when torture was used during interrogations. That description suggests that which of the following is not always an error in logic?

   a. hasty generalization

   b. slippery slope thinking

   c. circular argument

6. The author of the previous reading also cites Israel as a country that has used some form of torture during interrogation. Would you say the author of this reading uses Israel to illustrate the same

or a different point? _____ Please explain your answer.

_____

_____

7. Which of the following statements more effectively synthesizes, or combines, the main ideas of this reading and the previous one by Jonathan Alter?

   a. Jonathan Alter, the author of "Time to Think About Torture," strongly suggests that we consider the use of psychological torture, whereas Steve Chapman, the author of "No Tortured Dilemma," insists that if torture becomes a tool of law enforcement, it will eventually be misused.

   b. In "Time to Think About Torture," Jonathan Alter suggests that the time has come for us to consider the use of psychological torture during police interrogations; Steve Chapman, in contrast, insists that psychological torture will fail here, as it has in Israel.

   c. In "No Tortured Dilemma," Steve Chapman suggests that we can only use torture if a "ticking bomb" scenario arises, whereas Jonathan Alter insists that physical and psychological torture are necessary tools in the current war on terrorism.

8. The author says that "it would not be wise to formally authorize the use of torture to combat terrorism" (paragraph 12). What's the implied meaning of that statement?

_____

_____

9. How do you think Steve Chapman would view Alan Dershowitz's suggestion that judges should supply police with a "torture

warrant"?_____

10. In the concluding paragraph, the author describes a situation in which the police need to save New York City from a nuclear blast, and he concludes by saying, "I trust they'll do what they have to do, and forgiveness will follow." What does he mean when he says

the police will "do what they have to do"?_____
What does he imply when he says "forgiveness will follow"?

_____

Unlike the author of the previous reading on torture, this writer does not even imagine any opposition, let alone respond to it. Yet, some people will disagree with his point of view. Who might they be, and what might they say?

Reading 5 # The Truth About Confessions

GETTING FOCUSED

The author of this reading, Peter Brooks, suggests that individual rights are not being fully protected during interrogation procedures conducted by police. Intent on protecting the public good, the police may be exploiting guilt rather than uncovering a crime.

Textbook Features and Readers' Strategies	
Feature:	The title suggests that the writer is going to tell readers the "truth" about confessions.
Strategy:	Read with the intention of identifying the truth the author has in mind.
Feature:	Taken from the editorial page of a newspaper, this reading does not rely so heavily on topic sentences; instead the reader is expected to draw numerous inferences.
Strategy:	Newspaper paragraphs are often short. If you haven't found the topic sentence by the second or third sentence, start asking yourself what the author is implying.

Evaluating Your Background Knowledge

The author of this reading is relying on your knowledge of these words and terms. Look over this list carefully to make sure you know everything on it. *Note:* The number in parentheses indicates the paragraph where the word can be found while an asterisk accompanies the word's first appearance in the reading.

DNA testing (1): an extremely accurate form of testing that involves the use of genetic material

Rousseau (2): Jean-Jacques Rousseau (1712–1778), a Swiss-French philosopher famous for his *Confessions*, a work in which he seems obsessed with the need to expose his guilt

probative (3): serving to prove, test, or try

exonerated (4): proved innocent

propitiate (6): appease, please

absolution (7): forgiveness

consolatory model of religious confession (8): the process of encouraging the admission of guilt in order to be accepted back into the larger community

ruses (8): tricks

abjection (10): despair

1 How many people over the centuries have been executed or spent life in prison on the basis of a false confession? Eddie Joe Lloyd of Detroit, who in 1984 confessed to the gruesome rape and murder of a 16-year-old girl, was freed from prison last week [August 2002] because DNA testing* proved that he was innocent. He had spent 17 years behind bars.

2 The idea that one can confess to a crime one didn't commit seems bizarre. Confession is the most personal of statements. It is supposed to express the intimate truth of the individual, to reveal his lived experience and "inner dispositions," as Rousseau* put it in his *Confessions*. This truth, these dispositions, are obscure, shifting, illusive; most confessions are laden with unintended meanings.

3 In a legal context, a confession has for centuries been considered the "queen of proofs," the most probative* evidence one can have. And when courts in the United States have a signed confession from a suspect, they rarely question it. It's enough to convict, or to arrange a plea bargain without further ado.

4   And yet it's clear that people do make false confessions. The use of DNA testing by groups like the Innocence Project has now exonerated* 110 convicted felons, a number of whom gave false confessions. Other false confessions have been exposed by vigorous lawyering and the work of psychologists. There is no way to guess how many convictions in the past were based on false confessions.

5   Eddie Joe Lloyd was in a mental hospital at the time he was interrogated by the police. A number of the false confessions that have been brought to light come from persons with mental disturbances, with low IQ levels, or from minors. But it would be wrong to conclude that only those not wholly in command of their faculties make false confessions. The range of normal psychological functioning is broad, and it includes many persons who can be made to confess to things they didn't do. The human psyche is a fragile and still mysterious thing; subject[ed] to certain pressures, it can crack.

6   How can one make a false confession, absent torture or other physical abuse? Perhaps because the falseness of the "facts" confessed to has less importance during the interrogation than the need to confess in order to propitiate* your interrogators. They have locked you in a room, and they tell you the only key to your release is your confession. They claim to know you are guilty, and want merely to seek confirmation of how you did the crime. They tell you things will go more easily for you if you confess.

7   Interrogators understand that their main obstacle is a suspect's silence. If they can convince the suspect to talk, once he begins there's a good chance they can shape his story. In most human beings there are more than enough guilty feelings to go around, and pressures to confess those feelings. Confessions speak of guilt, but they don't necessarily name the guilt, the relevant crime. Suspects who confess falsely accept the story told by their interrogators because they have lost confidence in their own recollections or reached such despair that they will say anything to make the questioning stop. As the psychoanalyst Theodore Reik noted in *The Compulsion to Confess*, confession is often not an end in itself, but rather the means of an appeal to parents or authority figures for absolution* and affection.

8   Police interrogators are authority figures with a vengeance. They can use the consolatory model of religious confession,* implying that absolution will come from making a clean breast of things, leading to a reintegration with the community from which the suspect is now wholly severed. Courts have played along, permitting them to use all sorts of ruses,* including outright lies—claiming "proof" of guilt from

fabricated polygraph tests; false eyewitness reports; false findings of fingerprints, hair, blood or semen at the crime scene.

9   Even the Miranda warnings, designed to inform the suspect of the right to remain silent and the right to an attorney, have not prevented false confessions. An estimated three-quarters of suspects waive these rights, thinking they can talk their way out of their jam.

10   Most suspects are poor, often marginally literate, almost always terrified of the police. Their sense of "rights" in the face of authority can be minimal. Some even seem to assume that, one way or another, they will do jail time. At times a false confession may simply look like a way to hasten what seems to be a predetermined end. The impulse to confess is human, and in a state of dependency and abjection,* it is not implausible that we might say what we know our listeners want to hear.

CHECKING YOUR COMPREHENSION

Directions: Circle the letter of the correct answer.

1. Which statement most effectively expresses the main idea of the entire reading?

    a. Most confessions are completely worthless and have no place in our legal system.

    b. Eddie Joe Lloyd of Detroit was unfairly imprisoned and lost seventeen years of his life that can never be returned to him.

    c. A signed confession has for years been considered proof positive of guilt; but, in fact, confessions may not be as trustworthy as some people think.

    d. False confessions are usually the result of police brutality; therefore, they should not be admitted into evidence at a trial.

2. The transition opening paragraph 4 signals

    a. addition.

    b. time order.

    c. reversal.

    d. effect.

3. In paragraph 3, the author points out that confessions have for years been considered the "queen of proofs." In paragraph 4, however, he suggests that

   a. DNA testing is a better indicator of guilt or innocence.

   b. vigorous lawyering has been responsible for many false confessions.

   c. it's not a good idea to put complete faith in a confession.

4. Which statement best sums up the main idea of paragraph 5?

   a. People who have low IQ levels are the ones making false confessions.

   b. Eddie Joe Lloyd should never have been interrogated while he was in a mental hospital.

   c. The human mind readily cracks under pressure.

   d. It's not just those with low IQ levels who are likely to make a false confession.

5. In paragraph 6, the author poses a question. Which of the following statements most effectively paraphrases his answer?

   a. People give false confessions because they can't stand the idea of being locked up in the interrogation room for another minute.

   b. People give false confessions because they think they can go home once they confess.

   c. People often make false confessions because the police tell them they will feel better once they do.

   d. People sometimes confess because they are in despair and want to please the person asking the questions.

6. In paragraph 7, the writing of Theodore Reik is mentioned in support of which main idea?

   a. Police interrogators do not hesitate to bully suspects.

   b. While a confession proves that a suspect feels guilty, it does not necessarily prove that the person committed a crime.

   c. Most of us feel guilty about some area of our lives, but few of us are ready to confess to a crime we didn't commit.

7. In paragraph 8, the author suggests that police interrogators

  a. refuse to influence suspects when it comes to a confession.

  b. use their image as authority figures to manipulate suspects into confessing.

  c. may encourage a suspect to confess but will not in any way influence the story he or she tells.

  d. make up the confession and then tell the suspect to sign it.

8. What's the implied main idea of paragraph 8?

  a. The police don't realize that in their role as authority figures, they can encourage a suspect to falsely confess.

  b. The courts are largely to blame for the willingness of some suspects to make a false confession.

  c. Aided by the courts, the police are free to "trick" a suspect into confessing, and that trickery can sometimes lead to a false confession.

9. Which statement best expresses the main idea of paragraph 10?

  a. Some suspects confess because they are confused and scared.

  b. Some people confess because they believe once they confess they will be able to go home.

  c. Some people confess because they are convinced that they are going to jail no matter what they say, so they might as well speed things up by confessing.

  d. People make false confessions for different reasons, but the capacity to do so is in us all.

10. Overall, the reading is organized by which pattern?

  a. time order

  b. comparison and contrast

  c. classification

  d. cause and effect

DEEPENING YOUR UNDERSTANDING

Directions: Answer the following questions by circling the letter of the correct answer or filling in the blanks where required.

1. How would you describe the author's tone?

   a. concerned

   b. angry

   c. neutral

   d. disgusted

2. What would you say is the author's purpose?

   a. to identify for readers several of the many cases in which innocent people have falsely confessed

   b. to persuade readers not to put so much faith in a suspect's confession

3. In paragraph 4, the author says, ". . . it's clear that people do make false confessions." How does he support that claim? _____

   _____

4. Do you think the author's evidence for the reality of false confessions is

   a. adequate?

   b. inadequate?

   Please explain your answer. _____

   _____

5. How do you think the author wants you to feel toward the people who have made false confessions? _____

   Please explain your answer. _____

   _____

6. Which statement do you consider accurate?

   a. The author sides more with the police than with the people who make false confessions.

b. The author sides more with the people who make false confessions than he does with the police.

c. It's impossible to determine the author's personal feelings.

Please explain your answer. _____

_____

7. How do you think a police investigator would respond to the

author's description of police interrogation? _____

Why might the investigator have the reaction you describe?_____

_____

8. Think back to the unit on memory and ask yourself if what this author says confirms or contradicts what you learned about remembering. (If you need to refresh your memory, feel free to flip through pages 78–145.)

_____

9. Based on the reading, do you think the author believes that *any* innocent person interrogated by the police is likely to make a false

confession? _____

Please explain your answer. _____

_____

10. Using information gained in the reading, explain how suspects' rights could be strengthened so that more false confessions could be eliminated.

_____

_____

AIRING YOUR OPINIONS

1. Do you feel that the author has given you "the truth about confessions"? Why or why not?

2. Do you think there is any other "truth" about confessions than the one described in the reading?

Acknowledgments

Jonathan Alter. "Time to Think About Torture" by Jonathan Alter from *Newsweek*, November 5, 2001, p. 45. Copyright © 2001 Newsweek, Inc. All rights reserved. Reprinted by permission.

Lisa Belkin. "Just Money" from *The New York Times Magazine*, December 8, 2002. Copyright © 2002 The New York Times Company. Reprinted by permission.

Douglas Bernstein and Peggy W. Nash. From *Essentials of Psychology* by Douglas Bernstein and Peggy W. Nash, pp. 180–189, 199–202. Copyright © 2002. Reprinted by permission of Houghton Mifflin Company.

Elizabeth Bird. "Beyond Self: Invasions of the Mind Snatchers" by Elizabeth Bird from *Psychology Today*, April 1989, p. 64. Reprinted with permission from Psychology Today Magazine. Copyright © 1989 Sussex Publishers, Inc.

Peter Brooks. "The Truth About Confessions" by Peter Brooks from *The New York Times*, September 1, 2002. Copyright © 2002 The New York Times Co. Reprinted by permission.

Steve Chapman. "No Tortured Dilemma" by Steve Chapman as appeared in *The Washington Times*, November 5, 2001. Copyright © 2001. Reprinted by permission of Creators Syndicate.

Melvin DeFleur and Everett Dennis. "Electronic Democracy Through News Groups and Listserves" from *Understanding Mass Communication* by Melvin DeFleur and Everett Dennis, pp. 224, 406–409. Copyright © 1998. reprinted by permission of Houghton Mifflin Company.

Barry Glassner. From *The Culture of Fear* by Barry Glassner. Copyright © 1999 by Barry Glassner. Reprinted by permission of Basic Books, a member of Perseus Books, L.L.C.

Larry Leslie. From *Mass Communication Ethics* by Larry Leslie, pp. 185–194. Copyright © 2000. Reprinted by permission of Houghton Mifflin Company.

Richard A. Posner. "Security versus Civil Liberties" by Richard A. Posner from *Atlantic Monthly*, December 2001, p. 46. Reprinted by permission of the author.

Zick Rubin, Letitia Anne Peplaw, and Peter Salovey. From *Psychology* by Zick Rubin, Letitia Anne Peplaw, and Peter Salovey, pp. 149–160, 171–173. Copyright © 1993. Reprinted by permission of Houghton Mifflin Company.

Robert J. Samuelson. "Unwitting Accomplices" by Robert J. Samuelson from the *Washington Post*, November 7, 2001, p. A29. Copyright © 2001 Newsweek, Inc. Reprinted with permission.

Frank Schmalleger. From *Criminal Justice Today: An Introductory Text for the 21st Century*, 7/e by Frank Schmalleger. Copyright © 2001, 1999, 1997, 1995, 1993, 1991 by Prentice-Hall, Inc., Upper Saddle River, New Jersey 07458. Reprinted by permission of Pearson Education, Inc., Upper Saddle River, NJ.

Stuart Taylor, Jr. "Legal Affairs: The Media, The Military, and Striking the Right Balance" by Stuart Taylor, Jr. from *National Journal*, October 22, 2001. Copyright © 2001. Reprinted by permission.

Shibley Telhami. "Arab and Muslim America: A Snapshot" by Shibley Telhami from *Brookings Review*, Vol. 20, No. 1 (Winter 2002): 1–15. Reprinted by permission of The Brookings Institution.

Joseph Turow. From *Media Today: An Introduction to Mass Communication* by Joseph Turow, pp. 198–205, 423–428. Copyright © 1999. Reprinted by permission of Houghton Mifflin Company.

Barry Yeoman and Bill Hogan. "Airline Insecurity" by Barry Yeoman and Bill Hogan from *Mother Jones* (January/ February 2002). Copyright © 2002, Foundation for National Progress. Reprinted by permission.

Index